Cinéma Militant

Cinéma Militant

Political Filmmaking and May 1968

Paul Douglas Grant

WALLFLOWER PRESS
LONDON & NEW YORK

A Wallflower Press Book

Wallflower Press is an imprint of
Columbia University Press
Publishers Since 1893
New York   Chichester, West Sussex
cup.columbia.edu

Wallflower Press® is a registered trademark of Columbia University Press

A complete CIP record is available from the Library of Congress

ISBN 978-0-231-17666-8 (cloth : alk. paper)
ISBN 978-0-231-17667-5 (pbk. : alk. paper)
ISBN 978-0-231-85101-5 (e-book)

Columbia University Press books are printed on permanent
and durable acid-free paper.
Printed in the United States of America

Cover design by Elsa Mathern

Contents

Acknowledgments

This book could not have been completed without the assistance of the following film-makers, scholars, artists and workers, who were all very generous with their time: Jean-Pierre Thorn, Nicole Brenez, Jacques Kèbadian, Michel Andrieu, Jean-Denis Bonan, Roger Journot, Sebastian Layerle, Richard Copans, Robert Linhart, Nicole Linhart, Leslie Kaplan, Alain Nahum, Guy-Patrick Sainderichin, Jean-Paul Fargier, Gérard Leblanc, Pierre Buraglio, Guy Chapouillé and Front Paysan, Jean-Pierre Olivier de Sardan, Tanguy Perron, Serge Le Péron, Monique Martineau, the people at Ciné-Archives, Forum des images, the Cinémathèque Française, ISKRA, Les Films d'ici, Centre Culturel Populaire de Palente-les Orchamps, Ethan Spigland, the late Paul Ryan, Robert Stam, Dana Polan, Manthia Diawara, David Oubiña, the late Bob Sklar, Richard Porton, Martin Johnson, Dominic Gavin, Jihoon Kim, Priyadarshini Shanker, Greg Zinman, Rebecca Miller and finally my colleagues at the University of San Carlos School of Architecture, Fine Arts and Design for their patience during the writing of this project, especially Misha Anissimov, Joseph Espina, Araceli Culibra and my co-chair in the SAFAD Research Committee, Kimberly Gultia.

Special thanks go to Nicolas Dubost, who shared not only his incredible experience as an *établi* at Renault-Flins, but also his season tickets to PSG. And to Yann Le Masson; truly one of the highlights of this project was getting the chance to meet this incredible militant on his barge in Avignon along with his committed companion Catie, before he passed away in January 2012.

Lastly, none of this would have been possible without the support of my family, Maryann Douglas, Andrew and Roberta Grant, Pascale Wettstein, and Malcolm and Sidney Grant.

À Pascale, Malou et Sid

List of Abbreviations

ACO Action catholique ouvrière

AFO Association familiale ouvrière

AOF Afrique Occidentale Française

ARC Atelier de recherche cinématographique

ATTAC Association pour la taxation des transactions financières et pour l'action citoyenne

CCPPO Centre culturel populaire de Palente-les-Orchamps

CERFI Centre d'études de recherches et de formation institutionnelles

CFDT Confédération française démocratique du travail

CNPF Conseil national du patronat française

CoBrA Copenhagen, Brussels and Amsterdam postwar art collective

CPDF Coopérative de production et de distribution du film

CRP Les cinéastes révolutionnaires prolétariens

CRS Compagnies républicaines de sécurité

DEUG Diplôme d'études universitaires générales

FGERI Fédération des groupes d'études et de recherches institutionelles

FLN Front de libération nationale

FRELIMO Frente de Libertação de Moçambique

GONG Groupe d'organisation nationale de la Guadeloupe

GP La gauche prolétarienne

IDHEC L'Institut des hautes études cinématographiques

ISKRA Image, son, kinescope et réalisations audiovisuelles

JCR Jeunesse communiste révolutionnaire

LCR Ligue communiste révolutionnaire

MCF-ML Mouvement communiste français marxiste–léniniste

MEDEF Mouvement des enterprises de France

ML Marxist–Leninist

MLAC Le mouvement pour la liberté de l'avortement et de la contraception

MLF Le mouvement de la libération des femmes

MLP Mouvement de libération du people

OCI L'Organisation communiste internationale

OCT Organisation communiste des travailleurs

PAIGC Partido Africano da Independência da Guiné e Cabo Verde

PCF Parti communiste français

PCI Parti communiste internationaliste

PCR(ml) Parti communiste révolutionnaire marxiste–léniniste

PLOCC Palente-Les-Orchamps Centre Culturel

PSU Parti socialiste unifié

SDS Students for a Democratic Society

SFIO Section française de l'internationale ouvrière

SLON Société pour le lancement des oeuvres nouvelles

SRF Société des réalisateurs de films

UEC Union des étudiants communistes

UJCML Union des jeunesses communistes marxistes–léninistes

UNCAL Union nationale des comités d'action lycéens

UPCB L'Unité de production cinéma Bretagne

Introduction[1]

n the 74th issue of the French film journal *Écran*, Guy Hennebelle opened his column, "La vie est à nous", with "As you read this the Third Assembly of *Cinéma Militant* (excuse me: 'multimedia of social and political intervention' [l'audiovisuel d'intervention sociale et politique]) has already taken place [...] What is the future of this cinema we call militant? Is it destined to disappear or will it renew itself?"[2] The issue of *Écran* marked the tenth anniversary of the political upheaval in France during May 1968, and thus this somewhat mournful reflection was not entirely misplaced; in fact, the text pointed to a number of issues that had to some extent plagued this "cinéma dit militant" from its inception. For instance, did this filmmaking tradition have any future outside the immediate political context of May? Was the term *cinéma militant* the most appropriate description of this cultural practice? And how could this cinema reach a wider audience while still remaining faithful to the political context that gave rise to it?

Yet these questions were posed from within the milieu, addressing those filmmakers, theorists and militants of many stripes who had been wrestling with these issues in their film practice for at least a decade. However, for those not on familiar terms with *cinéma militant*, it was perhaps premature to begin mourning its possible death. It would seem, rather, that in order to articulate *cinéma militant*'s history, its aims, its aesthetic strategies and its potentials, it would be necessary to open the floor to some preliminary questions, particularly the question as to what exactly constituted this cinematic practice. Were there aesthetic similarities, political affinities, and organisational and production strategies which all aligned to give a discrete picture of *cinéma militant*? These are the questions that this book attempts to address, those nascent questions at the heart of a practice that remained strangely outside the purview of historians of cinema and radical politics alike.

Pascale Casanova remarked that Paris had long been "La République mondiale des lettres", but throughout the late 1960s and 1970s it was equally the capital of the "République mondiale du cinéma révolutionnaire". This book examines the French tradition of *cinéma militant*, which flourished during the immediate aftermath of the events of May 1968, producing a wide range of film work from underrepresented populations that included such varied groups as entry-level factory workers (*ouvriers spécialisés*, or OS), highly theoretical Marxist–Leninist collectives, and even the militant special needs community. Counteracting the dearth of attention paid to these militant film practices, which grew out of concrete historical circumstances, this book explores the diverse, culturally conditioned currents of militant aesthetics and theory that these practices absorbed and produced.

With the waning of *Les trente glorieuses*[3] and the political events that occurred in France during May and June of 1968, French cinema participated in a political transformation that has traditionally been narrated along a specific and seemingly immutable axis. The common narrative, as it is formulated in Anglophone film studies, articulates the unfolding of the events in relation to cinema as beginning with the Langlois affair. André Malraux, the minister of cultural affairs under President Charles de Gaulle in 1968, wanted to remove Henri Langlois, who was among the founders of the Cinémathèque Française, as the director of the cinémathèque. The reasons given were largely about Langlois's careless handling of the archival material, and his political intransigency with regard to running the cinémathèque, and in February 1968 he was asked to step down. However, Langlois had many supporters, particularly among the luminaries of French cinema, including the *Cahiers du cinéma* critics and French New Wave directors. Langlois' advocates were quick to organise a protest in front of the cinémathèque, where violent clashes with the police ensued. After months of protests against Malraux, Langlois was reinstated in April 1968.[4]

Following the Langlois affair, perhaps the best-known element of the relationship between May '68 and cinema was the shutting down of the Cannes film festival by filmmakers as a show of solidarity with the workers and students striking in Paris. The iconic image of Jean-Luc Godard pulling the curtain over a movie screen serves as a potent metonym for how the events and their relationship to cinema were to be historicised. These are the heroic moments of cinema in relationship to the events of May 1968. But as the events waned and '68 became '69, there were a few formal filmic hiccups, followed by the seeming prolongation of the French New Wave project, albeit with some mournful lessons imparted by the so-called failure of the events inscribed within that tradition.

While this rendition is somewhat deflationary, and seems to push the radical politics of the period to the back, the narrative still manages to contain many of the coordinates within and against which *cinéma militant* would define itself. For example, the slightly transformed melancholic New Wave saw the emergence of new auteurs such as Philippe Garrel, Jean Eustache and Maurice Pialat, who undertook the application of the various forms of realism and naturalism, as they had respectively understood them following the events. Yet there was also the continuation of the work of the New Wave filmmakers proper. Among others, Eric Rohmer, Claude Chabrol, François Truffaut, Jean-Luc Godard and Jacques Rivette continued their work, which had clearly been affected by this seemingly momentary but nonetheless pivotal interruption. Of the central figures of the New Wave, Jean-Luc Godard was the most directly linked to the Marxist–Leninist turn that had taken hold of the left in France. Even prior to these events, Godard had been increasingly vocal about his political inclinations, perhaps best (and most controversially) represented in his film *La Chinoise* (1967). After the events, Godard's film work with the Groupe Dziga Vertov and his political activism alongside La cause du peuple[5] attested to his militant affinities and has recently been well documented in a series of biographies of the filmmaker.[6]

Apart from Godard's explicit alliance with the ideas associated with the Marxist–Leninist turn, other directors of the New Wave were injecting into their films their own understanding of the political sea change the events had provoked. Jacques Rivette's work *L'amour fou* (1969) expressed the insights of '68 by articulating them, in the spirit of Thomas Mann's *Magic Moun-*

tain, as a finite group of people sequestered from real-world events, passionately living in circumstances that permit a carnivalesque eruption but that were ultimately doomed to come apart. Claude Chabrol was a consistent critic of the French bourgeoisie who frequently formulated his critique within the formal and narrative conventions of the thriller. He made his most explicitly May-inspired work in an adaptation of Jean-Patrick Manchette's *Nada*.[7] Yet in the far-left atmosphere following May, Chabrol's critique of the bourgeoisie (from the point of view of someone firmly anchored in that class) was not well received by the champions of the reigning militant politics.[8]

Nonetheless, it was Chabrol's use of a popular genre, namely the political thriller, as a means of allegorically representing the political concerns of the period that pointed to perhaps the most visible political tendency in French and, more generally, Western European cinemas. While in French literature the first instances of the *neo-polar* were surfacing, Western European cinema was simultaneously witnessing the production of films like Costa-Gavras' *Z* and *État de siège* (1972). Hennebelle ironically baptised those films "*série-Z*",[9] which differed from the *neo-polar* by dint of a certain political earnestness. The *neo-polar* was marked largely by narrative distanciation along with a self-conscious, self-reflexive, often ironic and darkly humorous commentary on its own form. Yet it clearly and avowedly had been created within the May paradigm of insisting on politics figuring within the work.[10] The *série-Z* expressed the contrary in seeking to make its form invisible. In this way, the spectator would be easily carried away by a seemingly verisimilar narrative, only to be injected with a political message that often recounted the horrors of repressive governments in developing countries.

One filmmaker who managed to mix the generic conventions of the *série-Z* with the self-reflexivity of the *neo-polar* was Yves Boisset. Although often dismissed by the critical press of the day, his early work, such as *Un condé* (1970), fell within this hybrid paradigm. Boisset even worked within a kind of subcategory of this tendency. Boisset took a didactically allegorical approach, exemplified in his *Dupont lajoie* (1975), where he relied on a different generic structure – that of the black comedy.[11] In general, these films and the *série-Z* had as their avowed mission to attract a wide and popular audience. What was politically progressive in these films was the *détournement* of a popular cinematic genre, most frequently the thriller, and its infusion with a politically engaged content. However, for many critics, an engaged narrative content was too bound by bourgeois conventions to be capable of politically undoing what its traditional structure imposed.[12]

While this cinema, the political thriller, served as a progressive left-wing cinema for the average post-'68 cinema-goer, there was another force of political cinema, a more demanding radical cinematic project explicitly mobilised by the experiences of May. This cinema was primarily a documentary tradition that took the vital expression of what had been articulated in the proposals of Les états généraux du cinéma français (see p. XXX) and produced an immense body of film work over the course of the decade following '68. This political cinema, unlike the *série-Z*, was interested not only in creating political films, but, as Godard had so often repeated, in creating films politically.[13] It is this tendency that is a proverbial blind spot in the general conceptions of, first, what occurred in French filmmaking during and after '68 and, second, how those events continued to form and inform film in concrete, realisable ways. This tendency is the tradition known as *cinéma militant*.

The purpose of this book is to move through this often dense period in French film history by using four specific film collectives to open on to a larger discussion of the phenomena. The primary collectives are ARC (Atelier de recherche cinématographique), an early film group that emerged from the French national film school IDHEC (L'Institut des hautes études ciné-matographiques) and began their work by documenting a miners' strike in 1966; Cinélutte, which was composed of former ARC members and whose work concerned largely the docu-menting and sometimes staging of strikes; Les groupes Medvedkine, a group of factory workers in Besançon who, under the guidance of professional filmmakers, learned to create films on their own as an effort at autonomous self-representation; and Cinéthique, a highly theoretical filmmaking collective, which emerged from the film journal of the same name. Aside from these collectives, a chapter is dedicated to the work of Jean-Pierre Thorn, whose influence on these groups in terms of both theory and practice is so foundational that his work must figure prominently in this project.

This cinematic tradition, both intentionally and unintentionally, set itself against some of the dominant theoretical positions of the period. The collectives and filmmakers worked outside of mainstream filmmaking, but equally rejected what might be considered the dominant auteurist traditions that were being created in more marginal areas of film production. In place of the variations on structuralism and psychoanalysis that informed some of the auteurist filmmakers (and dominated the film theory of the period), the practitioners of *cinéma militant* created their own set of theoretical wagers. To interrogate the question "What is a revolutionary film prac-tice?" these filmmakers turned to issues of film distribution, modes of production, control of the means of production, aesthetic parameters (particularly regarding the issue of naturalism) and, finally, putting the camera in the hands of the workers. Except for perhaps the questions around aesthetics, these questions did not figure prominently in the theoretical repertoire of the then contemporary political auteurs.

These cinematic questions should continuously be thought of in reference not only to the cultural criticism that was developing and exporting so well, but also, more specifically, to the political climate of the period in question. An at times almost pathological preoccupation with the idea of the failure of the May events did not just provide a challenge for cultural workers to figure out the best aesthetic representations for these concerns. It was equally a practical opportunity for conservative politics to step in and promise the settling of accounts with a generation that appeared to be bent on a drastic left-wing revolution. Clearly this atmosphere had repercussions in the domain of cultural work, and the combination of a sense of failure of the left (a leftist philosophy certainly being rendered more difficult with the revelations about political violence in Mao's China and the Khmer Rouge in Cambodia) and increasing pres-sure from the political right saw the splintering of the left into smaller "special interest" groups that for many appeared to be a thorn in the side of a unified, class-based political front. While occasionally over the course of this book these political and cultural conditions are evoked in relation to the specific film projects, they should be thought of as one of the primary underlying conditions that preoccupy this project from beginning to end.

Finally, one of the challenges of this study is the need to delimit the vast corpus of *cinéma militant* – a very telling challenge because it points to the massive amount of work created under this rubric. There is not sufficient space to do justice to the whole of this film movement, and I particularly regret the absence of so many important groups and filmmakers. I feel a certain obligation, however, to acknowledge certain absences. Those who figure only briefly in this study but who deserve longer treatment are René Vautier, Carole Roussopoulos and Yann Le Masson. While there are many collectives which emerged during this perhaps "golden age" of *cinéma militant*, these individuals were trans-collective and frequented many of the politically engaged film groups, thus having an impact on the milieu as a whole.

In a 2003 introduction to a new collection of his early writings on nineteenth-century proletarian culture, Jacques Rancière wrote, "There are certain words we no longer wish to hear … the people, the poor, revolution, the factory, workers, the proletariat".[14] This project goes back to these words and the way in which they were claimed, disputed and productively articulated by a committed cinematic project. The consideration of this work and tradition offered in the following pages is thus intended for at least two distinct yet interconnected fields: one is the history of French cinema, which needs simply to account for this gap; the other is the field of militant histories, which may recognise the need to tell a story that appears to have been obstinately ignored. This largely overlooked period of immense cinematic relevance deserves to be explored, not only to fill in a lacuna but also to pay respect to a tradition that itself sought, or rather struggled, to recount untold histories.

Chapter 1
Wildcat Strikes and Wildcat Cinema in May '68: ARC (Atelier de recherche cinématographique)

1.1 What is cinéma militant?

In the wake of May '68, the term *cinéma militant* was defined, redefined and debated in texts published in the film journals *Positif, Cahiers du cinéma, Cinéma, Écran, La revue du cinéma image et son* and *Cinéthique*, among many others. Over the course of the 1970s, participants in the debate tried to come up with new terms to account for the multiple forms of this political cinematic practice. At one point, writers like Christian Zimmer and Philippe Maarek used the term *cinéma parallèl*, an early designation that sought to provide a categorical space for a more inclusive definition of political cinema, that is, one not specifically *militant*.[1] Experimental, avant-garde, mainstream and even pornographic film could find its way into this loose generic paradigm, and in this ability to co-opt marginal genres, it diverged from the slightly more rarefied *cinéma militant*. Later on, terms like *cinémas de rupture* and *cinéma d'intervention* were used to capture the spirit of this type of political cinema. The focus on terms demonstrated an understanding within the militant milieu that this sometimes unnameable cinema was somehow insufficiently characterised and too limited in scope.

In tracking this seemingly constant mutation of terms, the film journal *Écran* emerges as one of the forums most interested in working out this question of designation. *Écran* was created in January 1972 by Marcel Martin and Henry Moret after a split with the Fédération Française des Ciné-Clubs' film magazine *Cinéma*, and devoted a substantial amount of writing to the many forms of political cinema, frequently under the direction of Guy Hennebelle. In the December 1975 issue of *Écran*, Hennebelle and Daniel Serceau defined *cinéma militant* succinctly, yet in an open enough way to eventually account for the various (and sometimes innovative) modulations this tendency would later absorb and undergo:

> This name [*cinéma militant* NB] designates films that generally present the double characteristic of having been shot on a very small budget, in the margins of the commercial production system, and of having the goal of short-term political intervention or long-term ideological intervention.[2]

While this definition may have remained relatively constant, the struggle for a term or generic configuration would continue to change across the pages of *Écran*. In the February 1974 issue of *Écran*, Hennebelle's column "La vie est à nous" appeared for the first time. The column was to be dedicated to films "made in the margins of the commercial production–distribution system, primarily shot on 16 mm, Super 8 or video".[3] The column always bore the stamp "La vie est à nous" in a large square at the top of the page. In a smaller font in the lower right corner was written the type of cinema under consideration. In the first appearance of the column, this text read "cinéma parallèle". Some of the films cited in the inaugural column were by Tor e benn, Vidéo-doux[4] and Front Paysan, each of which clearly adhered to the tradition of *cinéma militant*. By May 1975, in issue 36, the text defining the rubric (the subtitle of

Figure 1.1 *Écran: Dix ans après mai 68*

the column) read "cinéma militant". Over the course of 1975, the subtitle switched between "militant" and "parallèle", but it remained as "militant" from 1976 through 1978.

In 1978, a special issue of *Écran* was published entitled *Dix ans après mai 68... Aspects du cinéma de contestation*. This was the inaugural issue of *CinémAction*,[5] a journal that would continue, up to the present, to focus on cinemas created in the margins of dominant national productions. *Dix ans après mai 68...* took an increasingly comprehensive approach to *cinéma militant* and addressed the subject from aesthetic, practical and cultural vantage points such as the role of feminist filmmaking, fiction and experimental genres. In the May 1979 issue of *Écran*, a number of proposals for different terms were made in a long, collectively written article entitled "Vous avez dit 'Cinéma d'intervention'?"[6] The article offered "Seven propositions from *CinémAction* for new trends in French cinema".[7] Hennebelle and others from *CinémAction* (including the militant Breton filmmaker René Vautier) offered seven texts, each provocatively titled, to try to keep the flame of *cinéma militant* alive; each, however, wavered about its definition, its name, and its political and aesthetic missions.

In December 1979, "La vie est à nous" (the subtitle at this point being "cinéma d'intervention") saw its final publication. *Écran* was on the eve of not only a format change (colour cover and smaller format) but also a fusion with *La revue du cinéma image et son*, effective in January 1980. The final column featured an interview with politically engaged documentarian Jean-Michel Carré but also opened with a section entitled "À bientôt j'espère" (Hope to see you soon). The title was a reference to the documentary by Chris Marker and Mario Marret of the same name, which was the filmic spark for creating Le groupe Medvedkine Besançon. In this final column, Hennebelle wrote:

Today is thus the last time you will read this column [...] In issue number 22 of February 1974 "La vie est à nous" appeared for the first time. For almost six years, nearly every month we did our best to present the "life" of a cinematic current born of the events of May 1968 that attempted to breathe new life into the seventh art, to get it out of the rut of a certain kind of traditional, sclerotic and academic cinephilia. For us *Écran*'s greatest merit will remain its having welcomed this rupture. If from issue to issue we were able, if only partially, to account for the complex and moving reality of a cinematic movement confronted with the hazards of life, politics and the politics of life, this column, in hindsight, will have played a role that goes beyond the mere contents of its pages [...] Finally, "La vie est à nous" will have only been a beginning. We will certainly continue this fight. This is why I have entitled this short letter not "Adien [sic] aux armes" but rather "À bientôt j'espère", the title of the first film by the 1967 militant collective founded by Chris Marker.[8]

In the February 1980 issue of the new *Écran*, Hennebelle edited a dossier entitled "L'avenir du cinéma d'intervention sociale" (The future of the cinema of social intervention). Closing the 1970s with this title suggested that questions remained about this type of cinema, even if the magazine's editors had, in some sense, settled upon its name.

However, the parameters Serceau and Hennebelle described in the December 1974 issue of *Écran* remain relatively constant throughout the debate regarding what this type of cinema was to be called. In 1976, these parameters were further elaborated, resulting in the following definition:

We understand the term [*cinéma militant*] to refer to a cinema that generally presents the following three characteristics:

It is a cinema that, in capitalist, developed [the West] or exploited [Third World] countries, is primarily shot in the margins of the commercial system of production and distribution. This is not the result of a vain purism, but rather because everything has been done to make sure that it is confined to this purgatory. However, there can exist a *cinéma militant* in certain socialist or socialistic countries that have understood that this type of cinema maintains its utility in the context of a class struggle that, as the example of China demonstrates, continues after the revolution. It is precisely in this spirit that Vertov and Medvedkin worked in the young Soviet Union.

It is a cinema that, due to the order of things in a capitalist regime, is almost always produced with limited means: 16 mm, Super 8 or even video. This constraint weighs heavily on the fate of these militant films, which can rarely claim the technical sophistication of commercially made films. In France it's only the artful guile of the groups that ensures the successful completion of a film. Shorts and even features almost never make any profit.

It is a combative cinema that from the beginning and by definition puts itself in the service of the working class and other popular classes or categories by giving itself a function of counter-information, intervention or mobilisation. It is a cinema that struggles globally against capitalism and imperialism. There are many militant filmmakers who work voluntarily or who are satisfied with a symbolic payment, or at least one far inferior to that which they would be paid working on a union budget in a "big" production.

In broad strokes this is how, in our opinion, we define the cinema that we call militant.[9]

What this suggests is that relying on any single, discrete definition chosen from this period risks narrowing the corpus of militant cinema. However, Serceau and Hennebelle offer an inclusive yet specific description that will provide the working model for this study. In this book, the majority of the films placed under this rubric are extremely low-budget productions, created predominantly collectively and/or by filmmakers working outside the mainstream (meaning both mainstream industry as well as mainstream auteurist filmmaking) and which employ various strategies of contestation, particularly against the dominant systems of representation. Even more specifically, many of the films examined here issue from that sector of the militant cinematic tradition that was concerned predominantly with the factory and the political vicissitudes this domain experienced.

The choice to focus on the factory came in response to an increasingly derogatory narrativisation of the events of May. One of most striking elements of the films examined in this study is that they go against the idea of a purely student-led revolution, something implied by both the mainstream and the official left-wing press of the time. Instead, these films provide images of the concrete role that the working class (here composed primarily of factory workers) played during the events and the extent to which it was involved in the radical politics of the post-'68 political sphere. The reason for the astonishment at this working-class role is directly linked to the progressively impoverished accounts of the events. A wonderful, if anecdotal, expression of this narrative deterioration was relayed by Michel Andrieu, one of the founding members of the filmmaking collective Atelier de recherche cinématographique (ARC). After completing his film *Les Vacances de Clémence* (2008) (incidentally, about the wife of a factory worker in 1967), Andrieu was confronted by a journalist from the French Communist Party (Parti communiste français, or PCF) daily newspaper, *L'Humanité*:

> In 2008 I made a film at Saint-Nazaire and a young journalist from *L'Humanité* interviewed me. When the subject turned towards May, she began spouting off the well-worn rhetoric about May '68 being nothing more than a bunch of students and hippies having a party. I told her that I thought, given the fact that she was a journalist from *L'Humanité*, it was pretty ballsy to say such a thing. I was quite angry. It was a period of great reflection in which not the whole population, but at least a good section of the population, was taken by the "right to speak". It was entire factories, peasant groups, etc. So not only is it a ridiculous idea to tout, it is also fundamentally wrong.[10]

The trivialisation of the May narrative becomes particularly complicated when we look at the fact that the negative account stems from a number of differing historical viewpoints, some of which issue curiously enough from a position that would generally seem to be sympathetic to the events and their participants. One of the most extreme narratives traces the events' influence on former French president Nicolas Sarkozy, who is suggested to be the ultimate *soixante-huitard*.[11]

Another, more recent critical tendency comes from the children of those who participated in and were politically informed by the events. Virginie Linhart, the daughter of UJCML (Union des jeunesses communistes marxistes–léninistes) founder Robert Linhart, published a book entitled *Le Jour où mon père s'est tu* (The day my father stopped talking).[12] The book opens with an account of the author's experience of being raised in a far-left household, a place where the political trumped the familial, and the effect this had on her subsequent development as well as on the dissolution of her family. She then turns to a series of interviews/meetings with others from her generation, such as Samuel Castro (Roland Castro's son), Pierre Geismar and Ève Miller, the daughter of Jacques-Alain and Judith Miller. Each account characterises the culture and generation emerging from '68 as one made up of hedonistic, self-centred adults who were incapable of providing appropriately for their own children.[13]

The personal motivation behind Virginie Linhart's description is quite apparent, and yet it reflects a view that is at the heart of much of the re-evaluation. In 2008, the New York Public Library held a debate between Bernard-Henri Levy and Slavoj Žižek. Early in that debate, Levy brought up the subject of May '68 and went on to cite the Maoist slogan "Le moment est venu que la classe ouvrière prenne les drapeaux de la révolution des mains tremblantes des étudiants" (The time has come for the working class to wrest the revolutionary flag from the trembling hands of the students). He used it to suggest that Geismar and company had dominated the events.[14] Levy used the slogan to reinforce the imagined lack of participation of the working class in the near revolution, and the revolutionary cultural mutations that were occurring. This perception is one that emerges from a view that Paris and the students in the Latin Quarter were the principal actors in the events.

In a strange twist, a monumental work dedicated to the events, Hervé Hamon and Patrick Rotman's *Génération*, promoted this mythology.[15] While *Génération* is in many ways a reliable source regarding the history of the radical left that grew up around the events, it does have a limited scope, despite consisting of two massive tomes. The limitations are geographic and social, in that its account is almost entirely Paris-based and focuses on youth culture. The work has been addressed critically, most notably in Kristin Ross's *May '68 and Its Afterlives*.[16] However, what is perhaps more fascinating than turning to a textual response or debunking the myth through counterarguments is to look at the recorded documentation of both the events and the subsequent politicisation of the French working class. The films this study examines all feature (or were made by) union workers, independent workers, workers who had never been politically engaged to any extent, filmmakers, students and immigrant workers; perhaps most importantly, they are peopled with and created by women as much as with and by men. Even with the obvious caveat that these films were created through montage as the central concern of their project, their visual evidence alone bears witness to an empowered, radicalised working class, and thus flies in the face of any reactionary argument about the working class's marginality.

1.2 Interrogating the absence

At the height of its production, *cinéma militant* was confronted with a cliché that began to circulate among critics and seemed to point to one of the reasons for this tradition being left by the wayside in the history of French cinema: *cinéma militant, cinéma chiant* (militant film, boring/annoying film). Over the course of its expansion, *cinéma militant* had developed a reputation for being mere propaganda that had no real aesthetic merit or formal value. Later on in this study, in the chapter on Cinélutte, one of the filmmakers responds to this charge by asking, boring and annoying for whom? In other words, is this cinema boring for those who participated in it and created it and for whom it struggled? On the contrary, while it was a cinema rooted in the political language of its time, which may have had its limitations, we will see that it was nonetheless an extremely passionate cinema. It dreamed of changing the world with the assistance of a medium that its producers found exceptionally well suited to the task.

1.2.1 A hermetic subject
On the surface, *cinéma militant* might appear to be a too hermetically French subject, in turn posing the question of to what extent such a cinema could, or even should, interest those

outside of France (not to mention those outside the circle of left-wing interests). Despite the validity of such a question, the issue is not really one of why this cinema isn't very well known among the general film-going public. Rather, it is why the specialists, the film historians or even the historians of the French far left are not on more familiar terms with *cinéma militant*. The question becomes even more curious when we look at the massive amount of writing and attention that has been given to May '68 in English in terms of theory, politics, literature and mainstream film studies.

If we look to similar traditions in other regions (Latin America, for instance), the same sort of model of film (for example the work of Jorge Sanjines, Fernando Solanas and Patricio Guzman) is extremely well known and figures prominently in almost all histories of their respective national cinemas.[17] The hermetic argument is weak and even surprising, given the abundant, if at times suspicious, cultural exchange between the United States and France, particularly with regard to film culture.[18] However, there is another, very practical matter regarding *cinéma militant*'s reception in English-language film studies – the paucity of translated copies of the films. Clearly, the economic limitations of these films did not permit the kind of international distribution their producers may well have hoped for.

1.2.2 Propaganda

Cinéma militant filmmaking is popularly conflated with a cinema of propaganda. The PCF maintains an extensive archive of films made within its bounds.[19] However, this cinema and its films, generally speaking, respond to the dictates of the party, employ the aesthetic strategies of newsreels, and often circulate within the conditions favoured by the PCF. For example, although this has changed to some degree over the last decade, they were not frequently shown in film festivals, movie theatres or any of the other alternative spaces that the "nonpartisan" groups and filmmakers benefitted from. In fact, distribution was not as pressing a concern for the PCF as it was for those groups not attached to a political party.

At times, a crossover occurred between the groups examined here and those working within the framework of the PCF. This intermingling of the two tendencies would come prior to the far-left break with the PCF by the pro-Chinese Marxist–Leninists, and also at moments when the two tendencies would momentarily converge owing to cultural and political fluctuations in the continually shifting political field of 1970s France. We will see an example of this latter type of interaction when we look at the filmmakers of Cinélutte (self-described as Marxist–Leninist), who, working within the parameters of the IDHEC film school, momentarily aligned with others at IDHEC who were loyal members of the PCF. Similarly, as we will see in Chapter 3, a group emerged from the PCF, initially called Dynadia (later changing its name to Unicité), whose work came the closest to the non-Communist Party militant traditions.[20] But in general, the films, filmmakers, groups and theories examined here were, first, directly opposed to the PCF, citing them along with the CGT (the Confédération générale du travail trade union) as revisionist (as we'll see, this emerges as one of the predominant themes of the militant cinema examined in this study); and, second, as concerned with cinema as they were with politics.

1.2.3 Aesthetic quality

Against this backdrop, it is hard to conclude that the films are underrepresented as a result of their industrial, propagandistic approach to film, but a third possibility for their exclusion relates to the question of quality. This pointed issue was rigorously debated, and one of the questions that emerged within this framework concerned the longstanding issue of to what extent aesthetics were necessary to convey political ideas. For instance, in opposition to some vague notion about aesthetic acceptability for a certain class of viewer was the idea that it was perhaps just as important that the process of creating the film itself could serve as an object lesson precisely in the ideas the groups were attempting to transmit. Further, regarding the nascent work created during the events, the question of aesthetic quality, form and practice served as a critique of spontaneous production. While this issue of spontaneity (*spontanisme*) will return throughout this discussion, particularly in relation to the work of Jean-Pierre Thorn, it should for now be noted that the groups which approached this question sought to resolve the politics of practice, quality and form; these concerns were the driving force behind the collective Cinélutte.

1.3 Production eclipsed by theory

Of the many possible reasons for the seeming absence of *cinéma militant* within the historiography of French cinema, the eclipsing of production by the proliferation of theory is certainly one of the most interesting. What renders this aspect of the omission remarkable is that the theory that took precedence over production (and distribution) was itself an integral part of the far-left militant project as a whole. As we will see in looking at the literature (both Anglophone and Francophone) surrounding this period, much of the historicisation centred on the theoretical debates that dominated the period immediately preceding, and the decade following, the events. Jean-Pierre Oudart's "Cinema and suture" is one of the essays that most typifies this trend in film studies, in that it draws on Millerian interpretations of Jacques Lacan (Jacques-Alain Miller himself being a member of La gauche prolétarienne [GP] and its subsequent La cause du peuple) and an Althusserian approach to ideology. The text was published in France in 1969 and translated in 1978 into English in the periodical *Screen*.[21]

Along with the "suture" essay (and the many commentaries on it), the apparatus essays published in *Cinéthique* by writers affiliated with *Tel Quel*, and Jean-Louis Comolli's meditation on technology and ideology in *Cahiers du cinéma*, participated in this militant theoretical milieu.[22] These essays and this form of theorising were a shock to film theory. They were undone and left by the wayside only because of their seeming aporia and the introduction of cultural studies and its appropriation and development of the work of Lacan and Louis Althusser, as well as other trends (such as the groundswell of postmodern theorisation and cognitive trends in film theory). The double bind here is that while these theoretical methods began to wane, eventually becoming almost anathema,[23] their importance at the moment of their inception – and perhaps more important for this study, the moment of their translation – ensured that the field of French film studies and history was obscured insofar as political production was eclipsed by theory. One of the great overlooked ironies of this movement was that one of the principal and most faithful champions of this mode of theorising, the film journal *Cinéthique*, was a film production and distribution collective with a reasonably substantial body of work (see Chapter 5). At the same time, it was the mouthpiece for a theoretical tendency that suggested that the project of radical film production was always already bankrupt, given the tainted ideological perspective inherent in the cinematic apparatus.[24]

If, on the one hand, this focus on theory pointed to an indissoluble link between theory and practice, it also oriented the reception of this movement away from the productions themselves, and towards film's role in propagating Marxism–Leninism. While the efforts and effects of such an orientation were not without their merits (and indeed, they provided fodder for theoretical debates around politics and cinema that remain unresolved), they tended to obfuscate what was at the heart of the discussion: film. This loss of the principal object produced one of its most telling signs in the disappearance of images from *Cahiers du cinéma* during its Maoist period.[25]

When there is discussion of a politicised film production, it is in large part conducted in relation to film theory and criticism that was, during the period in question, particularly linked to *Cahiers du cinéma*, *Cinéthique*, *Positif* and the literary journal *Tel Quel*. Initially, the critics at *Cinéthique* and *Tel Quel* tended to look towards austere and difficult films like Jean-Pierre Lajournade's *Le Joueur de quilles* and Jean-Daniel Pollet's *Méditerrannée*[26] for instances of a materialist *cinéma militant*. Hennebelle described this tendency (pejoratively) as *telquelisme*,[27] which through the "desire to renew cinema and to make it an instrument of political combat produced a third form in post-'68 France: intellectual and aesthetic ultra-leftism".[28]

Hennebelle had a singular relationship with *cinéma militant*, his sensibilities being more in tune with the journal *Écran* than with *Cahiers du cinéma*, and certainly *Cinéthique*. Yet, in his associations with these groups, his outlook remained catholic in an effort not to alienate political groups working in the far-left milieu because of differing aesthetic sensibilities: his was an approach that sought to cast a net as wide as possible when considering *cinéma militant*. However, Hennebelle would occasionally enter into the critical debates surrounding the function of an effective political cinema in France, and in going after the avant-garde *Tel Quel*, he was effectively returning to a debate that had been initiated with Roland Barthes' *Writing Degree Zero* and Jean Paul Sartre's *What Is Literature?*

The question elaborated between Sartre's and Barthes' texts was that of the role of politically engaged or committed writing. For Sartre, writing honoured a commitment to the reader, and part of that commitment was one's responsibility to historically situate oneself as a writer in order to open up the possibility of one's freedom. It was largely a theory of commitment and literature that saw clear communication as the author's primary responsibility and emphasised the need for one to assume one's own historicity. A literature that did not communicate, that obfuscated its message with form, or that sought to write outside of its time, was ultimately a literature that refused to make a commitment.

While admittedly indebted to Sartre's concept of literature, Barthes responded to Sartre by pointing to what he saw as a lacuna in his text. Barthes, who was not a champion of the communicative model, saw the message as the aporia. Barthes, in a move would become common in structuralist and poststructuralist writing, pointed to a remainder in the text – something that existed beyond what was being communicated in content. To articulate this remainder, Barthes established working definitions for two elements in literature: language and style. Barthes posited that in the domain of language, the writer is fused to the socially fixed determinations of a given language and that in fact langauge "remains outside the ritual of letters"[29]: language is not "the place of a social engagement, but only a reflex without choice, the undivided property of man but not writers".[30] Style, on the other hand, comes from the experience the writer has as an individual, and Barthes was quick to propose that the historicity of the body of the writer had an influence on style: "Style is never anything more than a metaphor, that is, an equality between literary intention and the corporeal structure of the author."[31]

Neither idea (style or language) was sufficient to undertake an adequate elucidation of the Sartrean question of commitment in literature; in order to enter that realm, Barthes injected into the language/style dyad (the remainder) a third term, which was concerned with the *mode* of writing: *écriture*. *Écriture* was thus somewhat analogous to form, a subject that remained largely outside the argument Sartre had undertaken. (And, where it did appear, for Sartre it was historical "noise" that cluttered the author's message.) In this way, Barthes toppled the role of a committed writing that was diaphanously communicative by proposing the contrary. For Barthes, committed writing was decidedly anti-communicative. It was, he said, "the morality of form".[32]

This early work of Barthes established the groundwork for much of what would be accomplished at *Tel Quel* in its early incarnation. And it was within these bounds that emerged a period of film criticism and theory that rallied around the idea of *écriture* as political action. This meant that a challenge relating to form, and to "deconstruction", was being launched from within the far-left circle of critics, and it was upon this argument that Hennebelle pounced.

In a letter to *Cahiers du cinéma*, number 248, published under the title "Pratique artistique et lutte idéologique" (Artistic practice and ideological struggle), Hennebelle addressed the editors of the journal and elucidated, in often rabid terms, the ways in which he thought the journal was misguided regarding the issue of film production and its understanding of Marxism–Leninism.[33] While undoubtedly reading as a disapproving and at times condescending critique, the letter was not entirely divisive; on the contrary, it sought to locate the sites of intersection between his positions and those of the editors at *Cahiers*.[34] However, after opening with cordial gratitude for being invited to open up a dialogue in a time of "contempt", Hennebelle quickly announced that he was an adversary of the journal during its structuralist phase, during its revisionist phase, and during its so-called (*prétendument*) Maoist phase.[35]

Hennebelle further decides, before getting to the possibility of a working union, that it is necessary to enumerate the ways in which the journal has erred. He begins with a well-known debate that took place around the Jean-Marie Straub film *Othon* (1970) in which *Positif* attacked *Cahiers'* positive assessment of a film that the *Positif* critics believe typified *Cahiers*-style obscurantism. Disavowing any real aesthetic or intellectual alignment with *Positif*, Hennebelle opens his attack on *Cahiers* by stating that he believed that *Positif* had made the better argument, adding, "It is clear that the 'films' made according to your obscure conceptions during that period, apart from being generally stupid and boring [*nuls et ennuyeux*], in no way served the 'masses of workers and peasants' of France and Navarre."[36] Not only siding with *Positif*, Hennebelle went on to defend perhaps the most recognised nemesis during this period of the *Cahiers* critics: Jean-Patrick Lebel.[37] In this critique, Hennebelle distances himself and his sensibilities from Lebel in general but insists that Lebel got the upper hand in the argument. When finally addressing the issue of *telquelisme*, he describes it as another of the "errors" committed by *Cahiers*. For Hennebelle, *telquelisme* is similar to *Othon* as he characterised it: both prize hermeticism, obscurantism or obfuscation. But with regard to the relationship to militancy, he describes *Tel Quel*'s project as one that sees the work of revolutionaries as elaborating a Marxist–Leninist line "on the 'front' of the 'text' of language, of *écriture*".[38] For Hennebelle, such political practice would leave to the workers the "historic mission of struggling against the bourgeoisie in the factories and in the streets…"[39] For this reason, Hennebelle accuses the writers at *Tel Quel* of typifying "the fake artistic avant-garde and above all the fake political avant-garde".[40]

In terms of cinema, *Tel Quel* maintained the restrained canon described above. For a period, *Cinéthique* was in accord with the canon, as was *Cahiers*. The films they championed represented what they were calling a "materialist cinema", which sought in no unconditional terms to struggle against the "imperialist" impression of reality – what they referred to as the "original sin of the seventh art".[41]

1.4 Reception in English: Sylvia Harvey's May '68 and Film Culture

This focus on the theoretical implications of what was occurring in France after the events of May '68 is what was largely exported. In turn, it formed the Anglophone understanding of what the political cinematic topography looked like. Journals such as *Screen* gave voice to much of what was transpiring at the level of French theory following the events, while others, like *Cineaste*, *Jump Cut* and the Canadian *Ciné-tracts*, came the closest to dealing with the specificity of militant cinema in France. For instance, a *Ciné-tracts* article by Michael Ryan entitled "Militant documentary: *Mai '68 par lui-même*"[42] discusses some of the films produced during the May events, mentioning work created by ARC and Jean-Pierre Thorn (though never attributing the films to their producers), with a particular focus on Gudie Lawaetz's *Mai '68* (1974). This last film was created from images shot by ARC, Thorn, IDHEC students and others who filmed the events, and was largely dismissed by those who shot the footage as being legal plagiarism. As will be noted further on, many of these groups sold footage to television and other distribution platforms that could afford to purchase it in an effort to cover the costs of their projects. Ryan's text is something of an anomaly, as it is one of the few English texts to cite these works, although it does unfortunately return to a predominantly poststructuralist framework to discuss the work. Given the lack of access to the work and the filmmakers, the methods of production (which, as we will see, are at the core of the politics of much of this cinema) are not interrogated, and, again, theory dominates the discussion.

In 1978, a year prior to the publication of Ryan's *Ciné-tracts* article, Sylvia Harvey published one of the few books in English concerned specifically with the events of May/June 1968 in France and film. Harvey's book set out to consider the relationship between the events and "film culture" (as indicated in the title: *May '68 and Film Culture*). This focus meant that film production, while not without its place in the book, was treated according to the familiar theoretical logic and ceded its pages primarily to film criticism and theory and the debates that took place in film journals; the events captured on film and video received little attention. The orientation of the book is typified in a strange disclaimer in the introduction, in which Harvey announces that there is one aspect of particular importance she was unable to cover: developments in cinema semiotics.[43]

Despite its omissions, Harvey's research was historically in tune with the obsession already raging within the Anglophone world of the humanities. It lauded French formulations of the structuralist project, particularly reworkings and rereadings of Althusser's theory of ideology. Yet, while Harvey's book serves as a kind of perfect object lesson in how Anglophone film studies have understood the history of *cinéma militant*, or at least the issue of film and politics as affected by the events of May, it equally points to more global issues surrounding the reception, research and study of *cinéma militant*. First, as has been pointed out, the book reinforces the critical, textual side of the cinema emerging from '68: as the title states, it is concerned with film culture. Second, Harvey reiterates a historical trajectory that moves from the Langlois affair to Les états généraux. But of most interest for this study is another aspect of the (mis)conception of *cinéma militant* that becomes evident precisely at the moment when the book does address film production.

In a subsection of the chapter "The events of May and June 1968", entitled "The film groups and the film journals",[44] Harvey allows roughly three pages to account for the Groupe Dziga Vertov, Paul Seban, Chris Marker's SLON (Société pour le lancement des oeuvres nouvelles), the eventual Les groupes Medvedkine work and Dynadia. The majority of the references for these groups were culled from the usual sources, that is, *Cinéthique* and *Cahiers du cinéma*. But prior to closing the section on the film groups and turning her attention to the film journals, Harvey writes:

> One final group should be mentioned briefly, the *Cinéastes révolutionnaires prolé-
> tariens* (Revolutionary Proletarian Film-Makers). This group put forward the posi-
> tions and analyses of the Maoist left in France, and filmed the strikes and confrontations
> between workers and police at the Renault works at Flins; they also covered the trial of
> Alain Geismar. They speak of making films "under the direction of the workers" and
> were often forced to explore unusual venues for their screenings (in one case the street)
> because their films, often without visas from the censor and highly controversial because
> of the strong criticism of official trade unionism, could not be shown easily in public.[45]

The footnotes reveal that, apart from Seban (with whom *Cinéthique* had accorded a long interview that was included in a translation in Harvey's book), Harvey based her information about
these groups principally on a special issue of *Cinéma* in 1970 dedicated to film and politics.[46]
While the other groups appeared in numerous journals, primarily because of their affiliations
(PCF, Godard and Marker), Les cinéastes révolutionnaires prolétariens seemed to make their
principal appearance in this issue of *Cinéma*.

Les cinéastes révolutionnaires prolétariens appear to be a construct of Hennebelle and
Martin, who conducted the interview in *Cinéma*. Any reference to this group, even later references by Hennebelle himself, almost all inevitably return to this interview. They almost always
suggest something like "this group needs to be further explored" or state how little is known
of this group. The group was known principally for making a film about the Renault automobile factory at Flins, most commonly referred to as *Flins 68–69*.[47] But this film was actually a
re-edited version of Jean-Pierre Thorn's *Oser lutter, oser vaincre* (1968). The group is also cited in
the *Cinéma* interview as having made the film *La Palestine vaincra*. If we follow the unfolding
references to, for instance, *La Palestine vaincra*, a strange yet uncorrected metamorphosis takes
place. After the film is mentioned in *Cinéma*, Hennebelle's 1975 *Guide des films anti-impérialistes* cites it as being "produced by" Les cinéastes révolutionnaires prolétariens (CRP) but
directed by Jean-Pierre Olivier. A year after the publication of *Guide des films anti-impérialistes*,
Hennebelle co-edited the collection of texts *La Palestine et cinéma*. Here, *La Palestine vaincra*
again figures as a reference but no longer bears any trace of CRP, now being solely attributed to
Jean-Pierre Olivier de Sardan, who contributes a five-page text on the experience of making the
film (considered to be the first film in France to address the question of Palestine).[48]

In de Sardan's text, he describes the process of making the film, but never makes reference
to coordination or cooperation with Les cinéastes révolutionnaires prolétariens. Further, in an
interview with de Sardan in 2012, he claimed total responsibility not only for *La Palestine
vaincra* but also for the film *Flins 68–69*.[49] While Sardan was a member of the GP (for which
the CRP was supposedly the filmmaking wing), he stressed that he was not present at the
interview with Hennebelle and Martin for *Cinéma* and that, to his knowledge, a group known
as the CRP never existed.[50]

The emphasis placed here on this group is not an effort to verify the reality of its existence,
or to critique Harvey's citation of the group without establishing its legitimacy. Rather, the
important point for this study is that this case quite succinctly summarises the historiographical
situation of *cinéma militant*. That is, the paucity of historical documentation often led to the

repetition of certain narratives, which frequently were rife with discrepancies. On a perhaps different note, it also points to the immense influence of Hennebelle as *the* contemporaneous historian of *cinéma militant*.

Figuring in the appendix of Harvey's book is one of the few well-known debates surrounding militant production. Two films – Marin Karmitz's *Coup pour coup* (1972) and Groupe Dziga Vertov's *Tout va bien* (1972)[51] – were pitted against each other in an effort to call attention to two parallel tendencies in militant film production. The choice of these two films, however, was not as innocuous as it might have seemed; rather, there were other historical reasons for choosing these two films. One of the reasons, according to Antoine de Baecque, was that since the May events, Godard had been distancing himself from the *Cahiers* group (in large part because ownership of the journal was constantly changing, and he had a particular dislike of one Daniel Filipacchi).[52] At the same time, Godard was making common cause with the critics at the explicitly Marxist–Leninist *Cinéthique*.[53] The forceful defence of Godard's film by the writers at *Cahiers du cinéma* was an attempt to re-establish an alliance with the filmmaker.[54] Yet apart from this internal (if influential) aspect of the debate, the two films did serve to articulate, in a general way, the problems that militant film theory and criticism had been debating regarding film form in militant cinema.

Coup pour coup was the seventh and last film by Marin Karmitz as director. The project began as a collective effort, and Karmitz and his collaborators were largely sympathetic to, if not members of, the GP. Generally, *Coup pour coup* is about a strike at a textile factory and the sequestration of the factory management. The film was based on research at various strikes that the collective had participated in. There are very few professional actors in the film, and where they do figure, they play roles such as union delegates and shop steward. The result is that, in general, real factory workers populate the film.

Apart from this use of non-professionals in the film, another innovative aspect of this project is that Karmitz used video in both preproduction and production. Video was first used in the scouting and research for the film, as Karmitz would go to various strikes, participate in the demonstrations, interview the strikers, and so on. Video was also used for rehearsal, working on the script, auditions, and pre-shooting difficult shots; for example, the opening tracking shot was first worked out on video. Most interestingly, video was used as a tool of auto-critique. Scenes would be shot and taped at the same time, and then the tape would be shown to the actors, who were asked whether they felt they had been adequately represented. At the end of the day, the cast and crew would gather to look at the video of the day's shoot and debate the ways in which it could be improved. While this use of video constituted one of the inventive aspects of *Coup pour coup*, it was precisely this meticulous attention to detail – the attempt to work a perfected representation into narrative film – that the writers at *Cahiers du cinéma* launched their critique against. Such specific uses of video constituted a method that attempted to perfect the film's verisimilar aesthetic, they wrote; that is, they were an effort at perfecting naturalism.

What is notable about the debate surrounding these two films is not that it juxtaposed two exceedingly different films to interrogate political differences; instead, it addressed two films that maintained reasonably similar political positions. Both films claimed a Maoist theoretical heritage, both were collectively made, both were about a strike, and, further, both were about sequestration. But *Tout va bien* had mobilised Brechtian aesthetic strategies in a way that could find favour only with the writers at *Cahiers du cinéma*. The *Cahiers* writers' critique of *Coup pour coup*, meanwhile, was certainly not opposed to the analysis of writers over at *Cinéthique*. In her book, Harvey also includes a brief but telling "exchange" between two critics. Gérard Leblanc from *Cinéthique* had been invited by Hennebelle to contribute his assessment of *Coup pour coup* in the pages of *Écran*.[55] While Hennebelle opens his contribution with "I consider Marin Karmitz to be one of today's most important French filmmakers"[56], Leblanc ends his article with "Karmitz uncritically recreates a bourgeois film practice".[57]

In their critique, *Cahiers du cinema* suggested that an effective militant cinema had to employ aesthetic strategies that would seek to understand reality as a nexus of interwoven social, historical and ideological processes. It should further reveal these processes through its practice; that is, it should render the invisible visible. *Coup pour coup*'s direct documentary approach, with its empiricist assumptions, might claim to offer an unmediated window onto reality. However, because of its primarily descriptive method it was perhaps unable to account for the myriad economic, social, historical, ideological and aesthetic complications that were not immediately visible in the profilmic material. In this sense, the critics at *Cahiers* were demanding the use of what Eugene Lunn saw as the first unifying aspect of modernism: aesthetic self-consciousness or self-reflexivity.[58] Instead of providing a transparent reflection or representation of outer reality, a film should call attention to the media and materials with which it is working, or the process of creation in its own craft. The verisimilar or naturalist style of *Coup pour coup* relied on customary modes of perception, and in order to challenge these habits of understanding, it was thought, a new method of production and reception had to be created and mobilised.

The writers at *Cahiers du cinéma* also raised an issue that would become a cornerstone debate of the militant cinematic tradition: the so-called democratic issue of letting the workers speak for themselves. Godard was concerned with this, suggesting that although it was true that the French working class had been denied a voice, the real problem was that the communicative apparatus had been in the hands of the oppressors for too long. Godard believed that if the working class took hold of the means of communication, they might simply replicate the master's discourse: Godard wanted to let the workers speak and then to transmit their speech for them.

1.5 History in France

The French literature on *cinéma militant* is composed in large part of articles and short texts in collections that were produced at the same time as the films themselves. No book-length study had been written about the subject until very recently, and the texts that did appear were generated primarily by those participating in the militant project in general (filmmakers, critics, academics, and so on). As shown above, these texts appeared in popular film journals like *Cahiers du cinéma*, *Positif* and *Écran*, and in more specialist, political film journals such as *CinémAction*, *Cinéthique*, *Cinéma politique* and *Impact*. Among the publications of a more general popular press, *Le Monde diplomatique* ran a column on what it called "cinéma parallèle".

General histories of French cinema have predominantly glossed over this period, equating political cinema in post-'68 France with the *série-Z*, or occasionally citing the work that Chris Marker did with SLON or Godard's work with the Groupe Dziga Vertov. To some degree, this remained the case with the literature that set out to specifically address political filmmaking. One important exception to this rule was Christian Zimmer's *Cinéma et politique*, published in 1974. Zimmer's book is a dense and sweeping analysis of trends in explicitly political filmmaking that gave plenty of space to the cinema emerging out of 1968. *Cinéma et politique* upheld a tradition that stemmed from *Cahiers du cinéma*'s tendency to look to Hollywood filmmaking in order to detect the ways in which a politics that countered its own fidelity to hegemonic ideological structures could be located in popular forms. But Zimmer's work went beyond this approach and looked at minor, specifically political cinemas in the United States and Canada, as well as engaging with southern hemisphere cinemas and European political cinemas. French *cinéma militant* was of interest to Zimmer. However, the moment he discusses the subject, the work falters, presenting a series of wrongful attributions, mistaken names and historical inaccuracies regarding the groups, filmmakers and films in question.[59] When and where Zimmer is on sure footing regarding this period, he retells familiar stories about debates surrounding the quest for a materialist cinema or the analysis of *Coup pour coup*.[60]

In 1979, another work appeared, with the promising title *De mai 68 ... aux films x*.[61] The author, Philippe Maarek, examined the decade following May '68 in order to create a cinematic balance sheet. The first section of Maarek's book, entitled "Rupture et cinéma marginal", consists of

Figure 1.2 *Cinéma et politique*

two chapters, the first being "Le cinéma 'Parallèle' ou 'D'avant-garde'" and the second "Le cinéma 'perpendiculaire' ou 'militant'". Finally, it seemed that someone had taken up the task of including this tradition in the canon of French political cinema. In fact, this chapter concisely charts the degeneration of the tradition. Unfortunately, Maarek abandoned this work quickly and turned his attention to the issue of politics in commercial, independent and even pornographic cinema. The book, composed of two parts, gave avant-garde political cinemas 30 (highly illustrated) pages and then devoted about one hundred pages to the other tendencies.

The above discussion of the prevalence of the practice of seeking out politics in an arena where it is perhaps less obvious (that is, mainstream national cinemas) is not meant to detract from the importance of such an enterprise. However, it is meant to illustrate the ways in which even those texts specifically dealing with politics and cinema in a primarily French context have overlooked the practice of *cinéma militant*. The two works cited above, while not perfect, at least made the gesture of inserting a fragment of this practice into film history.

Another work that is perplexing in its treatment of the period is Antoine de Baecque's two-volume *Les Cahiers du cinéma: histoire d'une revue*.[62] De Baecque's work would seem the ideal place to find the history of this moment. Indeed, the second volume of this work does trace the history of the journal and its involvement in the debates cited above. In roughly one chapter, de Baecque outlines, in very broad strokes, the various inner workings of the debates that appeared across the pages of *Cinéthique, Tel Quel* and *Cahiers*, as well as the critical response of Lebel and *Positif* and other, less well-known counterarguments. There are several pages on Les états généraux and the extent to which *Cahiers* was involved. There is an equally interesting analysis of the effect of the political sea changes at *Cahiers* on the readership, describing the decline in subscription rates and quoting outraged letters from disillusioned readers.[63] But it is just as obvious that de Baecque's preference was for the history that preceded and followed the militant period. This preference is again made clear by the page count: the beginning yellow period (referred to the period from 1951 to 1964 when the cover of the magazine was yellow) up to the release of *Les 400 coups* in 1959 (8 years) is treated in an entire volume, whereas 1959 to 1981 (22 years) is also covered in only one volume, with the militant period receiving just over one chapter.

Since the early 2000s, a number of works have appeared in French that specifically deal with the various militant production collectives. Some of the first texts to emerge during this period focused on the workers' collective Les groupes Medvedkine. With the publication of *Le cinéma militant reprend le travail*,[64] as well as Colin Foltz's master's thesis on Les groupes Medvedkine,[65] a new interest in the militant tradition flourished. Subsequently there emerged a few new texts in France, along with a series of DVDs dedicated to movements, groups and single-author works.[66] The most global account that came out of this new interest is Sébastien Layerle's book on the cinema of May '68. While the book does cover some of the cinematic after-effects of the events, it is generally in dialogue with the films produced during the events. One problem with documenting this tradition is precisely the lack of historical record, and in particular the historical record created outside of those participating in the events. This meant that the historiography emerged primarily from those creating the history.

Despite divergences in political affiliations, aesthetic choices or exigencies, generally speaking, one almost always has to depend on those documents that come from the milieu. While clearly this is often the case (and can even be said to be the flaw of all histories), it is worth pointing to the number of consistently repeated fallacies that were instilled in the history because of the fragility of the sources. At any moment, one feels that any fact about the diachronic unfolding of this narrative could be challenged, and further, that mutations are still occurring. And there is some reason to believe this to be especially the case with this history, which is at once an "oral history" and a textual history based on these oral histories.

Certainly, while the dominant retracing of political values of, and reflections on, the events of May '68 can be found in both popular and academic histories, some have suggested that the discourse surrounding '68 has grown increasingly critical, while others have stated that the events need be understood in fresh terms. There is not much contradiction in the history about the facts (apart from one important debate that figures largely in this book – namely, the role and place of the workers versus that of students in the events). Rather, the discrepancies, deviations and departures are largely matters of interpretation.

This is not entirely the case with the history of *cinéma militant*. Because of the number of missing films, the many versions and names of films (Thorn's *Oser lutter, oser vaincre* being the epitome of such work) and, above all, the seemingly hermetic networks in which these films were not only produced but distributed, historical accuracy is compromised from the outset. This tendency is exemplified in *Cinéma et politique: actes des Journées du cinéma militant de la Maison de la Culture de Rennes, 1977–78–79*,[67] which documents a series of conferences on militant cinema held in Rennes in the late 1970s, similar to the conference held in 1974 in Montreal, "Rencontres internationales pour un Nouveau Cinéma".[68]

In *Le cinéma militant reprend le travail* (*CinémAction, 110*),[69] a collective work involving participants in the militant tradition as well as a new generation of scholars, French *cinéma militant* is examined in its past and present manifestations. Among the contributions there is Sébastien Layerle on ARC and its relationship to Les états généraux and Cinélutte; Guy Gauthier on the participatory nature of video and film collectives, focusing on Les groupes Medvedkine and SLON/ISKRA (Image, son, kinescope et réalisations audiovisuelles); and Gérard Leblanc on aesthetics and militant cinema.

Again, Hennebelle is behind many of these texts on *cinéma militant*, and while his contribution to the writing on *cinéma militant* was unparalleled in terms of sheer volume, it would be wrong to approach his work as that of an historian proper. Rather, he was first and foremost a critic, as well as a chronicler: in Serge Daney's term, Hennebelle was a *passeur*.[70] Although Hennebelle kept his distance from the theoretical empire of the largely post-

Figure 1.3 *Cinéma et politique*

structuralist debates, he did, on a number of occasions, take the debates and their critics to task, never formally aligning himself with a particular position. Further, Hennebelle was by no means concerned only with French political cinemas. His *Guide des films anti-impérialistes* and *Quinze ans de cinéma mondial, 1960–1975* (later reprinted as *Les cinémas nationaux contre Hollywood*) are encyclopedic and engage the militant tradition in world cinema. The former was, as the title suggested, a guide or directory, but the second bore the authorial stamp of Hennebelle and his own theoretical, aesthetic and political approach to the subject. Primary in much of Hennebelle's work was a total antipathy to Hollywood filmmaking. Indeed, he was an early critic of the celebration of the work of the French New Wave filmmakers, as well as of the *Cahiers* critics' laudatory work on American cinema. To mark this suspicion, Hennebelle dedicated a chapter in *Les cinémas nationaux contre Hollywood* solely to the work of Godard, in which he gives a highly ambivalent if at times enthusiastic, assessment of Godard's work.[71] On the one hand, Hennebelle wanted to do away with such work, but on the other, he expressed hesitation about this near-wholesale rejection of the militant avant-garde and the political modernist tendency. There is a suggestion that Hennebelle suspects there is something in Godard's work worth saving that escapes its formal obscurity.

Hennebelle had expressed his misgivings about this political modernism in his responses to *Tel Quel* and the *Othon* debate: he had little tolerance for the austere and obfuscatory political aesthetic of the work championed by *Cinéthique* or *Tel Quel*, or, again, much of what *Cahiers* feted. The work that Hennebelle championed instead came from filmmakers like René Vautier,

Joris Ivens and Marin Karmitz. However, most vital in Hennebelle's work was the engagement with even those tendencies that he would himself personally dismiss. This engagement was described above in relation to the debate between Hennebelle and Gérard LeBlanc around *Coup pour coup*, but when we begin to look at his work in *Écran*, *CinémAction* and his various published collections, we find that this tendency was pervasive.

Perhaps the first real articulation of Hennebelle's activity vis-à-vis specifically French *cinéma militant* of any magnitude was *Cinéma d'aujourd'hui*'s 1976 *Cinéma militant: histoire, structures, méthodes, idéologie et ésthetique*.[72] Not only was this Hennebelle's first in-depth engagement with the phenomena, but it was also the first lengthy engagement with French *cinéma militant* in general. The book is a collection of interviews, debates, distribution catalogues and texts that attempts to systematise the aesthetic tendencies of this tradition. One outcome of this book is that, in organising the texts around contemporary militant cinema, it simultaneously created the conditions for developing a "prehistory" of French *cinéma militant*. This, in turn, allowed for the development of a rich, if loose, French militant cinema canon.

1.5.1 The prehistory as institutional minor canon

From the birth of cinema to the end of World War II, the examples of a French cinema or filmmaking practice resembling the post-'68 *cinéma militant* are few and far between. While it might not be an

Figure 1.4 *Guide des films anti-impérialistes*

Figure 1.5 *Cinéma militant: histoire, structures, méthodes, idéologie et ésthetique*

exaggeration to cite the first political, even militant, film made as *La sortie de l'usine lumière à Lyon* (because of its focus on the factory and the working class, and its early realist framing of daily life), the film nonetheless falls short in its intention, and certainly in its mode of production. To locate the primal scene of French militant cinema, the criteria must at least encompass an *express* aspiration to militancy, and ideally also the organisation of a mode of production that is itself political. Perhaps the first real iteration of this tendency was found in a group written about by George Sadoul:[73] the 1913 anarchist film collective Le cinéma du peuple, which produced the films *La Commune* (1913) and *Le vieux docker* (1914).[74] It was not only the politically engaged aspect of the films this group made that gave them their status as the progenitors of a certain tendency in French militant filmmaking, but the fact that the political content was linked to a politicised mode of film production: the collective.

Two decades after the disappearance of Le cinéma du peuple, a collective emerged from the film production service of the SFIO (Section française de l'internationale ouvrière).[75] With Marceau Pivert and Germain Dulac, the SFIO film service made *Mur des fédérés* (1935), an early engaged documentary on a demonstration commemorating the fallen Communards.[76] This collective was a nascent incarnation of what is perhaps best-known example of an early precursor to *cinéma militant* – the interwar Front Populaire sympathisers. A collective under the name Ciné liberté was formed and produced *La vie est à nous* (1936), perhaps the most emblematic film emerging from this movement, directed by Jean Renoir.[77] The CGT also hired Renoir to direct *La Marseillaise* (1938), which while being an historical film about the French Revolution, functioned again as propaganda for the *Front Populaire*.[78]

With the onset of World War II, filmmaking in occupied France was limited almost solely to popular fare, with the occasional allegorical subversion. However, Guy Hennebelle identified two productions that could be considered to form part of a prehistory of *cinéma militant*.[79] The first example is Robert Godin and Albert Mahuzier's clandestinely shot *La caméra sous la botte* (1944), which showed daily life in occupied Paris.[80] The second is *Oflag XVII A* (1945). Hennebelle cites an article from *Écran*, number 29, by Paul Léglise:

> Situated between Linz and Vienna, the officers' prison camp Oflag XVII is famous for the 32 underground tunnels that were dug there between 1940 and 1945. Today we know something about everyday life in that camp thanks to a film made clandestinely by prisoners. Fourteen reels of 8 mm film were shot showing the work of digging as well as daily life in the camp. The camera was hidden in a fake dictionary that camouflaged an empty box with a retractable window for the lens and viewfinder. The name of the film is *Oflag XVII A*.[81]

While the occupation's paucity of militant production is predictable, the immediate postwar French cinema likewise has never been considered a hotbed of political filmmaking. It was precisely this period that gave rise to the famous formula about French film by François Truffaut and the critics at *Cahiers du cinéma*: *cinéma de papa*. Yet while the future New Wave filmmakers were eschewing the contemporary "quality" French film and fawning over American studio productions and Italian neorealism, the early 1950s saw the production of at least three films that epitomised a trajectory that was at once political and avant-garde: René Vautier's *Afrique 50* (1950), the Lettrist Isidore Isou's *Traité de bave et d'éternité* (1951) and Paul Carpita's *Le rendez-vous des quais* (1955).

Afrique 50, a film shot more or less clandestinely, was banned in France until 1996.[82] René Vautier had been a member of the Resistance and had just finished studying at IDHEC in 1949 when he was approached by La ligue d'enseignement to shoot a film on education in the French colonies.[83] The film was aimed at secondary school students (*lycéens*) in France and was intended to show how villagers in the AOF (Afrique Occidentale Française) lived and learned. And this is precisely how the film begins: Vautier opens his film as a slice of life in an Ivory Coast village, but he then takes a sharp turn provoked by his discovery that Africans were being used to operate a dam because their labour power cost less than electricity. The film thus becomes a document of the wreckage of colonialism. Vautier escaped the government officials who were accompanying him and began to shoot clandestinely and on the run across West Africa. When Vautier returned to France, he took the negatives and dropped them off at the Ligue d'enseignement, where the police immediately confiscated them. In 1951, Vautier was arrested and sentenced to one year in prison in Haute Volta (today Burkina Faso) for making his film.

Vautier continued to make films, and after *Afrique 50* is probably best known for his film *Avoir vingt ans dans les Aurès* (1972), based on the testimonies of Bretons who fought in Algeria. In 1971, along with Nicole and Felix Le Garrec, Vautier created L'Unité de production cinéma Bretagne (UPCB), whose goal was the creation of a committed regional cinema.[84] Although this production company would not commit itself to a particular party line, Vautier would always maintain his allegiance to the PCF and its capacity as a revolutionary party and a progressive political force in France.[85]

A year after Vautier's nascent militant and formal experimentation, the Romanian-born Lettrist Isidore Isou made his *discrépant* film *Traité de bave et d'éternité* (1951) (*discrépant* films used a methodological approach that sought to create disharmony between the image and the sound). The Lettrist movement held the germ, along with CoBrA,[86] of what would become the Lettrist International and eventually the Situationist International. Isou's *Traité* is a hybrid of contemporary films' international avant-garde tendencies and forms a tangential lineage with Dziga Vertov's *Man with a Movie Camera* (1929) and Walter Ruttmann's *Berlin: Symphony of a Metropolis* (1927). The film employs avant-garde formal strategies – using inserts of black leader, scratched and marked-up film stock, inverted images and, throughout much of the film, a pulsating, tribal, Lettrist poetic score that accompanies Isou's critically political and cultural diatribe.

Fellow Lettrist and future Situationist Guy Debord's cinematic output also began in the 1950s and was directly inspired by Isou's *Traité*. In 1952, Debord gave new meaning to "black and white" with his *Hurlements en faveur de Sade*, a one-hour film composed of black-and-white leader and occasional voiceover. The *hurlements*, or howlings, of the title did not refer to sounds coming from the diegesis, but rather to sounds that might be produced by the spectators of this film after sitting in front of an imageless movie for a few frames too long. In 1959, Debord made *Sur le passage de quelques personnes à travers une assez courte unité de temps*, and in 1961, *Critique de la séparation*. These films were followed by a period throughout the 1960s in which Debord's creative and theoretical preoccupations migrated to other media.

Debord and another Situationist, René Viénet, returned to film as the first generation of Situationists waned. In 1973, Debord adapted his monumentally influential book *Society of the Spectacle* into a film. Subsequently, he made *Réfutation de tous les jugements, tant élogieux qu'hostiles, qui ont été jusqu'ici portés sur le film "La société du spectacle"* (1975) and *In girum imus nocte et consumimur igni* (1978). Meanwhile, Viénet used the Situationist concept of *détournement* and produced three entirely "détourned" films,[87] the best-known being *La dialectique peut-elle casser des briques?* (1973), a black-and-white martial arts film dubbed with pro-Situationist dialogue. With the secession of Debord from the Lettrists to the Lettrist International (and eventually Situationists), Isou and Maurice Lemaître would carry on the Lettrist tradition, in both film and text.

With a critique of French colonialism serving as the subject of Vautier's project and a burgeoning critique of everyday life as that of Isou's film, prior to the events of 1968, the other major political backdrop that shaped cultural production in France was the war in Indochina, and only shortly after that the Algerian War. The Marseille-born resistant Paul Carpita, who had been working since the mid-1940s with an incipient counter-information group called Cinépax, began work in 1950 on his best-known film, *Le rendez-vous des quais* (1955). The film tells the story of a young dockworker in Marseille who refuses to join a union and ends up being exploited, all against the backdrop of France's military operations in Indochina. What gives *Le rendez-vous des quais* its cinematic and political power is, on the one hand, its narrative concern with the organised working class, but also, on the other, its aleatory and direct shooting style (the film appropriated documentary at the level of both aesthetic approach and film form). Carpita worked on the film until 1953, and shortly after its premier in 1955 the film was banned. *Le rendez-vous* was considered lost for 35 years, until it resurfaced in 1990. While Carpita would appear to be a significant precursor to the post-'68 filmmakers with their militant preoccupations, he is rarely cited as an influence, in large part due to the difficulty of seeing the film following its suppression. His importance is only today being assessed, after his death in 2009.[88]

Although by no means defining films by way of an expansive influence over the age to come, the work created in the early 1950s by Vautier, the Lettrists and Paul Carpita serves as a kind of filmic salvo for the following 20 years of filmmaking in the margins (many militant filmmakers came to these films – with the exception of Vautier's work – only after having already undertaken their own militant projects). Each film is in some way rooted in a particular strategy, for example Vautier's Eisensteinian approach to montage, the use of *détournement* by Isou, and the verisimilar-realism of Carpita. These strategies were to be built upon in the decades to follow.

Two other substantive projects from the early 1960s form part of a possible prehistory of *cinéma militant*: *Octobre à Paris* (1962) and *J'ai huit ans* (1961). In 1962, Jacques Panijel, a biochemist working at the CNRS (Centre national de la recherche scientifique), directed the documentary film project *Octobre à Paris*. *Octobre* recounts the massacre of peaceful Front de libération nationale (FLN) demonstrators by the French police in Paris on 17 October 1961. Although the French government quickly banned the film, it was Panijel himself who kept the film from being distributed or projected, even after the ban had been lifted. Sébastian Layerle noted that Panijel made this decision because the events of 17 October had never been recognised as a state crime.[89]

J'ai huit ans is an eight-minute collective production created by René Vautier, Yann Le Masson and Olga Poliakoff, with assistance from Franz Fanon. The film is a montage of drawings by Algerian orphans living in a Tunisian refugee camp, with a voiceover by these same children. The film was not distributed through standard channels but rather benefitted from an underground militant circuit. The film's production was accompanied by the nascent militant tract *Manifeste pour un cinéma parallèl* (Manifesto for a parallel cinema),[90] which enumerated many of the concerns and strategies for the political avant-garde cinema to come. In particular, it pointed to possible alternative distribution channels, such as community centres, factories and film clubs – organisations that could project whatever films they chose to, given that they were private enterprises. This focus on new modes of distribution, from which Panijel's film had also benefitted, was to be immensely important to the underground filmmakers of the coming decade, both in France and throughout the international underground, or parallel, film movement.

Although this brief periodisation leaves us in the early 1960s, what was to follow was a rapid development of the militant project proper.

1.6 The cinema of May 1968

In 2004, *CinémAction* published its 110th issue, entitled *Le cinéma militant reprend le travail* (Militant filmmaking gets back to work). Guy Hennebelle contributed an introductory essay to the issue, published shortly after his death, whose title made the suggestion, "Si ce n'est plus l'heure des brasiers, c'est peut être celle de la reprise" (If it is no longer the hour of the furnaces, perhaps it is that of the reprise). *CinémAction*'s inaugural issue, published in 1978 as a special edition of the film journal *Écran*, was itself about militant cinema and already offered a kind of balance sheet and interrogation along the lines of "Where are we now? What is to be done?" So in

Figure 1.6 "Beneath the sidewalk, the strike..."

2004, while reminding its reading public of the rich history of militant filmmaking in France, *CinémAction* was equally reminding its readers of how contentious such a project was.

Hennebelle's suggestion that it was no longer the "hour of the furnaces" meant, of course, that revolutionary fervor (and even a particular style of militant filmmaking) had ebbed and that the time of Getino and Solanas' Third Cinema had reached its end. But perhaps the time of the "reprise" (an explicit reference to Hervé Le Roux's 1996 documentary of the same name) meant that nearly 40 years after the events of May '68, militant cinema had still not found its resolution, and, in fact, had continued its history of being an aporetic project contested ever since its most nascent state. Le Roux's *Reprise* (1996, 192 min.) was a retrospective search through the militantism of the '68 generation, taking as its conceit the image of a young female factory worker who had been caught on film for ten minutes refusing, in the most explicit terms, to return to work after the strikes of May 1968. The ten-minute film *La reprise du travail aux usines Wonder* (The return to work at the Wonder factory) was shot under the direction of IDHEC students Jacques Willemont and Pierre Bonneau as a documentary about the students and workers of the OCI (L'Organisation communiste internationale).[91]

In 1997, Gilles Dauvé (a.k.a. Jean Barrot) opened his essay "Out of the future", which would serve to introduce a revised edition of his *Eclipse and re-emergence of the communist movement* (co-authored with François Martin) with "One of the best films about class conflict is a 10 minute sharp and biting shot, taken on June 10, 1968, outside the gates of the Wonder factory – a battery-maker – on the outskirts of Paris."[92] And French New Wave icon Jacques Rivette also referred to the film as the most interesting filmic document to emerge from the events. *La reprise du travail aux usines Wonder* was never intended to be a standalone film, but rather to be part of a longer student production made within the framework of reportages at IDHEC. However, all that remains of that project is the sequence originally titled quite simply "Wonder, mai 1968". This sequence shows the circumstances surrounding the end of a strike and workers were being ushered back into the factory – not only by the factory management, but, more dramatically, by union leaders from the CGT. The sequence takes form as it focuses on a young woman who refuses to return to work and a young student who intervenes and defends the woman and her refusal.

Le Roux said in an interview that he didn't consider *La reprise* to be *cinéma militant*.[93] Also, in a recent interview, Jean-Louis Comolli, one of the politically engaged writers of the '68 period *Cahiers du cinéma*, reflected on this period and its films. He remarked about these films that in watching them again (singling out *Oser lutter, oser vaincre*), he had to conclude that they were simply bad films.[94] Yet Comolli had, on the other hand, sung the praises of a film by Cinélutte, a film by Les groupes Medvedkine, and *La reprise du travail aux usines Wonder*.[95] One thing we can say about an approach that announces "Those films are bad ... but"[96] is that it returns to the obsession with auteurs. This obsession was seen in the nascent enunciation of the *Cahiers du cinéma* group (in their admittedly conservative beginnings), continued up through the article "Cinéma/idéologie/critique", and was reinforced in the famous editorial of May 1974 that sought to break with political militancy and return to cinephilia.[97] Nearly each of these invocations of good and bad beat a path backwards from what was an otherwise revolutionary project. If Marxism in the West, as described by Perry Anderson,[98] was principally an aesthetic project, then the critics at *Cahiers*, *Tel Quel* and *Cinéthique* were balking in the middle of their own Marxian aesthetic clarion call. It could be considered that in crying "poor quality", and in neglecting much of the militant cinema produced during this critical period, these critics were historically on the wrong side of their own argument. While they could lambaste the PCF for being revisionist and the GP for being *Spontex*(a cynical chide that invoked a French sponge manufacturer.[99]), the critics themselves needed to respond to their own "inner bourgeois" – that beast that could not let quality be wrested from its canon.

Figures 1.7–1.9 *La reprise du travail aux usines Wonder*

Further, this ambivalent response suggests a desire to separate politics from aesthetics. This is a view that sees in every meeting of the two a tiresome tract, which, should it move beyond the didactic, is inevitably bereft of politics. All of this casts a slight shadow of suspicion on the celebration of *La reprise du travail aux usines Wonder*. While the film certainly offers a quasi-empirical view of an aspect of the events, it is a film out of context, that is, the documentary that was left undone. If, on the one hand, the film denounces the flaccid yet bullying policies of the CGT, it also tells the story of an isolated single worker's challenge rather than that of the collective. Equally, the workers dismiss the young male student when he admits that he doesn't work at Wonder. But if we remember the initial impetus for this project, the goal was to demonstrate unity between students and workers. So with *La reprise*, what we are ultimately left with is a man and a woman on the cusp of their prelapsarian drift into the so-called post-'68 miasma.

While the film is invigorating to watch, with its portrayal of one woman screaming in the face of an unjust capitalist compromise, it is ultimately a document of failure – one that supports the ever-growing discourse around the failure of the events of May '68. What is absent, and what the film requires to retake its position as a politically militant film, is the historical context; that is, in more filmic terms, it needs a reverse shot. And yet such a context did exist. The fact that Willemont was working on this film within the framework of an IDHEC project was by no means an unusual or happenstance detail. IDHEC, occupied during the strikes, had made common cause with Les états généraux du cinéma as well as a number of militant filmmakers and collectives.

Figure 1.10 *Le Cinéma s'insurge* (publication of Les états généraux du cinéma français), issue 1

Les états généraux du cinéma français, while not explicitly a filmmaking collective, did associate itself with filmmakers and collectives producing work during the events. One of these projects was the series of anonymous films called *Cinétracts*: short, silent montage films composed primarily of still imagery. *Cinétracts* were projected in alternative spaces and expressed the immediate historical character of the events. The project counted among its participants unknown militants as well as the best-known members of the Parisian cinematic intelligentsia: Jean-Luc Godard, Alain Resnais and Chris Marker, to name a few.

But perhaps the most significant collective was Atelier de recherche cinématographique (ARC), comprising a number of figures, such as Michel Andrieu, Jacques Kébadian and Jean-Denis Bonan, who had been working in the margins of the film industry and who would go on to be well-known militant filmmakers, if not filmmakers *tout court*.

Figure 1.11 *Le Cinéma s'insurge* (publication of Les états généraux du cinéma français), issue 2

The filmmakers who would eventually constitute ARC began working together in 1963 at IDHEC, where they undertook a documentary film project about striking miners. One of the principal figures from this group was Jacques Kébadian, who was born to Armenian survivors of the 1915 genocide in Turkey. Kébadian's father moved to France in the early 1920s, later bringing his mother over. Kébadian described this family history as having had a direct impact on his later political reflection.[100] Kébadian went to IDHEC in 1963. His first job was as an editor on the children's programme *Bonne nuit les petits*.[101] It was working on *Bonne nuit les petits* that Kébadian met Robert Bresson. Claude Laydu, the star of *Diary of a Country Priest*, was also the writer and producer of *Bonne nuit les petits*, and he put Kébadian in touch with Bresson, who hired him as the assistant director on *Au hasard Balthazar* (1966), *Mouchette* (1967) and *Une femme douce* (1969). In 1967, Kébadian made a feature-length film entitled, simply, *Trotsky*.

Figure 1.12 *Le Cinéma s'insurge* (publication of Les états généraux du cinéma français), issue 3

Kébadian and Andrieu shot the miners' strike that lasted from 1 March to 3 April 1963. The film as it exists today is structured around the chronological unfolding of the strike and ends with a recitation of everything the miners accomplished and gained from the strike.[102] The rushes of this project were never edited by the IDHEC students but were instead purchased by the CGT. In the PCF's Ciné-Archives, the film is listed as *La grande grève des mineurs* (1963, 25 min.), and although it was often cited as being partially a collaborative project, in the archive it was ultimately attributed to Louis Daquin.[103]

In 1967, the same students filmed a demonstration for the Sécurité sociale that was finished with assistance from IDHEC. At this time, Kébadian and Andrieu began frequenting a group gathering around Jean-Denis Bonan and Mireille Abramovici.[104] Bonan, who figures prominently in the chapter on Cinélutte, was known by Kébadian and Andrieu for his surrealist short film.[105] Bonan was born in Tunis, Tunisia, in 1942. He cited his experiences growing up there (having had a too-early vision of the injustice of the soft apartheid in place in Tunisia) as influencing his later political militancy.[106] After completing his military service in 1965, Bonan started training as an assistant editor. He was hired by Les Actualités Française, where he was in charge of, among others, Les Actualités Françaises Tchad, Senegal, Algeria and Tunisia.

Bonan began making experimental films, and eventually, in 1967, he and his companion Mireille Abramovici, along

Figure 1.13 ARC

with the filmmaker Marco Poli, went to the experimental psychiatric clinic La Borde. There they
joined CERFI (Centre d'études de recherches et
de formation institutionnelles).[107] That year, Bonan
made a film with Poli about the patients/boarders,
called *IXE*.[108] The research and work at La Borde,
along with this film, were part of a project rooted
in the anti-psychiatry movement as well as the
work of Fernand Deligny,[109] Felix Guattari and
Jean Oury. The work being accomplished sought to
undo the boundaries between patient and doctor,
filmer and filmed. This meant that, at this stage,
the political and social occupations of the coming
collective *cinéma militant* were already being established.

Also working at La Borde was Jean-Claude
Pollack, a young psychiatrist interested in filmmaking
and its psychiatric potential.[110] Given that Guattari
and others had created the FGERI (*Fédération des
groupes d'études et de recherches institutionelles*), Pollack
encouraged the filmmakers to set up a similar group
dedicated to filmmaking.[111] Pollack introduced
Bonan and Abramovici to Kébadian, Andrieu,
Françoise Renberg and Renan Pollés, and together
they established ARC at La Borde that year.[112] The
group was formalised during the final trimester of
1967, and Kébadian immediately relayed his interest
about what was happening in Berlin at the time. He
convinced the group to film the German student
movement activist Rudi Dutschke in February '68.
In the first trimester of that year, ARC went to West
Berlin with members of the Trotskyite organisation JCR (Jeunesse communiste révolutionnaire, or
Revolutionary Communist Youth)[113] and shot what
would become *Berlin 68* (1968, 41 min.),[114] the first
formal creation of ARC.[115]

Figures 1.14–1.16 *Berlin 68*

With regard to a specific political ideology,
ARC was to the left of the Communist Party,
but the conflicts that would arise later between
the PCF and the far left had no impact during
the initial establishment of the group. In general,
ARC was politically heterogeneous and relatively
inclusive. Kébadian was, prior to '68, a Trotskyite,

Figure 1.17 Rudi Dutschke, *Berlin 68*

Andrieu was a pro-Situationist and follower of Socialisme ou barbarie,[116] Abramovici and
Bonan were anarchists, and the other participants identified, in general, with some mixture of
these tendencies.

Kébadian has remarked that the two principal factors that kept this politically heterogeneous group from splintering were the shared desire to make cinema and the unanimous agreement about the war in Vietnam.[117] After May, however, the political tensions would become more exigent, each member growing more sectarian and pursuing separate political paths. But over the course of May/June '68 ARC's political views were much like the events themselves: wide, wild, but generally anti-capitalist and anti-imperialist. As we'll see, ARC's method of filming also tended to mirror the anarchic aspects of the events. The unifying factor was a collective desire to break with the dominant cinema and cinematic practice in order to create a "parallel cinema of combat that received no aid from the system".[118]

ARC functioned both as what they referred to as a "reflection group" and as a collective grounded in film practice. Prior to undertaking a film project, the group would reflect collectively on the problems that the subject of the film presented.[119] This reflection was a practice that allowed those participants in the group who were not filmmakers to express and discuss the political, social and cultural aspects of the endeavour. Apart from the filmmakers at the group's core, ARC's fellow travellers included psychoanalysts, sociologists and architects; even future *nouveau philosophe* André Glucksmann was a participant.[120] This meant that the preproduction stage of reflection was not just an interrogation about the technical approach to producing a given film but a reflection on *what* should be filmed and how to approach filming from a social, cultural and political standpoint. The collective would temporarily cede to individuals the responsibility for each project at the moment of a given technical stage of the film. During a shoot, one member of the collective would take responsibility for directing, with perhaps a number of people filming. The rushes would be screened for the collective in order to discuss the direction that the editing would take, and then an editor would undertake the editing with the occasional critical discussion about the project over the course of the editing process.[121] Andrieu has said that the organisation of ARC, in essence, was much like an editorial board of a magazine, meeting every day, brainstorming and editing.[122]

During the events of May '68, ARC's approach to filming also mirrored the events themselves: they employed a wildcat, and occasionally spontaneous, method. Just as almost every sector went on strike, from football leagues to textile factory workers, ARC quite simply tried to shoot everything that was transpiring. And while during the early stages of Les états généraux ARC didn't maintain a very close relationship with them, once Les états généraux moved its base to the Parisian suburb of Suresnes, ARC became more involved and began to regularly send a representative.[123] While the collective created films such as *Nantes Sud Aviation* (1968) and *Le droit à la parole* (1968),[124] much of the footage from these works was sold to television. However, the footage was also incorporated into two film projects: Gudie Lawaetz made unauthorised use of it in his *Mai '68* (1974) and Godard made authorised use of it in his *Un film comme les autres* (1968).[125] *Nantes Sud Aviation* was made under the direction of Andrieu and Pierre William Glenn and chronicles the workers' participation in the May strikes at French aircraft manufacturer Sud Aviation. *Le droit à la parole* was a project undertaken by Andrieu and Kébadian which looked at the way the May strikes opened up spaces for participatory dialogue, focusing largely on the unity being forged between students and workers during the events.

While most of ARC's projects reflected some inclination towards spontaneity, taking on the loose organisation of the events themselves, one film in particular suffered from, or at least was the clearest articulation of, this tendency: *Le joli mois de mai* (1968). Jean-Denis Bonan was primarily responsible for this film and has commented often that it was a project that was ultimately both useless and dangerous.[126] Bonan's informal assessment points to two issues: one is the question of spontaneity, and the other is a question that plagues some of the mythology surrounding the idea of the collective film. Regarding the collectivity, Bonan has said that the project became particularly compromised during the editing stage owing to conflicts stemming from the collective attempt to edit the material into a coherent film.[127]

Le joli mois de mai shares the sensibility of *Flins 68–69* (cited above), which was created out of Jean-Pierre Thorn's *Oser lutter, oser vaincre*. Though not the reworking and re-editing of a previously existing film, *Le joli mois de mai* is composed of a series of shots of demonstrations and confrontations in the street. It differs from other ARC productions particularly in its near total lack of interviews. Bonan provides a voiceover that confirms the spontaneous and generically left-wing positions of the film (and, to some extent, ARC as a whole), calling for a "liberating revolt" and the destruction of the "electoral illusion". The film also relies on footage from *Berlin 68* and intercuts footage of Vietnamese demonstrators. If there is one aspect of the film that need not be dismissed so easily (given the confines of the militant political and cinematic project to come), it is its capacity to represent the movement as collective and to offer a vision of the events of May that sees the varying sectors of French society participating. This collective aspect is unfortunately countered by Bonan's voiceover, which tends to foreground a single author and lessens the collective aspect apparent in the images of the film.

Apart from its production work, ARC developed its own distribution network during the events, and it equally benefitted from the existing distribution circuits of Les états généraux du cinéma français and other established companies like ISKRA (see Chapter 4). After the events, the films continued to be distributed through the established militant networks, which had shifted emphasis away from film production to focus on distribution as one of the key militant strategies.

Figures 1.18–1.21 *Le joli mois de mai*

ARC ceased to exist soon after the events, and different groups were established in its place. After the dissolution of the JCR and the establishment of the LCR (La ligue communiste révolutionnaire), Kébadian distanced himself from the strictly Trotskyite current and joined the Comité de base Censier and then the GP.[128] Kébadian also participated in the early stages of Marin Karmitz's *Coup pour coup*, but he was quickly disenchanted with the way that the collective aspect was undermined by Karmitz's individual aspirations and recuperation of the film.[129] He eventually became an *établi* (see Chapter 2) at Valentine[130] at the end of 1969, and was arrested and imprisoned for political violence. In 1970, Kébadian, along with Andrieu and others from ARC, developed the Groupe Eugène Varlin, but only one film was made and the collective dissolved quickly.[131]

For ARC and other militant filmmakers, one of the most frequently cited influences (after Godard) was Jean-Pierre Thorn. His cinematic output inaugurated and closed a certain period and style of *cinéma militant*, the opening salvo being the almost vituperatively Marxist–Leninist *Oser lutter, oser vaincre* (1968). *Oser*'s subject was a strike at the automobile factory Renault-Flins, an important hub of militant activity both during the events and long after.[132] It was thus that Bonan and Abramovici began to pursue the Maoist cell Ligne rouge, in which Jean-Pierre Thorn was a central figure.

The work of ARC, along with that of Jean-Pierre Thorn, began to map out a practical cinematic territory that challenged some of the dominant theories about to unfurl across the far-left film journals of the period. Although people like Jean-Patrick Lebel critically went after the apparatus theory and its various mutations, the mode of critique was principally that of attacking the theory on its own terms and was therefore reactionary. What we will see with the collectives, filmmakers and films to be examined is the development of a critical practice that moves away from issues of technicity and the apparatus, in favour of positing social formation and interrogation as a challenge to bourgeois ideology.

Figure 1.22 *Valentine la révolte*: the newsletter published by the Revolutionary Workers of Valentine

Figure 1.23 Jean-Luc Godard's note of support to Jacques Kébadian, sent while the latter was in prison

While some critics focused on the apparatus and debated whether Quattrocento optics confined cinema to the spread of a perspectival "stain" (or whether filming was always already the re-presentation of a representation and thus a reflection of dominant ideology), the militant filmmakers examined here attempted to attack on a different front and with different theoretical and practical concerns. Less interested in the question of inescapable aesthetic ideological traps, they militated via organisational forms, attempting non-hierarchical collectivisation, questioned whether or not the camera should be put in the hands of the workers, and found ways to construct a political line through film distribution. Even *Cinéthique*, having forged their momentary alliance with *Tel Quel*, sought out ways of organising a film that would attempt to flee the cinematically ideological constraints they themselves had articulated.

Chapter 2
Jean-Pierre Thorn: "No investigation, no right to speak"

2.1 Jean-Pierre Thorn and *Oser lutter, oser vaincre*

Jean-Pierre Thorn's first feature-length film, *Oser lutter, oser vaincre* (1968, 88 min.) is an elaborately constructed documentary about a strike and occupation at the Renault-Flins automobile factory between 15 May and 18 June 1968. The film is the expression not so much of the anarchistic politics and wildcat student actions that had taken hold in the Latin Quarter, but rather of a far-left movement, identifying itself as Marxist–Leninist, which had its roots in a dramatic split with the French Communist Party.

Prior to *Oser lutter*, Thorn's earliest cultural engagements were in 1965 and 1966, when he directed two theatre pieces by Bertolt Brecht: *Saint Joan of the Stockyards* and *Señora Carrar's Rifles*.[1] His first short film, *Emmanuelle* (or *Mi-Vie*), was made in 1966 and was clearly influenced by Godard, particularly his *Masculin Féminin* (1966). Like Godard's film, *Emmanuelle* was about the state of French youth in the face of military action in Vietnam. While the film is generally outside of the militant domain, the experience of creating it did coincide with an early attempt at establishing a film distribution collective called Cinéma-Liberté, with which Thorn and other filmmakers tried, unsuccessfully, to screen *Emmanuelle* (or *Mi/Vie*) at the Avignon festival in 1967.[2]

Thorn's next project, *BT.E4.10.N.103, No Man's Land* (1967), was a short film shot in Villeneuve-la-Garenne and his first collaboration with the composer Jacky Moreau, who would later work with Thorn on his film *Le dos au mur* (1980). *No*

Figures 2.1-2.2

Man's Land was inspired by one of Moreau's compositions and recounted a French teenager's sense of entrapment in the spectacularly modern world. Again, while these early projects were not examples of the Marxist–Leninist-informed cinema that would be the hallmark of Thorn's output for a decade to come, they nevertheless expressed a generalised political consciousness.

Following this brief experience with Cinéma-Liberté, Thorn developed an interest in the idea of making a film collectively.[3] He began frequenting the meetings of the Union des jeunesses communistes marxistes–léninistes (UJCML)[4] at rue d'Ulm in Paris, where the students in charge of *Servir le peuple* (UJCML's journal) suggested that they make a film about class struggle in Brittany. The UJCML was a particularly dogmatic and highly theoretical group of far-left students who had split with the Union des étudiants communistes (UEC) over issues of revisionism within the PCF.[5] Robert Linhart was the leader at the UJCML and was considered Louis Althusser's prize pupil.

The idea for this film project coincided with the May events. The influence of the UJCML on Thorn's political ideas concerning the events translated into "economism" and a strict workerist dogmatism that culminated in a rejection of the student uprisings in the Latin Quarter.[6] Both Thorn and the UJCML, while pro-Chinese from the outset, were now consistently drawing on the thought of Mao Tse-Tung and considered the "revolting" students to be part of the bourgeois elite, and their actions at the barricades no more than a ludic party.[7] Instead, these young Marxist–Leninists turned their attention to the working-class strikes and demonstrations taking place in the factories of France.

Inspired by the occupation at the Renault-Billancourt factory and a march he participated in leading to that factory, Thorn approached a CGT director to ask whether he could help the cause by filming. While the director expressed some interest in the project, nothing ever came of it. Instead, members of the UJCML told Thorn, "Go to Flins, there's a comrade there; interesting things are going on in that factory."[8] Effectively, Jean-Michel Normand,[9] founder of the Syndicalistes prolétariennes de la CGT and a first-wave *établi* from the UJCML, along with about fifty young workers all ready to revolt, were able to get Thorn into the factory to shoot the film. This film would ultimately become *Oser lutter, oser vaincre*.

2.2 The strike at Flins, as told by Jean-Pierre Thorn/Ligne rouge

Opening with a kind of militant *Sortie de l'usine Lumière à Lyon*, *Oser lutter, oser vaincre* begins with a strike march inside the Renault-Flins automobile factory on Wednesday, 15 May 1968. While a worker from Flins discusses the movement through the factory and the lack of union participation, Thorn presents the procession of strikers across the various shop floors, gathering more and more workers. The film immediately introduces what will be its subject, as a diegetic voiceover explains that the strike and occupation were not the initiative of the unions; rather, it was a workers' movement dominated by workers. And, because of the large number of participants, the unions were ultimately forced into a position in which they had to follow the workers.

While the primary targets of the film's critique are the CGT and the PCF, there is a recurring figure in the film, a Confédération française démocratique du travail (CFDT) delegate, who, early in the film, critically suggests that a factory occupation during a strike is merely supplemental to the strike itself. In the delegate's view, the only real concern at the level of factory management and ownership is that production has stopped. Pushing this idea further, the delegate insists that stopping production should be the only concern of the striking workers. In response to these assertions, Thorn inserts a title card that poses the question, "And for the worker?" While in terms of the narrative this intervention reinforces the film's political position vis-à-vis the unions, it is also a formal announcement. According to Tangui Perron, the film has upwards of 250 title cards,[10] and these inserts work consistently to reiterate, contradict or narratively reinforce the shots with which they are inter, juxta or counterposed.

Figure 2.3

In looking for a new film form, Thorn was initially under the influence of the direct cinema tradition, despite its naturalist tendencies. Yet his distaste for the naturalist tendencies of direct cinema pushed Thorn, although not entirely, in the direction of *cinéma vérité*, which revealed its artifice in the manner of a film like Jean Rouch and Edgar Morin's *Chronique d'un été* (1961). While Thorn was suspicious of voiceover, suggesting that it was a formal tactic that denied montage and the image their rightful place in the dialectically materialist process,[11] *Oser lutter* did have recourse to a modest use of voiceover. But the principal strategies, both extradiegetic and formal, Thorn most

Figure 2.4 A militant *Sortie de l'usine Lumière à Lyon*

frequently employed to articulate the contradictions of the reality being filmed were the use of title cards and montage.

Oser lutter was created (particularly in the post-production phase) under the sign of Sergei Eisenstein's *October* (1928) and Brechtian epic theatre. For Thorn, the title card was a method of interrogating the image, the audience and the subject(s) of the film – a technique faithful to Brecht's objectivity or distance. In *Oser lutter* (as well as in *Margoline* [1973], and certainly the later *Le dos au mur*), the Maoist principle of the *enquête*, or investigation, was the basis for a cinema that could point out the contradictions of the reality filmed. It stood against naturalism and sought to refute the idea that filming a revolutionary event was enough to make a revolutionary film. Even in his later films, Thorn remained preoccupied with the ways in which he could continue to keep the spectator in a state of activity, often repeating that "ambient naturalism is a game society plays in order to make us accept reality".[12] He supported this position by citing Brecht's "Consider nothing natural so that everything may be considered subject to change".[13]

One of the aleatory technical issues that arises in *Oser lutter, oser vaincre* is the sound quality and the cacophony resulting from the multitude of voices and discourses. For example, there is frequent use of asynchronous sound in the film, provoking the question as to how, in Thorn's search for a kind of "workers' truth", we are to understand the asynchronous recording. Perhaps, as much as it is a technical limitation resulting from economic circumstances, there is another effect produced, which pertains not just to the aesthetic "quality" of the film (good versus poor quality) but equally to the film's political mission to break with naturalism and establish a critical spectatorial distance. It poses a question that underlies much of the militant filmmaking during and after '68: how is a marginalised and often suppressed speech recorded or registered? Thorn's serendipitous filmic response is that such speech does not occur naturally; rather, it is constructed, forced and continually in need of "synchronisation".

This move between voiceover, title card, asynchronised sound and synchronised sound forms a methodological approach to posing the various questions of the film from different perspectives. For example, in one sequence a voiceover announces that the CGT launched an offensive against the militants at Renault. As a response to this announcement, the film returns to the CFDT leader insisting on the uselessness of the occupation, while a title card asks "What are they afraid of?" The answer to this question arises in a discussion between a CGT representative and a Renault worker, where the worker poses the question that is at the heart of the impetus to make this film: if there had been no student movement, would there have been a workers' movement? A chorus of voices responds, "Certainly not!" and the workers announce the necessity of a student–worker alliance. This aural mosaic, while heavily constructed, points to the use to which Thorn is putting cinema, meaning that this project cannot be critiqued for trying to obfuscate its own elaboration. In fact, it is precisely this struggle against vulgar naturalism that moves Thorn's project from a document, or tract, to a work that engages cinema on its own terrain.

Given its reputation as a particularly dogmatic film (made by the Maoist Thorn and later attributed to Ligne rouge, or Cinéma ligne rouge; see below), it is worth noting that, thus far, the Marxist–Leninist line of *Oser lutter* has yet to be fully mobilised. In this way, there is a kind of seduction that seems to be taking place. The film positions itself strongly, both in its explicit discourse and its formal elaboration, on the side of the striking workers. At the same time, it distances itself radically from the unions and the PCF, which cannot, based on the opening of this film, be perceived as being portrayed as anything other than traitors to the working class. Thus, Thorn paves the way, in a political and cinematic bait-and-switch, to fill the void of the unformed and somewhat tenuous speech of the workers with the speech of Marx, Lenin, Mao and Stalin.

Not until 13 minutes into the film do the explicit political alliances make their first appearance, via the title card "We are always correct to revolt – Mao Tse-Tung". This is a distancing device and a political enunciation that is separate from the perhaps more anarchistic, workerist tone that has been dominating the film up to this point. Even more intriguing is that this introduction of the specific political position is made within the discursive boundaries of cinema: the line is issued via title card and does not emerge from the interior world of the film, that is, from the striking workers. This gesture offers an insight as to how Thorn takes a political subject and cinematically constructs the narrative of the unions betraying the striking workers.

In terms of the narrative of the CGT betrayal, there is a particularly illustrative sequence in *Oser lutter* featuring a group of militants from the CGT preparing banners and pickets for a demonstration. A CGT delegate wanders across the lawn where young workers paint their slogans and their demands on the pickets. Thorn edits this sequence by using a series of stills taken from the scene. The film freezes on the slogan "Capital à l'humanité", while the CGT delegate simultaneously comments on the slogan, insisting that it is nonsense. The delegate ends up telling the strikers which pickets they can and cannot use during the demonstration. The camera pans down over a still image of the portly CGT leader, which is followed by an analogous shot of a much thinner worker. The result of this juxtaposition is not the cliché of the overfed, moneyed bourgeois class next to the undernourished worker, but rather a caricature of the fat, PCF-affiliated CGT delegate next to the undernourished worker.

This caricature is shored up by Thorn's insert of a precedent-setting title card for the film that reads "PCCGT", an illustration of the collusion between the two organisations (the CGT and the PCF) and the first expression of the idea of a unified front against the workers. Thorn follows this sequence with scenes from the demonstrations, which effectively show that the workers have chosen to use precisely the slogans that the CGT delegate forbade. As well as establishing the opposition to the role of the CGT, expressed in the popular manner, these pickets point to the way in which Thorn formally begins to draw on other communicative strategies. These strategies fall within the purview of the unity of opposites: freezing on an image and letting the dialogue continue and setting up counterpoints, not just through title cards but also through the various forms of diegetic writing (for example, banners with demands filmed while a contrapuntal dialogue is heard and anti-unionist graffiti is seen).

Following the Grenelle agreements (*accords de Grenelle*),[14] the film documents the so-called "return to work" and the immense disappointment felt by many of the workers. The strike at Flins actually intensifies in response to the accords. Whereas up to now the film has portrayed the chronological unfolding of the strike in relatively broad strokes, it now shifts to a method that details the chronology, intensifying as the strike continues. Formally, this means that the film becomes extremely "text-heavy", and these texts are in the multitude of

Figures 2.5–2.7 *Oser lutter, oser vaincre*

forms that we have seen so far, that is, title cards, placards and newspaper headlines.

A title card announces the 21st day of the strike as a labour official comes to Flins to meet the strike committee. The unions and management organise a vote to see who agrees to the return to work, and the strike committee immediately calls on the workers to refuse a vote organised by the bosses. A CGT car announces a meeting by megaphone, trying to round up workers. The meeting of the CGT shows the portly delegate screaming into a megaphone that they are in favour of a reduction of work hours, increase in pay, and so on, essentially stressing that they are on the side of the workers. Meanwhile, Thorn films the workers at this meeting themselves holding a megaphone and responding to the delegate's speech by singing "The Internationale".

This sequence of events, apart from the punctuation of the anthem, is shot in the most direct style, and is a clear demonstration of how propaganda functions through the seemingly autonomous shots of a verisimilar documentary style. When the audience is confronted with what might be considered more traditional propagandistic images – Marx quotes, images of Mao – those elements might actually foreground the aesthetic approach to such an extent that their transparency closes off the possibility of a natural reception. Such formal punctuation does not articulate the epistemological basis of the dominant ideology: I see it as I am supposed to see truth; therefore it is true.

However, while these unambiguous formal elements point to a clarity in Thorn's cinematic project, we are occasionally confronted with a moderately confused formal and stylistic remainder. In a scene reminiscent of the "Bourse" sequence in *Le dos au mur* (see discussion later in this chapter), following the vote the workers bring out the ballot boxes and throw them on the ground. It is an absolutely ludic moment, both cinematically and in terms of the strike itself – a moment filled with laughter. Thorn chose to freeze on the image at precisely the moment when the ballots are thrown in the air. A montage of stills showing different stages of the ballots falling follows, while "The Internationale" continues to be sung and the strikers burn the ballots. An aerial shot of the demonstration accompanied by quotes from Mao announces structurally what resembles the end of the second act.

But this sequence with its numerous formal interventions ends up serving as a counterpoint to the *apparent* autonomy of the shots leading up to this scene. The freeze-frame and the Mao quotes – all those elements that serve to create and transmit a specific political line without obfuscation – end up being the most transparent aspects of propaganda, and preclude the communication of the naturally occurring or spontaneous truth. The appearance of these strategies points to some of the remaining aesthetic confusion about political cinema in Thorn's early work.

In terms of the move from asynchronous to synchronous sound, the film frames these two modes within special structures. Thus, when the film moves into the occupied factory and focuses on discussions with the workers about previous experiences with strikes, suddenly the sound becomes synchronised, which in turn changes the tone of the film. The synchronous sound gives a calm lucidity to the workers' speech, which has thus far been represented in the chaotic cacophony of the events of the strike. Even with this simple transition of audio technique, the film formally moves

Figure 2.8 The CGT speaks

Figure 2.9 The strikers respond, singing "The International"

Figure 2.10 Destroying the ballot boxes

Figure 2.11 Throwing the ballots

from the general (the mass of often unformed voices) to the particular (the clear articulation of the workers' speech).

One of the significant events in the history of the French Marxist–Leninist movement issuing from May '68 was the death of Gilles Tautin. Tautin was a 17-year-old student and member of the UJCML who participated in the uprising at Meulan on 10 June. Tautin, along with other demonstrators, was chased by police in Meulan onto a bridge over the Seine, at which point, in an effort to escape, he jumped like others did into the river.[15] While the others survived, Tautin drowned. Thorn includes this event in *Oser lutter*, inserting the text "Gilles Tautin est assassiné". A voiceover describes the police chasing a group of students and the eventual discovery of Tautin's body, which was found in the river. The voice says that when he climbed back up the banks, he turned to the police and said, "There you go, you won, he's dead." This is followed by a long tracking shot and the funeral procession for Tautin.

Figure 2.12 Burning the ballots

Figure 2.13 Funeral procession for Gilles Tautin

Following a vote, in which the majority choose to go back to work, the film shows the workers returning unenthusiastically as someone selling *L'Humanité* shouts that it is the voice of the PCF, the only journal of the working class. As he says "*L'Humanité*", Thorns shows a group of depressed workers returning to work, emphasising the perceived irony of the journal's title. The headlines read "Renault. They broke the veto of power. 66,000 workers return this morning." This is followed by the title cards "Did the PCF poorly Direct the Workers' Strike or Perfectly Direct the Bourgeoisie's Strike?" and "The Truth is the PCF doesn't Want the Revolution; the PCF has gone over to the side of the Bourgeoisie; the PCF entirely revised Communism; That's Why We Call Them Re Vis Ion Ist."

A final voiceover yells out, "Vive la revolution communiste!" As the footage from the film plays, images of Marx, Lenin and Mao are dissolved over them; and finally they are dissolved over the title card "WE WILL WIN".

As Perron has pointed out, the closing of this film in particular poses problems for historians because of the re-editing that Thorn did to remove some of its more abrasively dogmatic elements.[16] In addition to the two versions of the film in circulation, Thorn's original and the re-edited CRP *Flins 68–69*, Thorn created a third version in 1978 in which he removed a number of intertitles as well as the images of Stalin in the closing credits. In assessing the current version of the film, the absence of Stalin's visage lessens the ideological force of the original film. While the bias against the CP and the CGT is blatant in the choice of who speaks, what is shown and how the film is edited, the current version of the film's most forceful dogmatic expressions are those title cards that bear quotations from Mao.

Thorn has said of *Oser lutter* that when he arrived at Flins to shoot, he had no preconceived plan for the film, and he suggests that the film was ultimately a demonstration of "an incredible thirst to understand".[17] Over the course of the shoot, Thorn and his principal cameraman Bruno Muel (who was a member, if sceptical, of the PCF) began to see that the party and the unions were betraying them at the end of the May movement.[18] Even if Thorn had been politically and theoretically formed by the UJCML at the beginning of the movement, he and the crew of *Oser lutter* had maintained productive alliances with the members of the PC within the Les états généraux du cinéma production commission (Chris Marker, Jean-André Fieschi, Antoine Bonfanti, et al.).[19] The relationship was more than just a theoretical alliance, because it was this production committee that provided Thorn with a whole team of technicians, editing tables, stock and other resources.[20] It is an impressive moment in the history of French cinema, given that Thorn was only 20 years old, and the luminaries of French film production were working to support the shoot at Flins. However, what transpired over the course of the shoot and in the editing process changed the film and the filmmakers drastically.[21]

Figures 2.14–2.15

The initial project was organised by the production commission of Les états généraux du cinéma, those from the PC within Les états généraux du cinéma, and the students and teachers at IDHEC. It was to be a film that grouped together the whole of the worker–student–peasant movement: the quintessential *film de synthèse*.[22] But when Thorn undertook the editing process, it became apparent that ideological conflicts were brewing within the PC. There was a critical movement taking place within the UJC(ml) as well, a movement that would result in a splintering of the group into a number of *groupuscules*. These events, together with the realisation that the workers' movement had been betrayed by the CGT, triggered in Thorn the idea that he had made a political error and that his film was merely a kind of diffuse leftism. Based on this idea, Thorn re-edited the film collectively with a group that eventually went on to become *établis* at Sochaux.[23]

Thorn's explicit intention with *Oser lutter* was to work against the so-called "spontaneous" tendency (see below), using Lenin's texts as support.[24] His was a struggle against the idea that one could merely film an event, project it, and call it a revolutionary film. Thorn and those he was working with in post-production were cultural Leninists, for whom political consciousness could come only from exterior economic conditions, and they thus believed their role as filmmakers was to make this exterior world understandable. *Oser lutter* was for Thorn a just film with regard to the positions he held at the time; it was a film that sought to render history comprehensible and to transform it.[25] Again, in keeping with his admiration of Soviet cinema, Thorn was ultimately setting out to make contemporary militant agitprop.[26]

Describing some of the formal accomplishments of *Oser lutter*, Tangui Perron has pointed out that while there is an immense debt to and influence of Russian formalism, particularly the work of Eisenstein, there is equally, in the use of black-and-white stock, an evocation of the best of *cinéma direct*. The influence of the latter is not solely felt in the use of the stock, but articulated in a seemingly liberated worker's speech and a framing that captured the faces and movement of those same workers. For Perron, the film "condenses the best of the militant cinema from the 1960s – personal but magnificent references to the masterworks of Soviet cinema – and the worst propaganda films".[27]

However, instead of the *cinéma direct* tendency, with its inclination towards the naturalist strategy of self-effacement, Thorn (while not necessarily using the term) worked closer to the *cinéma vérité* tradition, foregrounding select elements of the cinematic apparatus. *Oser lutter*, in particular, quite effectively works within the *vérité* paradigm in the sense that it attempts not a verisimilar representation of truth, but rather a meeting with a truth. The *vérité* strategies in *Oser lutter*, such as alternating between documentary footage and title cards, open up a space for the audience to understand that the film is, in Philippe Dauty's words, an "attempt to analyze what is being shown, that is, an interpretation".[28]

But to stop at such a discrete definition betrays something at the core of the Marxist–Leninist project. This project posited that analysis and the capacity to make bold statements based on concrete belief left little room for what might be called the vacillations of interpretation. It did so even in the face of the increasing tendency towards an interpretive relativism, which was rampant during the period after '68. Such vacillations cannot rightly be said to be evident in *Oser lutter*. Rather, Thorn's comments and the increasingly dogmatic filmmaking wing of Ligne rouge attest to an analytic certainty, as opposed to an openness to interpretation and the rubric of the postmodern shibboleth that each truth is as valid as any other. This latter relativist position would be untenable in the political framework in which Thorn and the other far-left filmmakers were working. How could a term like "revisionist" work in any sense other than negatively in such a climate? It was, in fact, the contrary of interpretive tolerance that was in question: one need only think of the rigidity with which far-left political cells fractured based on political certitudes.

Oser lutter, as it was presented in its time, maintained a conviction that is perhaps at the root of the famous slogan *cinéma militant, cinéma chiant*. Dauty saw the contagion of the images because the slogans on the title cards were interpretive. However, it is equally worth considering that this strategy was an attempt to give the images the formal truth they required while abandoning wildcat shooting and, in turn, wildcat interpretation. It was an effort to wrest the images from their seemingly neutral and natural occurrence and to place them within this specific historical moment.[29]

Thorn has since refuted the "interpretive" analysis of *Oser lutter* while being entirely critical of this early effort, referring to it as unbearable or even unwatchable. He has suggested that the key to the dogmatic certainty the film expresses is a certainty of youth, a youth that yells, "The revolution and Marxism have been hijacked! We're going to bring you the truth!" It is what he has referred to as the "messianic will", often expressed in the term *au service...* (in the service of...), for example, in the service of the revolution, in the service of Marxism, in the service of the working class. And in this "service of", the individual appears to cede to the collective.[30] "What I dislike about *Oser lutter* [...] is the fact that everything is white, everything is black, there is no detailed analysis; it is this lesson/moral/pedagogical side that exasperates me."[31]

Reading *Oser lutter* in terms of its political commitments, and its formal use of Brecht, Eisenstein and other Soviet filmmakers to combat the naturalism and aleatory action of the *spontanistes*, is highly useful and representative of the cultural and political period in which it was made. Focusing on these aspects makes it easy to draw a line between the intentions of the filmmaker vis-à-vis the film and the critical reception and interpretation of the film. And yet there is another aspect that gets overlooked but that is equally important in the combat against naturalism – and that is the way in which the film plays with generic structure.

With his later film *Le dos au mur* Thorn took a Western-like approach (see below), and "Western" is a generic categorisation applicable to *Oser lutter* as well. While a specifically Western aspect is present in the film, the use of a narrative structure also orders the action and the tension that it relies on. By creating a narrative, regardless of its resolution, the combat against naturalism is foregrounded. This is accomplished not only by the traditional means of emphasising the construction of the event (through revealing the means and modes of production), but also by implicating the spectator in a narrative. While *Oser Lutter* sees Thorn add a strategy that is traditionally associated with fiction filmmaking, the ideas about the film's fidelity to a given truth and Thorn's hope to give birth to that truth through cinema still hold true.

Offering a nexus and hybrid of formal strategies, the film represents an immense vehicle of cinematic polyvocality. It combines documentary, epic theatre, diegetic and nondiegetic text, a multitude of voices, strategies of communication, generic shifts, formal shifts, direct cinema and Russian formalist Soviet cinema. These all combine into a great motor to combat the increasingly dominant cinematic (and political) strategy of wildcat naturalism within the militant paradigm. And yet it is "the worst [aspects of] propaganda films" that carry the film and keep it from tipping into some sort of prelapsarian postmodern pastiche. It is the fidelity to realism in its most critical manifestation that removes it from the simple mould of propaganda and puts it into a productive relationship with the medium of film and all its attendant conventions.

This transformation produced a film that articulated the need to build a new revolutionary party, and it stated in no uncertain terms that the PCF and the CGT were entirely revisionist entities. More recently, Thorn has attributed the dogmatic aspect of the film to youth. The belief at the time was that Marxist–Leninist theory should not be confined to the contexts of the economic struggle, and that filmmakers needed to inform the masses and to make films as a means of popular education. Through Thorn's understanding of the PCF, he ended up moving closer to groups like ARC, which were, as we have seen, composed primarily of Trotskyites and pro-Situationists. But eventually Thorn, Jean-Denis Bonan and Mireille Abramovici, along with Jean Lefaux, who made *Écoute Joseph, nous sommes tous solidaires* (1968),[32] worked together to establish the Marxist–Leninist cell Ligne rouge.

2.3 Ligne rouge

According to Christophe Bourseiller, Ligne rouge, which formed in 1969, stemmed from two tendencies in the Maoist movement. On the one side was the MCF-ML (Mouvement communiste français marxiste–léniniste), a group that refused the transformation into the PCMLF (Parti communiste marxiste-léniniste de France).[33] The other group was the UJCML, which had three major offshoots: one developed into the GP (La gauche prolétarienne), another became Vive le communisme, and the third became the so-called *Toulousains*, who undertook the creation of Ligne rouge. The group had a reputation for being particularly dogmatic and positioned itself squarely against the PCMLF. They established groups throughout France, including a cell in Sochaux, which would have consequences cinematically in relation to Les groupes Medvedkine's project.[34]

Ligne rouge developed a discourse largely critical of populism.[35] This idea made itself evident in the film practices of those who refused to adopt an idea common during the period – that of turning the camera over to the workers to allow them to film themselves (see below). While we will see ways in which this practice was undertaken and enacted with impressive results (notably with Les groupes Medvedkine), we will also see over the course of this period a group of film-makers (particularly those associated with ARC, Thorn and Cinélutte) who refused this practice for various reasons. And each of these groups maintained some link with Ligne rouge.[36]

2.3.1 Vive le cinéma, arme de propagande communiste

Ligne rouge developed their political position, along with their cinematic philosophy, in an influential text entitled *Vive le cinéma, arme de propagande communiste*. Originally produced in 1969 as a pamphlet by Thorn and others at Ligne rouge, the text was re-edited and printed in *Cahiers du cinéma*, numbers 245–246.[37] *Cahiers du cinéma* attributed the text to Prolétaire ligne rouge (perhaps mistakenly, given that PLR was yet another split that emanated from Ligne rouge) and acknowledged the fact that critics at the journal had rewritten the text. *Cahiers'* intention with the project was not only returning to but rewriting the tract, acting on the belief that the original text needed to be adapted to contemporary historical and cultural circum-stances. Although the text is multifaceted in both its theoretical position and its description of practice, it was also a tract that had, at its origin, a specific economic goal.

Before writing the text (which would not be published officially until nearly a year later), Thorn and a group of filmmakers, primarily composed of those from ARC, along with Lefaux and Ligne rouge, grouped themselves within Les états généraux du cinéma as a counterforce to the anarchistic tendencies manifested by Jean Charvein. The Charveinist tendency was articu-lated in the wildcat approach to shooting. This approach wasn't all that distinct from the initial method Thorn had used when creating *Oser lutter* (at least in the shooting stages – that is, arriving at the scene of the strike and shooting whatever could be shot). However, the result was that the filmmakers and Les états généraux du cinéma (even with the assistance of IDHEC and recourse to the black market, where the costs relating to the massive amounts of film stock development and printing were lower) accumulated large amounts of unsecured debt to the film laboratories. Given that the negatives were housed in the labs, the growing debt could have potentially resulted in the seizure of the films.[38]

Under these conditions Thorn, Kébadian and the others set up a "reflection group", which would articulate the need to move away from trying to create popular counter-television and instead push for and create projects with specific political orientations. While this period was very productive for the *Cahiers du cinéma* (and militant cinema more generally), the many scis-sions and the fragmenting of a unified political project were well under way: a class-based analysis of the then contemporary situation gave way to analyses based on struggles over micro-political and cultural issues. The reprinting and updating of the text was intended to rede-fine the cinematic task at hand, which was being confronted with these shifting cultural and historical circumstances.

To articulate the reasons for returning to this text, the writers at *Cahiers du cinéma* wrote an introduction that cited two specific qualities of the Ligne rouge thesis that remained pertinent for Marxist–Leninist critics at the magazine in 1973:

> The text offers a number of coherent and systematic responses to the following questions: […] what films are to be made at the current stage of the revolution in France […]? How to overcome empiricism in terms of distribution? What is the assessment of the experience on the cinematic front? What does practising the mass line mean in terms of the production and distribution of films?

Further, the text is the only one we know of that comes from a Marxist–Leninist organisation which formulates a point of view on the entire cinematic front. It thus constitutes a good example of what could be a specific base for the engaged discussions by the magazine, with the purpose of uniting with Marxist–Leninist organisations: a specific base that wouldn't be a substitute for the political discussions themselves, but that would represent an important support and point of departure for such discussions.[39]

One of the issues that the editors had to address was, precisely, what was the actual "revolutionary stage" they were living in? To facilitate the interrogation of this rather unstable periodisation, they had to ask what characterised this age and what were the tasks and responsibilities of Marxist–Leninists (not yet specifically ML filmmakers). To respond to the first question, regarding the characterisation of the epoch, the text provides a list of seven perspectives.[40]

First, the characterisation focused on the collusion between social and US imperialists to repress national liberation movements as well as urban revolutionary movements that were developing in the imperialist countries themselves. The text also cited China and Albania as the revolutionary bases of the contemporary world. The second issue was the specifically French situation, which it characterised primarily as a crisis of the bourgeoisie. Third, it decried revisionism, particularly as it was expressed by the CGT and PCF (the "C" almost always in quotation marks, invoking the idea that the PCF was communist only in name – that is, the "so-called communist party").

For Ligne rouge, this revisionist tendency countered spontaneous workers' movements. This situation would be rendered more complex when the editors/writers took on the *spontanistes* of the GP. Ligne rouge, along with a number of other Marxist–Leninist (ML) groups, took issue with the idea of the GP as *spontaniste*, labelling them, for instance, *Spontex*. This insult, in turn, likened a serious ML movement to a minor advertising scheme, that is, a relic of the so-called spectacular world. This issue created a significant split within the far left – a contentious sectarianism that pitted Marxist–Leninists against each other. Within the context of this tract, however, given that this is as much a treatise about film as it is about the political position of the group, "spontaneity" is not always about a working class coming to consciousness through experience and events, but also about the dismissal of cinematic naturalism, which stands in well for an aesthetic iteration of spontaneity. This critique of spontaneity dominated the rest of the points, and the text finished by characterising the period as being one dominated by *spontanisme* and economism.[41]

According to Thorn and Ligne rouge, the tasks of the Marxist–Leninists were to disseminate communist ideas to the masses in order to create communist cadres (a kind of nucleus of party personnel that could easily be expanded) and to conduct a concrete analysis of the situation in France in order to elaborate a tactic for revolution.[42] These positions bring us back to the vote within Les états généraux du cinéma to create specific film projects, which in turn would prepare the way for a revolutionary film project. The reflection in the text on the specificity of the film medium is also pertinent, given that it addresses the issue of "the masses". That is, a mass medium like film would be an effective means for communication aimed at "the masses"; and it has at least a twofold nature, in that it can analyse as well as be an object of analysis.

One of the principal questions that emerges from this text is what would be the specific role of the militant filmmaker within such conditions? The response is that "the work of communist intellectuals working with film is to transmit communist ideas to the masses so that they are then able to organise themselves as Marxist–Leninists and construct their party; and to popularise the ideas of the far-left workers through Marxist–Leninist critique".[43] The manifestation of such a project would be anti-capitalist, anti-revisionist and anti-imperialist (included here is a critique levelled not just at US imperialism, but equally at Soviet socialist–imperialist cinema). This cinema would point to the bond between national liberation struggles in the Third World and the revolutionary left in the urban centres of imperialist countries.

To further root itself in the specific role of a political cinema, the text makes an historical detour to examine the ways that militant cinema has thus far accomplished the tasks it has outlined. The analysis takes as its point of departure the militant cinema since '68 and what it sees as one of its dominant tendencies: the "myth" of counter-information. The myth of counter-information involved not only the simplistic formula of showing up at a strike, filming the demonstrations and interviewing a couple of workers, but also the theoretical positions that legitimised such an approach. These positions were articulated as an a posteriori theory about how the people being filmed (namely the militant demonstrators and the revolutionary working class) were never seen on TV, and how counter-informational film had finally captured and presented this overlooked reality.

Such a formula was antithetical to what Thorn had tried to accomplish, particularly in the post-production stage of *Oser lutter*. It was a formula that repeated the problematic notion of bourgeois objectivity, whereby the events are able to autonomously recount their own truth. Such a principle posed a problem for the filmmakers of Ligne rouge. It did so not only within the theoretical or aesthetic domain, but also quite practically, given that this position (that of counter-informational, naturalist objectivity) was the "negation of the need for a conscious intervention on the part of Marxist–Leninists".[44]

The critique of this counter-informational tradition emerges from those filmmakers struggling against naturalism or any variation on the verisimilar impression of reality model. Simply put, the critique is that the facts say nothing by themselves. This critique however could be issued from any ideological position, meaning we can imagine a far-right project that would equally stress that what was easily captured on film did not represent the totality of the given social and political conditions. Thus such a position needed to be qualified within the Ligne rouge political paradigm. Their response is that the masses don't need simply to see an event such as a strike; they need, instead, to see the way in which communist ideas are enacted in the events. In the spontaneous, naturalist, counter-television model, the active role of the filmmaker is reduced to a kind of uncritical loudspeaker circulating information generally considered to be outside the parameters of traditional film and television distribution circuits; in short, the filmmaker is aligned with "the distribution policy of Cinéma Libre".[45]

Another critique of *cinéma militant* centred on its recording and distribution of "spontaneous" films about political struggle that didn't reveal contradictions. This critique brings us back to the criticism of Marin Karmitz's *Coup pour coup*; here, the writers similarly point out that such films show an uninhibited solidarity among all the workers, that revisionists are entirely outside of the working class, and that the struggle develops without any contradictions.[46] An important question for militant filmmakers is can a film like *Coup pour coup* bring anything to a working class that experiences the struggle? Such films could be considered anti-dialectical, given that they refuse the requisite methodological approach for provoking an understanding of internal contradictions. The result of Karmitz's approach, and others like it, is the wildcat shooting of counter-informational films that never achieve any kind of synthesis.

Another example, one that is closer to home for Ligne rouge, concerns Thorn's own *Oser lutter*, a copy of which had been stolen from a screening by members of La cause du peuple. This group re-edited the film, creating *Flins 68–69* (1969), which stripped *Oser lutter* of its Marxist–Leninist analysis (the crushing of revisionism, the necessity of destroying the state apparatus, the necessity of a party, and so on). The revised version merely presented the sequences of violent confrontation between the workers and the police.

While Ligne rouge cites La cause du peuple as the party responsible for the *détournement* of *Oser lutter*, the group who undertook this project of re-editing Thorn's film was supposedly called Les cinéastes révolutionnaires prolétariens (CRP).[47] As Thorn has said, during a screening at rue d'Ulm, members of GP/CDP stole a copy of *Oser lutter* and created an internegative, which was turned over to the CRP to re-edit. The CRP, in describing this project, remarked that it was born of a concern that they needed to show the revolutionary workers at Flins that their struggle was continuing.[48] They wanted to make the film under the direction of the workers and claimed that this was precisely what had occurred.[49]

Practically, this re-edit posed certain technical problems, given that the workers were outside of Paris and the large majority of the materials necessary to undertake this project was located in Paris. To resolve this difficulty, the filmmakers of the CRP videotaped the work they were doing and then screened this working process for the workers to critique (a precursor to Marin Karmitz's use of video in *Coup pour coup*). While this process was somewhat laborious and ineffective, as it once more posed problems regarding materials (for example, the use of a cumbersome video projector), the next practical step necessary to ensure the participation of the workers concerned was to select a number of shots of May '68 at Flins from the film and edit them together. This assembly was then screened for the workers, and the commentary that was spoken during the projection was recorded. The group then shot footage in 1969, focusing primarily on a tendency of left-wing journals like *L'Humanité* and *Aurore* to treat revolutionary workers as fascists, revisionists, and so on.[50]

The CRP considered this film to be a perfect example of the kind that corresponded to the desires of the masses. The fact that they were unable to find a legal screening space for this film led to them projecting the film in the courtyard of a public housing project, "literally protected by the masses". This so-called protection translated into chasing away the police, who came to break up the screening. The result, according to the CRP, was that the film had two soundtracks: that of the film and that of the mêlée that was occurring during the screening.[51]

In a rather interesting twist, during the interview with Hennebelle and Martin, the CRP filmmakers were asked about their position on censorship. They decried the repression of freedom of expression, citing the quotidian confiscation of the newspaper *La cause du peuple*: "It's up to the masses to revolt and give rise to their own films and assure their distribution."[52] Further, they discussed another of their films, *La Palestine vaincra*,[53] which was again, somewhat ironically, seized by police during a screening.[54] Again, what renders these comments somewhat contradictory is the fact that this same "group" effectively acted like Maoist censors in their stealing and re-editing of Thorn's work.

For a group like Ligne rouge, the spontaneous approach of the CRP was anti-Marxist and denied the specific characteristics of the epoch. Film should not merely follow the spontaneous uprisings as they occur. If film is based only on these spontaneous uprisings, without developing a Marxist–Leninist line, then it will disarm the masses. These films, they suggested, merely gathered together the masses, but what, asked the writers of the tract, would we think of a political tract, a brochure or a pamphlet that maintained such characteristics? Approaching film this way – allowing spontaneous emotion to dictate the debate – renders the projection of militant films synonymous with the proceedings of a ciné-club. However, it is worth remarking that in outlining their position on spontaneity Ligne rouge took a bold step by citing the proponents of this model as anti-Marxist. Rather, the more correct criticism would seem to be that spontaneity is anti-Leninist.[55]

Turning to the issue of formalism, Ligne rouge suggested that, while not as pernicious as those issues cited above, it does nevertheless need to be eliminated from the practice. It was, to their mind, a "petit-bourgeois deformation"[56] that gave formal experimentation a revolutionary value in itself. The example they gave was filming the Eiffel Tower and then projecting it upside down. The so-called revolutionary value would be the rupture with traditional bourgeois forms. Considering these two claims in combination with the previous critique is useful: they not only point to the discursive tendencies refuted by Ligne rouge but equally demarcate the often reductive discourse of Ligne rouge itself. While appearing slightly before the fragmentation of the left-wing political terrain (on which many struggles would begin to take place), the text reveals a reliance on binary principles (even if coded by recourse to what they referred to as "dialectical thinking"). That is, it remains a discourse that thinks in terms of working "inside" and/or "outside" the system, with the caveat that merely being "outside the system" does not constitute a radical revolutionary project.

Ligne rouge pointed to a final type of film they deemed ineffective: the didactic or dogmatic film. They cited those films that mechanically attach a dogmatic voiceover to the film, examples being *Pravda* by the Dziga Vertov Group and Joris Ivens's *Le peuple et ses fusils*. The writers suggested that the pedagogic value of these sorts of films was quite limited because, again, to simply place an ideologically dogmatic voiceover onto a film would not connect with the masses but would instead render the ideas all the more unreadable.

In a section entitled "Towards a communist propaganda cinema", the group posed the question: "what films need to be made today?"[57] Thus began the programmatic section of the text. Ligne rouge cites as imperative "Films of political analysis and propaganda that are not content simply to show a struggle and glorify it, but rather analyse it by showing the internal and external contradictions, which are a weapon of communist education."[58] They pointed to a hypothetical example of such a project – a film about the demonstration at Pierre Overney's funeral.[59] A number of films had tackled the subject, but according to the criticism of Ligne rouge, these films only showed the demonstrators and Geismar's speech.[60] What was necessary was a film that could demonstrate a host of issues: the role revisionism had played in the narrative of Overney's assassination (perhaps in the way that *Oser lutter* did with Gilles Tautin); the response of the demonstrators; the various political positions held by the demonstrators (they cite the Trotskyites, who refused to yell an anti-revisionist slogan); and finally the number of people at the demonstration who did not normally militate alongside the far left. They suggested that such an example illustrated the difference between the specific, concrete approach that they were advocating for and the approach of the *spontanistes*.[61]

The question that follows is this: if these are the films to be made, how does one go about making such films? The first necessity when approaching a subject to film is to acknowledge the limitations of a single film; that is, no single film can represent the entirety of problems of the class struggle. So while a film needs to maintain its pedagogic or didactic aspect, it is imperative that the film also delimits its subject. While this approach gestures to the limitations of film as a medium with which to transmit political content, Ligne rouge suggested that there is a counter-capacity of film, which enables it to take very complex and abstract ideas and render them readable and concrete. They cited the example of undertaking a film project about French imperialism: the approach should not be to attack the whole of the phenomena, which would quite simply result in a mess. Rather, it should be to focus perhaps on the struggle of illegal immigrants, and, in interrogating this phenomenon, to begin to render visible/readable a specific aspect of French imperialism.[62] *Oser lutter* functions again as an example:

> The film is centred on the revisionist betrayal of the workers at Renault-Flins during May and June of 68: this is the framework of the film, but the other aspects of revisionism are shown based on the concrete example of Flins (the myth of the "pacific transition to socialism", the betrayal of the P "C" F at the political level, etc.). With cinema we must understand how to move from the specific (the concrete experience, an aspect of a problem) to the general.[63]

In practical, pedagogical terms, the text detailed the way in which the stages of production must unfold, beginning with the investigation: *enquête*. (In fact, this section of the text opens with a quote usually attributed to Mao but here credited to Stalin: "No investigation, no right to speak".[64]) As we will see in the discussion of the *établis*, below, this issue of the investigation will take on a profound meaning for Thorn and his political practice. The initial investigation is the most important aspect of the filmmaking process, according to the tract. And here the authors cited the waste of film in situations where the militant filmmakers show up to a demonstration and start shooting film aimlessly; they likened this technique to the method adopted by bourgeois journalists. They also cited the problem of film crews which show up to a demonstration or strike but have no affiliation with the workers involved, and so end up seeming antithetical, even alien to them. This approach is reminiscent of that adopted by those creating counter-television: the result is a slightly more progressive news story than that which one is used to seeing on television.

The investigation begins with the question, "why are we filming this particular struggle?"[65] In concrete practice, filmmakers are meant to respond to this question by going to the place of the struggle, familiarising themselves with the conditions and making contact with the militants leading the strike, demonstration, and so on. It is from this initial point that the subject of the film can be organised and the shooting can begin.

Ligne rouge finally addressed the issue of montage – which is as much about post-production editing as it is something that occurs prior to shooting, during the investigation stage of the film. Montage comprises the choice of subject and the choice of what to shoot (the images). These elements are organised after the shoot to make the film beneficial to as many people as possible – the issue that was really at the heart of Thorn's experience with *Oser lutter*. Again, prior to this text, Thorn's approach to making the film about the strike at Flins had, in the stages before editing, been rooted in precisely what the group were now expressly condemning. Thus the filmmakers at Ligne rouge had yet to practise the investigation, which they extolled, as intensely as they had practised (and theorised) montage. And, in turning to montage, the group began by quoting Eisenstein:

> Thus montage is characterised by contradiction, by the conflict of two elements opposing each other […] [T]o the conception of montage as a linkage of elements, the amassing of bricks to develop ideas, I oppose my idea of montage as a collision: a concept according to which the contradiction of the two factors creates a concept.[66]

During this period, and within the militant milieu, Eisenstein was not a neutral or universally heralded figure. The debate was evidenced in the choice of Godard, Gorin, Jean-Henri Roger and others to call their collective the Groupe Dziga Vertov. The ambiguous relationship to Eisenstein is also emphasised within the layout of the text, where the quote is juxtaposed with a sidebar critique indicating that, while they are in agreement with the dialectical aspect of the quote, they find that Eisenstein has erred: while montage as a confrontation with contradictions may give rise to readability and comprehensiveness, it must be noted that "films do not create concepts".[67] For Ligne rouge, montage is the organisation of the real and the facts according to a given political line, which is an interesting, if perhaps contradictory, way of formally presenting their arguments. Such a presentation leaves open a kind of interpretive space, meaning that the facts are presented within the framework of Ligne rouge's position (i.e., montage). However, this does not exclude the possibility of montage presenting the same reality and the same facts according to an altogether different ideology.

Ligne rouge used a Mao quote to neatly summarise what they saw as their production method:

> Take the ideas of the masses (scattered and unsystematic ideas) and concentrate them (through study turn them into concentrated and systematic ideas), then go to the masses and propagate and explain these ideas until the masses embrace them as their own, hold fast to them and translate them into action, and test the correctness of these ideas in such action. Then once again concentrate ideas from the masses and once again go the masses so that the ideas are persevered in and carried through.... Such is the Marxist theory of knowledge.[68]

Thus, Ligne rouge's working philosophy was, in their eyes, the Marxist understanding that the real hero *is* the masses. While a debate regarding simple binaries such as form and content may seem naïve today, their focus could nevertheless be reduced to an element of what they referred to as the film's "content", and they expressly set out with every intention to unify form and content. For Ligne rouge, there was no neutral form, and they insisted on the idea that revolutionary content needs a revolutionary form. Thus, their concern was not so much the narrative continuity of the film. The group was not interested in showing the adventures of a bourgeois hero; rather, its concern was to demonstrate the contradictions of the class struggle and to make these contradictions apparent to the masses: effectively, to arm the masses. Regardless of whether their films were exercises in direct cinema or fiction films, their foundation was always communism and the struggle against the bourgeois class.

Again, Ligne rouge cited Mao in a particularly paradoxical formulation:

> We must have consideration for our specialists, they are very important to our cause. However ... it is only in being the representatives of the masses that they can educate them, only in being their students that they can become their masters.[69]

This quote opens up the discussion surrounding what was then the controversial practice of putting the camera in the hands of the workers. This issue is dealt with in more detail in the discussions of Cinéma Libre, Cinélutte and certainly Les groupes Medvedkine. However, it is important to point out here that Ligne rouge understood this practice to be an unadulterated passing of the technical means of production to a group of factory workers or to workers in some other sector of the revolutionary class.[70] Ligne rouge wrote:

This explanation [the Mao quote] is important because a dominant current idea is: no specialists, cameras in the hands of the workers. This is only demagogy and an anarchistic deviation from the mass line. This "workerist" conception is extremely dangerous, reducing the role of revolutionary filmmakers to a mutual assistance committee of cameras, techniques, film and a work force, without foregrounding the political choices that will determine the film to be made, its orientation, the line that will guide them, the choice of militants with whom they choose to side, their function in the mass movement, and so on. Again we find here the desire to stop this conception's revolutionary use as the mere trailer of the spontaneous movement. These spontaneous ideas by our demagogues are as grave as, in cinematic terms, the idea of a communist avant-garde that is attacked. In effect if it suffices today to give the cameras to those leading the struggle to create a communist cinema, that would mean that the communist would have no role to play whatsoever, that there is no need for Marxist–Leninist theory to synthesise the ideas of the masses.[71]

This passage proves to be one of the most inflexible iterations of the argument against putting the camera in the hands of the workers. And, even though this text would serve as an inspiration to groups like Cinélutte, such groups would articulate the problem in much less dogmatic terms.[72] Further, the formulation regarding the need for a Marxist–Leninist theory and the possibility of its uselessness may provide some insight into Thorn's imminent abandoning of cinema, in an attempt to participate in, and fully understand, the experience of the working class (see the section below on the *établis*).

Ligne rouge attributed a kind of erroneous faith to the *spontanistes* in their practice of giving the cameras to workers, suggesting that films made in such a way have no educative value and ultimately remain the "blind follower" (*remorque*) of the masses. But their text gives way to a discussion of another controversial topic that challenges the notion of a "pure" and entirely democratic/egalitarian film collective. There remains the problematic role of "specialists" working within the most advanced sectors of the working class.[73] For Ligne rouge, the specialist's role involved "creating a close relationship with the masses during the investigative stage of the filmmaking process, using Marxist–Leninist theory to synthesise the findings of the investigation and creating historical investigations according to a Marxist–Leninist line".[74] There is a suggestion that certain militant filmmakers had the experience of being *spontaniste*, but they realised the difficulty of such a project when confronted with the montage stage of production. Though the writers do not cite any single group or filmmaker, it is possible to attribute this "evolution" in a Marxist–Leninist understanding of filmmaking not only to those filmmakers at Les états généraux du cinéma, but more precisely to those filmmakers writing the text, the filmmakers from ARC, and, more specifically, to Thorn and those who participated in the creation of *Oser lutter*.

The final section of *Vive le cinéma* turns to distribution – a subject that would later be stressed repeatedly with the emergence of groups like Cinélutte and Cinéma Libre. Ligne rouge suggested that the issue of distribution posed the same questions as the issue of film production. Whereas with production, the question is what film is to be made, with distribution the question is which film is to be projected, which is to be distributed. Further, the question of method had a role in this discussion as well – that is, *how* is the film to be distributed?

The cardinal rule for Ligne rouge was that distribution should entail the dissemination of films that educated and mobilised the masses. An aspect of this pedagogical emphasis was manifested in a common practice within the milieu of *cinéma militant*: namely, the production team (or a single representative) travelled with the films and attended screenings in order to present their own critiques of the films, to clarify the political line and, more generally, to stimulate discussion. For Ligne rouge, the idea of reckless (wildcat) screening and distribution was considered both a *spontaneous* practice and a "terrorist" practice. They saw in such practices the articulation of a revisionist disdain for communist work, as well as a refusal to accord "revolutionary" cinema the same place as other forms of propaganda. In keeping with the idea of a specific political line, just as a film cannot be produced "correctly" if it does not have a concrete and precise goal, neither can it be received "correctly" if it does not have such a goal. Where the *spontanistes* gave credence to the idea that a film can get the masses talking, Ligne rouge logically responded with a counter-interrogatory: if the masses are talking, what exactly is it that they are talking about? For Ligne rouge, this kind of spontaneous generalisation expressed the diminution of the value of the communists' role in educating the masses and directing their struggles.[75]

The group critiqued a number of *spontaniste* beliefs, one of which was that certain films shouldn't be distributed because they are too difficult for members of the working class to understand (Ligne rouge held that this simply played into a myth about the working class). They also disagreed that films representing violent struggles would provoke violent struggles. To this latter idea they responded that it is untenable, as it suggests that any film with any political line will be adequate. Again, their critique was that this thinking denied the role of the revolutionary communist filmmaker. In a succinct summary of their thoughts on the practice of merely showing violent struggles on film, Ligne rouge noted that "for a while now we've been showing films of the barricades and violent confrontations with the CRS, and yet we haven't had a new May of 68".[76]

A film's distribution, then, must always take into account the role of distributors as communist propagandists. Given that the films are but one moment in the work of propaganda, there is a need to have texts prepared for the discussions following screenings – texts that will help lead the direction of the debate, to clarify the film. As an illustration, Ligne rouge supported the idea of distributing revolutionary tracts along with the films. The examples they provided were *State and revolution*, to be read alongside *Oser lutter*, and *Where do correct ideas come from?*, to be read alongside *Le dieu de la peste* (Farewell to the god of plague, 1969–1971), a Chinese documentary about a bilharziasis epidemic:[77]

> To those who suggest that overly difficult films should not be used, we respond: from now on we can say that a film is a work analogous to that of a tract; its particularity is that its concrete power renders it a vibrant medium; it is a very particular type of brochure in that it can be read by many people simultaneously, it can be distributed to a larger mass [audience] without being of an inferior theoretical quality.[78]

They believed that films needed to be shown to the most resistant element in the working class, not just those already in tune with the given political line. In response to the argument that progressive films – not just Marxist–Leninist films – needed to be distributed, the group agreed, but added that it would be necessary to direct the discussions of the films within a Marxist–Leninist framework.

2.4 Cinéma Libre

While distribution was a prime concern of Ligne rouge and a large part of the activity of Cinélutte, it was such an integral aspect of *cinéma militant* that certain collectives were created with the sole objective of distributing films. Apart from some minor forays into production, Cinéma Libre was just such a distribution collective. Issuing from the movement of May 1968, Cinéma Libre was pejoratively considered a mailbox (*boîte aux lettres*) for the distribution of films made by far-left film collectives (indeed, Thorn and Cinélutte often levelled this charge at them). And yet the group had an elaborate and well-articulated position with regard to distribution and took as a kind of working motto the idea that "the distribution of a film is not only a moment of political intervention, but also a political intervention in cinema".[79]

Bernard Clarens and Klaus Gerke of Secours rouge[80] created Cinéma Libre in December 1971. Its primary goal was to create a distribution network that would help to move militant cinema from its marginalised status (the leftist "ghetto"), enabling it to reach the masses and become an "arm of propaganda [and] agitation and [able] to popularise struggles".[81] They pointed to the poor circulation of films like *Octobre à Paris* and *Sucre amer* leading up to May '68, and then to the insular and sectarian distribution of films in the immediate post-'68 period.[82]

For Cinéma Libre, militant filmmaking, and particularly what they would go on to characterise as post-'68 *cinéma militant à l'extrême gauche*, became a reality that needed to be dealt with on a more advanced level than it had been up this point. The concrete manifestation of militant filmmaking's rise in status was found in the prevalence of cinema as a political tool in just about every left-wing and far-left organisation, as well as in all cultural groups. And, while recognising this proliferation of *cinéma militant*, Cinéma Libre were quick to point to the reductive tendency of certain organisations with regard to their use of cinema as a political tool. Citing Unicité (formerly Dynadia), the PCF's filmmaking wing, Cinéma Libre, much like Thorn and Ligne rouge, saw a tendency to subordinate film to the status of an "appendix" to political action. That is, such organisations made the mistake of not recognising that cinema itself could be a political action.[83] Further, the group found that in this jumble of political discourses and practices, the only unifying characteristic that emerged was a deflationary, negative definition of *cinéma militant*: militant film was anything that was *not* a part of dominant or commercial cinema.[84]

In their analysis Cinéma Libre outlined "three modes of *cinéma militant*": propaganda, agitation and artistic supplement to political intervention. First, propaganda films are attached to a particular political line; that is, the spectators, as well as the film's makers, participate in a homogenous discourse that sees in film merely a potential to "illustrate" a given political line. This standpoint has two obvious weaknesses: that film remains the lapdog of the discourse, and that discourse must admit a weakness, given that it cannot stand on its own (that is, it requires an illustrator). In the end, the limitations of this kind of film are revealed by the self-legitimising character of the relationship between film spectator and the producer or filmmaker.[85] Second, agitation films seek to transmit information to the largest number of spectators, that is, to popularise a particular struggle through film. The third mode uses film as an artistic supplement to political intervention. This last position points towards a fundamental question that troubles militant cinema more generally: that of the spectacular aspect of the medium, that is, enjoyment.

Cinéma Libre's initial project had been to struggle against bourgeois production and distribution in the form of a struggle against spectacular consumption. The group's objective was to transform the relationship between film and individual as passive spectator into a collective and active relationship:

collective through a political critique of the idea of the audience [*publique*], through a particular way of leading debates following screenings, transforming the relationship between the audience and the cultural-filmic object, and *active* through research on the film screened and the communal practice – effective or potential – of the "collectivity-audience".[86]

And yet while wanting to create these "engaged relationships" between the film and its audience in order to undo the bourgeois practices of consuming film as mere spectacle, Cinéma Libre was also aware of the simplistic and mistaken aspects of this critique. So they sought to redress the issues by adopting an analysis of the spectacular function of cinema that went beyond the reductive formula "spectacle = bourgeois tool". In this sense, Cinéma Libre did not want to rid cinema entirely of its spectacular nature; rather, the militant cineastes

> needed to take responsibility for the cultural question both politically and without guilt. It needs to be recognised that *cinéma militant* should also be thought of as cinema, that is as a cultural object, an object of pleasure: precisely what an entire period of "leftism" refused to see, blinded as it was by its workerism and its defiance towards all that belonged to the "intellectual" domain and consequently the artist.[87]

Yet there was a problem with this understanding of, and approach to, militant film: it could never be universally adopted by the militant collectives or individuals as long as cinema remained a mere "artistic supplement".[88]

Cinéma Libre sought to carry out its programme of distribution within three specific domains. They favoured traditional far-left organisations (they cited La Ligue communiste, the GP and the Parti socialiste unifié [PSU]), groups emerging as part of the expanded cultural front (for example, Le mouvement de la libération des femmes [MLF], Groupe d'information sur les prisons [GIP]) and ciné-clubs, where they could move from the fetishistic/cinephilic approach to cinema to a politically engaged and conscious one.[89] These organisations pointed to the changing political tide, which was advancing towards the breakdown of a strictly Marxist–Leninist line within the far-left political milieu. Specifically, they pointed to the new struggles emerging in the domains of women's rights; lesbian, gay, bisexual and transgender (LGBT) rights; opposition to psychiatric incarceration; and advocacy for prisoners' rights and housing issues. Such a diverse tendency within the far-left community required, according to Cinéma Libre, a centralised distribution network for the mass of films. Centralisation was also necessary to assist those militants who were working within one of the various cultural frameworks that included the cinema in their activity, for example ciné-clubs, MJCs (Les maisons des jeunes et de la culture), high schools and regional associations.[90]

Cinéma Libre's position vis-à-vis general far-left organisations was that they were unexplored political terrain or "new fronts on which to struggle".[91] They maintained a position that was anti-cellular, which clearly made them vulnerable to criticism launched by various political cells. And yet their expansionist policy did not signify that they had renounced all positions or remained neutral with regard to the dominant far-left political tendencies of Trotskyism, Maoism, anarchism and other movements. Rather, their quasi-antisectarianism pointed to the necessity of maintaining a distance from particular groups in order to escape what they saw as an increasingly prevalent "*groupusculisme*".[92]

Cinéma Libre elaborated their position on an issue that was being debated by the militant filmmakers of the period, an idea closely adhered to by the group Cinélutte: production should be in the service of distribution (the counter-slogan, adopted by the Groupe Dziga Vertov, was "We produce, distribution will follow"[93]). Cinéma Libre suggested that their role as a distribution collective put them in a position to see the limitations of such a practice:

> The outcome of our practice has also brought us to no longer consider distribution as a means of investigation for the production of militant films. The experience has shown us the limits of "production in the service of distribution". In fact, the investigation runs into a nearly insurmountable problem: the debate in which it proposes to engage is already *delimited* by the conception of the militant cinema conveyed by the films that serve as its foundation, even if the "investigators" have a critical attitude with regard to the films. Since the practice of filmmaking (the relation of production among the crew, the place of the camera with regard to the reality reflected, the relationship between the "filmed" and the "filmers", etc.) has an effect on the form of "knowledge" conveyed by the film and therefore on the relationship to this knowledge that it will establish with its audience.[94]

And:

> Effectively the practice of creating a film (the relations of production within the crew, the placement of the camera in front of the reality to be reflected, the relationship between "filmer"/"filmed", etc.) has a direct repercussion on the form of "knowledge" conveyed by the film, and therefore on the relationship to this knowledge that will be established with "its audience" [...] it is these relationships to knowledge, these relationships between the discourse of a film and the spectator that reveal the political role in play during a film screened within the militant distribution framework.[95]

The response to this problem in the framework of Cinéma Libre's position is twofold. Either films need to continue the project of a *film de synthèse*, no longer specifically related to the movement of May 1968 but more generally "synthesising the experiences of the struggles of the masses" while pointing to some of the contradictions that occur within the struggles, *or* films should organise the discourse of the masses in order to bring out the political line within it, again with an effort at pointing to some of the contradictions that arise in such struggles, movements, masses, and so on:

> It is the relationships between the discourse of the film and the spectator that reveal the political role a film plays. These relationships help [us] to understand one of the most paralysing contradictions in the distribution of *cinéma militant*: that which brings us to irreducibly oppose "militant distribution" and "commercial distribution".[96]

The politics of Cinéma Libre were invested in creating a film distribution project that would provide a body of work that described the contemporary political environment. In turn, this would give way to a description of the everyday functioning of society:

> Such a project is not the result of chance. It responds to three problems that have come about as a result of our last few years of work: (1) the contradiction between artistic work

and collective work, (2) the relationships between political discourses and artistic work, and (3) the place of the intellectual within social reality.[97]

Regarding the first point, Cinéma Libre pointed to the limitations, even failures, which they had confronted when trying to make a collective film about the Resistance. The initial hopes of this project were that they would be able to create a collective that didn't mirror a traditional division of labour, and in which everyone would be able to participate in every aspect of the production. The fact that the project was never realised under these conditions resulted in their reformulation of the principal of collectivity. This new viewpoint had a distinctly Fourierist appeal – those most passionately attracted to the preparation, creative aspects, and so on, should take on a more directorial or even managerial role in the creation of the film.

In reference to the relationship between political discourse and artistic work, Cinéma Libre again drew on their experience with a failed project, this time a feature-length documentary on the Lip watch factory. The film, as they understood it, suffered from amateurism. While the project's failure stemmed from their own inability to come up with a sufficient theory to inform the Lip movement, more concrete reasons related to production also played a role. For instance, montage had not taken the primary role that it could have, and the conception of the project was not specific enough:

> As filmmakers we weren't at Lip or elsewhere for ourselves, but to transcribe an event. The problem is no longer just to see but to reflect upon the manner in which we would transcribe that which we chose to shoot. It is a question of finding a specific filmic language.[98]

Cinéma Libre thus sought to break with the amateurism they saw as plaguing much of the militant cinema of the time.

Cinéma Libre's critique of amateurism was a provocation to address the perennial issue of *la caméra aux ouvriers*, and the group aimed their criticism of this practice towards all those who extolled the strictly workerist perspective. Their concern was that a camera in the hands of a worker who has not reflected on the problem to be filmed will end up simply producing a representation analogous to the numerous TV news reports by which that worker has been conditioned.[99]

Along with this position on amateurism was a concern with *specialisation*. In terms of production, Cinéma Libre cited three levels that determine the elaboration of the political line of a film: the relationship between the crew and those being filmed during the creation of a scene; the place of the film or the camera within the struggle; and the relationships that are established among the crew themselves, particularly in relation to specialists.[100] On this last point Cinéma Libre refused the role of being a mere intermediary between politics and militants, meaning that the films that they would make/distribute would have to be more than mere "documents" about feminism or unemployment. The group was equally contemptuous of the direct approach of showing up at an event and merely filming the "heroic moments".[101] In fact, Cinéma Libre finished their self-description by suggesting that they were more interested in shooting the banal and the everyday than creating images that recount dogmatic truths.[102]

Ultimately, Cinéma Libre's aim was to interrogate the relationship between the revolutionary movement and *cinéma militant* – a relationship that was in need of both positive and critical analyses. On the positive side, they hoped to make it possible to bring film to groups who were not yet aware of the power of cinema as political action. On the critical side, the films themselves needed to be analysed from the standpoint of film criticism proper, which risked calling into question the cinematic quality and integrity of the films.

2.5 Les établis

Preceding a crisis in 1969 within Ligne rouge, Thorn and a few others established a critical movement that was triggered by Thorn's growing frustration with the apparently unceasing series of ideological debates (this crisis would ultimately splinter the group into different factions: Drapeau rouge and Prolétaire ligne rouge).[103] The thrust of this new venture was that the focus on theory needed to be abandoned in favour of an immersion in social reality. Given that the group had begun to split up, Thorn left and undertook the project of becoming an *établi*.

The history of *établissement* is a particularity of the French far left, primarily Maoist but with some Trotskyite and independent participants as well. Outside of France, the phenomena had a sporadic existence. For example, there is a written account of an *établi* in Germany,[104] a tendency within the Québécois Maoist movement[105] and even at least one American case.[106] But in general, what is referred to as the movement of *établissement* is a French Maoist practice. The genesis of *établissement* can be located in a French translation of a Mao Tse-Tung quote:

> *Puisque les intellectuels sont appelés à servir les masses ouvrières et paysannes, ils doivent tout d'abord les comprendre et bien connaître leur vie, leur travail et leur mentalité. Nous recommandons aux intellectuels d'aller parmi les masses, dans les usines, dans les campagnes. Il serait fort mauvais qu'ils ne se trouvent jamais, de toute leur vie, avec des ouvriers et des paysans. Nos travailleurs de l'État, nos écrivains, nos artistes, nos enseignants et nos travailleurs de la recherche scientifique doivent saisir toutes les occasions possibles pour entrer en contact avec les ouvriers et les paysans. Certains peuvent aller dans les usines ou à la campagne juste pour jeter un coup d'oeil et faire un tour; cela s'appelle "regarder les fleurs du haut de son cheval", ce qui vaut toujours mieux que de rester chez soi et ne rien voir. D'autres peuvent y séjourner plusieurs mois pour mener des enquêtes et se faire des amis; cela s'appelle "descendre de cheval pour regarder les fleurs". D'autres encore peuvent y rester et y vivre longtemps, par exemple, deux ou trois ans, ou même plus; cela s'appelle "s'établir".*
>
> [Since they are to serve the masses of workers and peasants, intellectuals must, first and foremost, know them and be familiar with their life, work and ideas. We encourage intellectuals to go among the masses, to go to factories and villages. It is very bad if you never in all your life meet a worker or a peasant. Our state personnel, writers, artists, teachers and scientific research workers should seize every opportunity to get close to the workers and peasants. Some can go to factories or villages just to look around; this may be called "looking at the flowers on horseback" and is better than doing nothing at all. Others can stay for a few months, conducting investigations and making friends; this may be called "dismounting to look at the flowers". Still others can stay and live there for a considerable time, say, two or three years or even longer; this may be called "settling down".][107]

The movement of *établissement* wanted students and intellectuals to give up their career aspirations and plant themselves within the working class. Practically speaking, this meant getting hired (in general, clandestinely) at a factory. This was not the first movement of intellectuals to take up factory work, and nor was it even the first French movement of intellectuals in the factory. In France, the tradition dates back to the Saint Simonians at the beginning of the nineteenth century, who incited the polytechnicians to get hired in the foundries in order to teach the proletariat how to take control of the factories.[108] Jules Vallès, in his novel *Le Bachelier*, describes a phenomenon similar to that of the *établi*. Also, in the early twentieth century, there were individual occurrences of intellectuals working clandestinely in the factory; writers like Jacques Valdour, Michèle Aumont and Jean de Vincennes all wrote of their experiences on the factory floor.[109] But perhaps the best-known individual experiment in this practice was Simone Weil's working undercover alongside the proletariat, summarised in her book *La condition ouvrière*.[110] France also saw movements that were less individual, such as the movement of the *prêtres-ouvriers* (worker priests) and the postwar Trotskyites at Voix ouvrière/Lutte ouvrière.[111]

But the movement of *établissement* proper begins with the UJCML. In 1966, at the 19th congress of the UEC, an Althusserian tendency (the Ulmards) within the UEC announced its position as Marxist–Leninist (the term was a stand-in for "Maoist" or "pro-Chinese" before these terms became popular). Headed by Robert Linhart, Louis Althusser's prize student, the faction was ejected from the UEC and went on to establish the UJCML. The following summer, in 1967, a year after the creation of the UJCML, the second congress was held before the scholastic break.[112] The theme of this congress was the importance of the *enquête*. The significance of this concept for the group is highlighted by the editorial in issue 5 of *Garde rouge*: "Whoever has not conducted an investigation [*enquête*] has no right to speak."

> Contrary to intellectual spontaneity, the Marxist–Leninist analysis of French social reality in its diverse aspects requires a patient work of concrete analysis and investigation, a solid basis on which we can construct the line, undertake partial analyses of the conjuncture, and progressively put into place the diverse elements of the programme [...] But it seems, given the specificity of our situation, that the investigation has another fundamental value. By means of it we can respond to the question: how do we ally ourselves with the working class? To merely have contact with a few workers isn't enough. To inform workers, to incite them to organise, that is a long-term project that we must undertake.[113]

The "*enquêtes*" of the summer of 1967 were divided into three separate events. The first and most spectacular was the invitation of members of the UJCML to travel to China and meet with the Communist Party and witness the Cultural Revolution first-hand. The delegation that went to China was composed of, among others, Robert Linhart and Jean-Pierre Le Dantec.[114] While this group lived the dream of being in China during the revolution, another delegation, led by Alain Monchalbon, was sent to Albania, a less prestigious affair by far.[115] Finally, while these two delegations were conducting their investigations abroad, a third delegation had been established to investigate the political climate among the working class in France. One of these groups, led by Nicole Linhart (Robert Linhart's wife), went to Vergèze to meet with workers from the Perrier factory and found that there were workers who supported both the Chinese and Albanian theses.[116]

When the three groups reconvened in the fall of 1967, the collective research of the delegations was presented at the "Conférence sur les enquêtes". It was here that they formulated "La ligne d'établissement". At a meeting in November 1967, the first of three primary waves of *établissement* began. Young students, *lycéens*, and intellectuals were incited to abandon their studies and careers to work and militate in factories. The aim of this practice was, in particular, to develop a militant Marxist–Leninist group within the CGT.

This was the first wave of *établis*, and there were roughly two more to follow. During the summer of '68 and the participation in the events, many students were content to express their political engagement at the barricades in the Latin Quarter or supporting striking workers. After the events, a second wave of *établi*s began and continued through the period of the GP. This is the period in which Thorn entered the factory.

One of the stumbling blocks for students wanting to become *établis* was that any young person showing up at a factory looking for work whose employment history didn't include factory work immediately raised the suspicions of the employers. So to become an *établi* was to get hired clandestinely. Such was the case for Thorn, who was a student and had to find a way to get social security. In order to erase his past, he worked a number of jobs in the textile industry, eventually getting social security. It was finally in 1971 that he became an *établi* at Alstom-Saint-Ouen, where he stayed until 1979. Thorn suggested that there were two main reasons for choosing Alstom: one was quite simply that the metro went directly there from Paris. The second, more political reason was that Alstom was ripe for *établissement* because the management was interested in employing members of the far left in order to destabilise the very powerful CGT.[117] According to Perron, Alstom was a factory that had a bad reputation for entry-level workers. It was low-paying, it offered poor benefits, it employed very strict management and its working conditions were rumoured to be awful.[118]

When he decided to become an *établi*, Thorn did so (somewhat contrary to common practice) independently and without the direct influence of a party. Although Thorn remained in contact with the remnants of Ligne rouge, his practice as a militant was initially focused on distributing pro-Chinese tracts, initiating cultural activities with his co-workers, such as screening films (*Kafr Kassem* [1975] and *Salt of the Earth* [1954]), and creating a book based on *Oser lutter* with stills from the film (Figure 2.16). But Thorn's militant activity would be carried out largely as a trade unionist.

When Thorn first arrived at Alstom, the CGT at the factory immediately denounced him, saying that he was the boss's lapdog.[119] His initial project was to create a Maoist line in the factory by organising *comités de base*. After a year of trying to organise the *comités de base*, Thorn founded, along with an Italian and an Algerian co-worker, a section of the CFDT within Alstom. The creation of the CFDT section was largely guided by the idea of organising the *ouvriers spécialisés* (OS), composed principally of immigrant workers who had no voice within the unions. According to Thorn, at that time, all the union delegates were white and higher-level workers (*ouvriers quali-fiés*).[120] The CFDT was such a success at Alstom that by 1975 their membership was exactly equal to that of the CGT membership.[121]

While at Alstom, Thorn became particularly aware of strikes involving immigrant workers. In 1973, racist attacks in France were on the rise, and they included assassinations. A Maoist organisa-

Figure 2.16

tion called Mouvement des travailleurs arabes called for a day of strikes in France against racism.[122] The CGT at Alstom refused to participate, saying that the immigrants never went on strike when they were asked to, and were in fact the bosses' allies. Thorn and the CFDT organised all the immigrants from each shop floor and called for the strike that the CGT refused. Out of 2,000 workers at Alstom, 600 went on strike.[123]

Around the same time, two strikes in the vicinity of Alstom were of interest to Thorn. One was composed almost entirely of immigrant workers who were striking against saturnism (an illness related to lead poisoning). This was the strike at Pennaroya,[124] and by participating in this strike, Thorn and the others saw how these immigrant workers were organizing. The other strike of interest took place at Margoline, a factory where the workers were almost all undocumented workers.

2.6 *La grève des ouvriers de Margoline* (1973, B/W, 41 min.)

Thorn made the film *La grève des ouvriers de Margoline* while he was still an *établi* at Alstom, and it was one of the first films to deal with the issue of immigrant workers, and in particular undocumented ones *(sans papiers)*.[125] While Thorn was an *établi*, he had more or less abandoned filmmaking, although he maintained a connection with it by occasionally participating in Cinélutte meetings, and even assisting in the editing of *Bonne chance la France* (see below). But in May 1973, joined by members of Cinélutte, Thorn made *Margoline*, a film that he edited in the evenings after work. Cinélutte produced the film (Figure 2.17) and went on to distribute it paired with their film *Jusqu'au bout*.[126]

The subject of *Margoline* is a strike by undocumented immigrant workers in response to the Fontanet–Marcellin memorandum, a law articulated across *Margoline* and transformed by the end of the film. While the subject matter, namely a factory strike, is clearly in line with Thorn's political sensibilities, *Margoline* does not place its primary emphasis on the unions in the strike. However, by the end of the film, the CFDT is foregrounded, but presented in a very different tone and perspective than that of *Oser lutter, oser vaincre*.

In general, the political method of *Margoline* is different from that of *Oser lutter*, but there are still a number of similarities in Thorn's approach to documenting a strike. From the outset, there are two similar formal strategies: the use of title cards and the construction of a clear narrative. *Margoline* opens with the announcement that on 21 June 1973, the French government used its police to protect a racist meeting by the fascist group Ordre nouveau ("New Order") (Figure 2.19). The announcement is juxtaposed with a sequence from the meeting in question and the virulent anti-immigration speeches that accompany it. The sequence cuts back and forth between this footage and footage of the police combating the counter-demonstration being held outside the meeting.

To explain the details of the Fontanet–Marcellin memorandum, Thorn relies on a title card in French and Arabic (accompanied by an Arabic voiceover, as is the

Figure 2.17

case with all title cards in the film): the card tells us that on 15 September 1972, the French government had reinforced immigration control under the guise of combating rampant immigration by means of the memorandum. This memorandum stipulated that every immigrant worker who entered France would be required to do so with a contract from the national bureau of immigration already in hand; the contract bound the immigrant to one year, with one employer, in one region and in one profession, with the decision regarding renewal made according only to the needs of the employer.

Figure 2.18

The film explains that at the border, police allowed undocumented workers to enter knowing full well that their papers would be refused. The Fontanet–Marcellin memorandum further forbade any and all retroactive normalisation of the immigrant worker (OS or labourer). This meant that those who were already in the country and employed, but without the newly ordered documentation, would be forcefully expelled and allowed re-entry only after acquiring the appropriate documentation.

Figure 2.19

In these sequences of explication one of the subtle differences in approach between *Margoline* and *Oser* emerges, the difference between a propaganda film and a pedagogical film. Where *Oser* sought to develop a unified and programmatic ML consensus about the strike at Flins and the events of May more generally, the use of title cards in *Margoline* gestures more towards a kind of case-building pedagogy. In this sense, while *Margoline* may figure as a more minor work in Thorn's oeuvre, it nevertheless has a much less emotionally driven approach to its politics and is rooted instead in a concrete presentation of the legal situation of its subjects. As the film continues, its position between *Oser lutter* and *Le dos au mur* is clear in that its aesthetic approach is somewhere between the film that speaks (*Oser*) and the film that listens (*Le dos*).

To articulate the tenuous status of these workers, Thorn employs a title card to explain that once the workers' status becomes undocumented, the only hope for them is to turn to those employers who "specialise" in hiring undocumented workers (*sans papiers*). This is the case in the paper recycling plant Margoline. The film shows images outside of Margoline, with its mass of paper debris strewn about, while a voiceover recounts the details of the factory – its location, the number of employees and the large number of mostly undocumented immigrant workers (80 per cent). We also hear how the owners promise the undocumented workers that they will get their papers, and yet a year after being hired at Margoline, they still have received nothing. Once the film enters the factory, the interior of Margoline is revealed to be almost identical to the exterior: brimming with piles and piles (not stacks) of paper. While the miserable working conditions are shown, a voiceover describes the massive amounts of paper to be unloaded off the transport truck, the unbearable paper dust and the fact that there is no sink to wash in (Figures 2.20, 2.21 and 2.22). This list of problems is punctuated with the remark that the undocumented workers are obligated to work on Sundays.

During the strike at Margoline between 21 and 23 May 1973 (at both Nanterre and Gennevilliers), the strikers demanded working papers and regular pay. Thorn uses a series of voiceovers to explain their demands, and the sequences include the audio in Arabic by an interpreter, as well as a score of continual drumming in the background. This emphasis on sound and music, something not foregrounded in *Oser lutter*, functions as a prelude to the work Thorn would accomplish not only with *Le dos au mur* but also in the late 1980s and up to the present. Much of Thorn's later work was about the use of "rebel" music (principally hip-hop and punk) as the continuation of the militant projects of the 1970s. That is, he integrated into his later films music and culture composed by the children of the generation of striking workers he portrayed in his early films.

The film continues along these formal lines, introducing what become almost stock characters and events of the tradition, namely the police intervention, the bosses and administrators, and the workers who struggle courageously against them.

Figures 2.20–22

The film ends by announcing that with the increase across France of strikes, hunger strikes and other forms of protest, the government modified the memorandum. Now, workers who entered France before a certain date will be considered documented. The workers at Margoline all received one-year contracts and their *cartes de séjour*. The final images of *Margoline* are of a CFDT poster with four ethnically diverse arms forming a block of solidarity accompanied by the text "Cancel the Fontanet–Marcellin memorandum; end the *cartes de séjour* and work permits that enslave immigrants; for every immigrant with work, a permanent identity card upon entering France, and valid in all regions and all professions! Equal social, union and political rights for all workers" (Figure 2.24). The last title card of the film explains that in September 1973, all the workers at Margoline became documented. Following that, in October 1973, the workers undertook a second strike and again were victorious, receiving an 80-franc salary raise to 6.00 francs per hour. In December 1973, a third victorious strike garnered the workers 6.50 francs per hour with bonuses. And finally, in March 1974, workers were preparing to struggle for a new raise and rotation at the work-stations.

Figure 2.23

The conclusion of this film is on the one hand formally similar to *Oser lutter, oser vaincre*; that is, the last images are graphic and textual. *Oser* employs the famous still image of Marx, Engels, Lenin, Mao and Stalin with text calling for Marxist–Leninist revolution. While those sentiments may underlie *Margo-line*, the graphic conclusion here is one of concrete statistics and the election of a union delegate. Without wanting to make value judgements about either of these approaches, it is hard not to sense a dramatic change in the militant land-scape, at least in relation to Thorn's work,

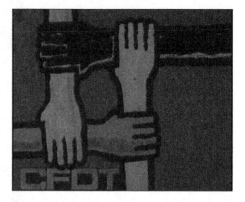

Figure 2.24

but also in relation to a broader picture of the French far-left political terrain. This type of modification, whether stemming from disillusionment or merely a feeling that a new approach was called for, will figure as prominently and even more explicitly in *Le dos au mur*.

Thorn's experience making *Margoline*, along with his support of the Pennaroya strike, found him taking an increasingly active role in using his position in the union to organise the immigrant workers. In 1977, Thorn organised a strike that started with a demand to get the forklift drivers proper winter attire. They were almost all Moroccan, worked outside without winter jackets, and were all completely sick. The rallying cry of that strike was "Padded jackets for everyone!"[127]

The strike in '77 was tactically different for Thorn. By then, he had rejected the idea of an occupation (counter to the adamant/militant insistence on such a tactic in *Oser lutter*) in favour of other forms taken from Maoists (guerrilla warfare) and even anarchists (work to rule). In an effort to upset production, the strikers worked out a strike tactic whereby every hour, a different work-shop would cease production and strike. The result of such a tactic was that the workers weren't hit so hard in their payments but effectively caused a serious slowdown in production. The strike drew a lot of attention and was composed of *établis* from Lutte ouvrière at the CGT and some from Humanité rouge in the CFDT.[128] Far-left groups would install themselves at the factory gates and pass out tracts to the workers as they arrived in the morning. The striking workers then began wearing masks (based on the apes in the film *Planet of the Apes*), partly to be anonymous, but also to introduce a ludic aspect to the strike, something that had been part of the May '68 movement, but not necessarily in the domain in which Thorn had participated.[129] Furthering this effort, the workers created musical methods by banging on the steel in the factory in a rhythm that was counter to that of production. These methods introduced a cinematic element into the strike – costume, soundtrack and entertainment. Ultimately, the management won this time, and the strikers managed to avoid getting fired. But the period after 1977 was a turbulent one for Thorn.

A series of personal blows changed Thorn's relationship to the life he had created for himself in the factory. In an ironic twist, Thorn was harshly criticised for not having organised an occupation of the factory during the strike, and there was an effort within the CFDT to take away his influence. In 1978 he quit his union position and returned to his work as an OS. On top of this setback, after the death of Lin Piao and the trials of the Gang of Four, Thorn was confronted with his own doubts about China. All of this led to Thorn leaving Alstom in 1979. For those who knew Thorn as a filmmaker, this break with factory work was long past due. However, Thorn's co-workers, particularly the immigrant community that he had grown close to in the factory, never really understood; they felt that he had abandoned them.[130] Thorn spoke of this period, saying:

> By leaving the factory I broke with everything that constituted my universe up to that point. I separated from my wife and returned to live in Paris, which I adored. I wanted to live as I desired, make films again, stop playing the role of a family man, and love the woman I chose to. I had spent all those years with an extraordinary super ego, stuck to the image of a model revolutionary worker.[131]

2.7 *Le dos au mur* (1980, colour, 105 min.)

On 1 October 1979 a new strike began at Alstom; it lasted until 26 November. The strike was an attempt to gain what the workers at the factory had been unable to achieve with the strike of 1977. Given the failure of the previous strike, the idea was to engage a method of striking that was much more aggressive. This seemed possible, given that the ideas of the militant workers had progressed since the previous strike. The strike at Saint-Ouen was initially undertaken in response to, and in solidarity with, the workers at the Alstom factory in Belfort. The latter, at the end of September 1979, had gone on strike following a showy centenary celebration that many of the workers found offensive, given the low salaries they were paid.[132] The workers' primary demands at Belfort were for an increase in salaries, including a 13th month pay. The case of Belfort received a lot of media attention because of the tawdry aspects of the centenary celebration and because of the large number of employees working there. Saint-Ouen, on the other hand, was too generic and small to be able to draw the kind of attention that Belfort would receive.[133] In any case, the workers of Saint-Ouen also demanded the 13th month salary, and after just over a week of striking, on 10 October, militants in the boiler works welded the doors shut.[134]

After leaving the factory, Thorn almost immediately fell ill and spent a month in hospital with meningitis. Six months later, when the workers at Alstom went on strike, they approached Thorn about the possibility of his filming it. For Thorn, this was the first step towards reconciliation with his factory experience:

I had never told them who I was, they didn't know I was a filmmaker, and they asked me why I hadn't told them earlier. It was then that they finally understood what all my baggage was about. And there I was filming the people who were my friends, and I was able to be who I really was – no longer hiding.[135]

In an interview, Thorn described his experience upon arriving at Alstom:

The first time I stepped [sic] foot onto the shop floor of Alstom I was fascinated: a sort of greenish atmosphere with a few yellow lines, smoke, light filtering in through the glass panels[,] a deafening noise and a very specific odour.... I worked on that shop floor with real aesthetic pleasure[;] I was finally happy. A few years later while scouting locations, I had this sudden flash. I opened the doors and I knew that we would shoot there: that smell. I [had] found the factory for my film.[136]

Thorn also remarked that while he was working at Alstom, particularly during the transportation of his work across the shop floor, he felt that he was living a kind of tracking shot. Life, politics and film were of an entirely lived order.[137]

Having perhaps learned the importance of the festival element with the strike of '77, Thorn opens *Le dos au mur* on a ludic note, with a lack of urgency and an assuredness in the manner of transmitting the strike information. Yvonne Chaillo[138] (who participated in a strike for the first time in 1979[139]) explains to someone on the telephone that the workers are on strike, that the factory has been occupied and that, of course, the person the caller is looking for is also on strike. She details the striking workers' demands, and the way she responds to the caller's questions suggests that even the caller understands the reason for the strike.

While the setting and the subject (a factory, a strike with occupation, union participation, and so on) clearly align *Le dos au mur* with Thorn's previous films, the first images immediately demonstrate the way this film differs from his earlier efforts. Again there is the ludic tone, and the relaxed and non-dogmatic characteristics of Yvonne's speech. By contrast, in *Margoline*, even if the film jettisoned a rigid Marxist–Leninist vocabulary, its tone was still austere in a way that matched that of *Oser lutter*.

Further, the fact that the film's first central figure is a woman was a substantial change from the largely masculine portrayal of the militant working class that dominated Thorn's cinematic representation up this point. In making this film, Thorn was, in some sense, at a crossroads, given that the filmmaker had been exposed to a number of cultural and even militant cinematic shifts since *Margoline*, and especially since *Oser lutter*. These shifts are evident in films like *À pas lentes*, *Classe de lutte* and the work of militant feminist organisations and filmmakers like Carole Roussopoulos (all discussed below). While, as we will see, much of *Le dos au mur* participates in a discourse of a working-class population largely dominated by men, this insistence on opening

Figure 2.25 Yvonne Chaillo

the film with a woman points to a significant cultural shift.

Thorn has repeated the idea on a number of occasions[140] that *Le dos au mur* can be read as a Western. In the credit sequence that follows Yvonne's telephone call, the use of harmonica and a kind of Alamo figure waving a red flag on the factory roof already point to the homage to the Western genre (Figure 2.26). There is also the storming of the Bourse (see below) and the sound of coyotes howling, added by Thorn during post-production.[141]

Figure 2.26

"The factory is a kind of Fort Alamo occupied by Indians who attempt rapid attacks, take up a position in their camp, are chased from it following an attack by the CRS, take it over again, but eventually give up due to exhaustion and hunger."[142]

In *Le dos* interviews are one of the principal strategies for narrating the strike, and providing the various positions of those involved, whereas *Margoline*, which did employ interview footage, was heavily dependent on voiceover to narrate the film. One of the interviewees, Henri Onetti, a CGT delegate, describes the occupation of the factory's first floor, where the workers locked out a manager. The manager was inside and didn't believe the workers were serious about the occupation; he thus refused to leave his office. When the manager left for lunch, the workers locked him out. Following this brief interlude with Onetti, the first insertion of something resembling a title card occurs. However, here it comes from within the diegesis of the film, through a poster made by the strike committee that states "la grève ça s'arrose" (there is an at least double meaning: the strike needs to be nourished/watered, but it also needs to be celebrated) and features a picture of a worker hosing down the clichéd image of a "fat cat" capitalist (Figure 2.27).

One of the early ludic elements of the film is the taking hostage of an enormous transformer in the factory, upon which sit three men, the hostage-takers (Figure 2.28). Following this there is a long overhead tracking shot of the factory while a voiceover recounts the details of Alstom's production. At one point he states that the strikers "effected a *coup d'état*". This line has been cited by Thorn and critics as an important moment in the film, because, following the announcement, the next sequence is of a worker showing his family the factory – something unthinkable during normal working conditions.[143] As the family move through the various factory floors, they come across another worker, who is also giving his family a tour.

One of the ideas *Le dos*'s shift in political tone begins to gesture towards is that there are no political stakes in this film, or

Figure 2.27

at least not in the same way as there were for the workers of *Oser lutter*. In *Oser lutter* workers were struggling not only against a corrupt management, but equally against a seemingly corrupt union and communist party – all against the backdrop of a near national revolution. While the established tone of *Le dos* does transform over the course of the film, the portrait of the strike thus far has less in common with militant Marxist–Leninism than *Oser lutter*, and is closer in tone to the anarchist Hakim Bey's loose concept of a TAZ (Temporary Autonomous Zone).[144] What has shifted,

Figure 2.28

and what critics will point to (as we will see later), is that it is very hard to be a militant of a Temporary Autonomous Zone. As a result, the film remains a militant film but appears to have been depleted of its reasons and resources for militating. While it might be easy to see this political aesthetic shift as a mere expression of Thorn's personal experience or way of representing the strike at Alstom, it is worth noting that this approach was entirely in accord with the cultural and political shifts that had been occurring in France at the end of the 1970s.

As remarked repeatedly, the most explicit nemesis in Thorn's work wasn't the CGT, the factory management or the Communist Party, but rather what he identified as naturalism. Up to this point in *Le dos au mur*, the combat against naturalism has not been made as apparent as it was in his previous efforts. Whereas montage and the use of title cards kept the viewer of Thorn's previous films constantly in a state of Brechtian observational and analytic distanciation, the text in *Le dos au mur* has been, up to this point in the film, almost exclusively diegetic, consisting of graffiti, picket cards and other profilmic writings. The use of nondiegetic music has managed to keep a hypnotising naturalism at bay, and such music will continue to play a role in the film. But equally, the ludic, carnivalesque aspect of the strike's organisation works against a naturalist grain: it suggests that the workers are creating circumstances and situations, that they are not merely thrown into the world as it is, unconditioned and ideologically unbiased. A further aspect of Thorn's fidelity to his anti-naturalist aesthetic in *Le dos au mur* is the successful foregrounding of the relationship between the filmmaker and the subject that results from the personal relationships between Thorn and his co-workers.[145]

In an interview, a physically run-down worker (he has a large goitre and one eye appears to be seriously damaged), who is still an OS after 45 years at the factory, discusses his low wages. Here Thorn introduces a technique he will use repeatedly throughout the rest of the film and that serves his anti-naturalist approach. At one point the worker says in discussing his paycheque, "Y a des haricots, y a pas de gigot" (There's some beans, but no meat). He then turns to the camera, and the image freezes as the worker smiles and the text of this last line is displayed underneath him (Figure 2.29). This formal choice is in keeping with the approach Thorn had used in previous films, and it injects a kind of "cinematic" quality into the film. That is, it announces an approach to filming that seeks to represent a particular perspective on the strike – one that does not claim to be the only perspective.

Thorn's portrait of the factory, particularly in the long tracking shots of the family moving across its shop floors, presents it as a kind of junkyard of history, full of antiquated machinery, the machinery that was disappearing in the same way the working class was disappearing. This representation creates an image of a kind of militant "kingdom of ends" – not only the end of the militant politics that have guided Thorn and *cinéma militant* thus far, but even the end of the industrial Western European working class. Yet during this stroll through the wreckage of the working-class experience, Thorn finds new ways of employing text: banners hanging from the archaic factory ceiling pass by in the tracking shot the same way that title cards might

Figure 2.29

have unfolded in Thorn's previous films. One banner is filmed initially in close-up, filling the majority of the frame. But as the camera zooms out, the space around it contextualises the meaning and to some degree collapses notions of diegetic and nondiegetic space.

This representation is furthered by the use of Jacky Moreau's compositions, which produce a high-modern score, with an ominous and sometimes invigorating rumbling bass. One question the music provokes is: for whom is this world ominous? These diegetic title cards are all clearly threatening the factory management, but there is also a visual suggestion that the workers and their slogans are themselves being threatened. On this dilapidated factory floor, the family appears to be under siege; it seems threatened by the space, whose banners and post-'68 strategies are no match for an increasingly ignominious and powerful capitalism that has mutated substantially since the days of easy Maoist epithets.

Writing about this interweave of discourses in *Le dos*, Dauty rightly sees a political and cinematic complexity that was not necessarily present in the "unity of opposites" approach to montage in *Oser lutter*. As an example, Dauty notes the polyvocality that occurs in the mixture of images, strikers' voices and music, and the fact that the montage does not reduce the importance of the singularity each of these elements possesses on its own.[146] Where the unilateral, dogmatic expression of *Oser lutter* seemed more politically assured, the questioning in *Le dos* gives rise to its characterisation as a film that listens as much as it speaks. Its ability to hear many voices and many modes of speech adds layers of possible understandings or readings that are absent in the sometimes monological presentation of *Oser lutter*.

One of the most commented upon sequences (and that held great personal significance for Thorn) is an interview with three striking workers. Although the film portrays the participation of CGT and CFDT members and delegates in various lights, it has distanced itself from the dogmatic, anti-syndicalist rhetoric of *Oser lutter*. Even so, about a half-hour into the film, Thorn employs a title card for the first time. It is modelled after silent-film title cards, with mildly ornate embroidery around the text, which reads, "Interview with three *Tartempions* who don't belong to anything" (Figure 2.30). The text comes from someone shouting the same line at a meeting about the role of the union delegates in the strike, at which point it is accompanied by a woman saying "Silence please!" followed by the pounding of a judge's gavel.

The three workers are presented as those who "don't belong to anything". They do not belong to a union (or they did previously but have since left), yet each has been elected to serve as a representative of a sector of the strike. The interview opens by focusing on the ways that the union's goals do not correspond to their individual aspirations. There are remnants of the critique from *Oser lutter* regarding the fact that the CGT remains firmly in the control of the PCF. They criticise the CFDT for what they perceive to be its disorganisation, largely resulting from the cells within the union, the extreme left positions of those cells, and the unproductive arguments that such *groupusculisme* provokes.

There is a moment in the interview when one of the *Tartempions* reformulates the thesis of *Oser lutter*, but in entirely

Figure 2.30

different, non-dogmatic (more impartial) terms. Far from being a union obsessed with stale workerism, the CGT-PC has in fact opened itself excessively to higher-level employees, effectively becoming a representative of middle-class aims and aspirations. The speaker identifies his own political aspirations as being on the left, but doesn't find representation for that position in the parties or unions. As the interview continues, it moves away from their rejection of unions and parties and turns to the larger question of revolution. Their various analyses of the present contemporary political situation maintain a derogatory tone, citing Third World revolutions that never fail to devolve into authoritarian regimes and dictatorships. The *Tartempions* also bring up the hope that Chinese communism had incited revolt and how, even there, the model collapsed. For these workers, the struggle boils down to the demand for a 35-hour workweek and the 13th month salary, that is, the practical demands of the workers and nothing more. This moment exemplifies the assertion made by Guy-Patrick Sainderichin that *Le dos* is a militant film stripped of its politics; its political models are no longer valid.[147]

The *Tartempions* "articulate an analysis of the political limits of their action, a bitter reflection on the decaying workers' movement".[148] By including these three figures, Thorn chose subjects that represented "the best of the tradition of the workers' movement, and those who point to its eventual future, leaving something to doubt".[149] On the one hand, Thorn received criticism for the amount of screen time he allotted these figures, though one critic found that

these three had the most important voice in the film (see below). In terms of *mise-en-scène*, it is worth noting that Thorn chose to shoot these three with their backs against the wall.

A more dramatic episode, yet one that maintained a fidelity to the playful approach established by the film, was the storming of the Bourse on Monday, 29 October, the 19th day of the strike. Shot by Bruno Muel,[150] this scene recalls the carnivalesque burning of the votes in *Oser lutter* as his camera follows the workers entering the Bourse. What is striking in this

Figure 2.31 *Les Tartempions*

sequence is the way that the camera itself generates political situations (Figures 2.32, 2.33 and 2.34). Alain Nahum from Cinélutte said of this sequence that it exemplified the idea of how *not* to be theoretical, but instead to provide a cinematic representation of the reality filmed. When filming a struggle, the camera needed to share the territory of that struggle.[151] Once inside, the workers throw leaflets with their demands into the air and raise a banner. What is particularly remarkable in this sequence is the way the camera manages to remain largely unperturbed for a long period during this storming. And then, two men in suits approach the group and the camera, the volume and pitch of the chaos rise, and one of the "suits" points his finger at the camera, at which point Thorn chooses to freeze. The film then cuts to sepia stills of the workers carrying their demonstration onto a train, all in a sequence resembling the still images of the workers at Flins throwing their voting ballots in the air.

The film winds down by chronicling the final days of the strike. On 14 November, the 35th day of the strike, the CRS arrive and expel the occupiers. The strikers say they are going to try to reoccupy the factory. In each sequence of strike meetings shown, there are fewer participants, and the strike begins to weaken. The debate among those striking becomes whether to continue to strike or do they return to work and agitate once they are back inside? There are still police outside the factory. The music is melancholic in tone. Someone proposes a strike every day for half a day. There is almost no one left in the hall discussing what to do. The feeling this sequence evokes is not just the desperation regarding the end of the strike, but more generally the desperation about the end of the post-'68 political movement.

On the 40th day of the strike, the camera follows the workers back into the factory as one of the workers explains that this is the reoccupation of the factory. The speech he gives is about holding out until the end. Outside, they close off the entrance to the factory by backing up a truck in front of the factory gates. The police arrive again, and the shrinking group of strikers decides not to reoccupy the factory.

Figures 2.32–2.34

A series of black-and-white stills of the factory gates being opened is accompanied by a voiceover explaining that the pickets have been taken away. Jacky Moreau's harmonica music continues dejectedly as the strike deflates. The workers on the 42nd day of the strike move through the factory demonstrating, heckling the management and carrying red flags, in a way reminiscent of the end of *Oser lutter*. Speeches are made within the factory, the strikers storm the bureaucratic offices, and then maybe 50 striking workers walk by the exterior wall of the factory singing "The Internationale" (Figure 2.35). An entirely distorted guitar version of the anthem (much like Jimi Hendrix's famous version of the US national anthem) accompanies a text on the screen that reads:

> The result of the negotiations
>> An increase in the end-of-the-year bonus from 75% to 84% of the salary at the end of '79 (100% at the end of '81)
>> Weekly reduction of one half-hour transformed into a payment in three installations without recovery
>> One extra day of paid yearly vacation
>> 27 francs of complementary commuting bonus
>> No general raise

On the 43rd day of the strike, a small meeting is held inside the factory acknowledging the insufficiency of the response to the strikers' demands. Those assembled insist that they have not given in, but rather that they were coerced by police and their own misery, and further that they were forced to struggle worker against worker. Shot in an extreme close-up, Onetti speaks directly into the camera and explains that they did not get what they wanted, that they were one against all. He says that the unions did not behave as they should have, given the situation. The ludic tone has disappeared from the film, and the menacing score now seems to define it. If there was ever any doubt as to whom was threatened by the ominous score, it becomes exceedingly clear by the end of the film. Onetti says that the capitalist wins because he has the power, but Onetti hopes that one day capitalism will explode; he won't fire the first shot, but he will fire the second, if it doesn't explode... The last word written on the screen is *sinon* (if it doesn't).

The last text of the film is a long scrolling account of what happened after the strike and the return to work. A large number of workers are fired, including Gérard (one of the *Tartempions*), and many workers choose to quit. There are a number of trials held against the strikers and the CGT and CFDT for illegal occupation. Some workers and strikers are interrogated by the police after the presidential elections. A song written by Thorn, "Les lendemains qui chantent", continues into the black leader.

Figure 2.35

• • •

Tangui Perron has called *Le dos au mur* a requiem for the revolution,[152] and one of the "best and most beautiful documentaries made about a strike in France".[153] While the film is in many ways a document of a failure, both the specific failure of the strike and the impasse of the more general project of post-'68 militancy, *Le dos au mur* counters this failure with a kind of perfected version of the militant cinema touted by ARC, Cinélutte and Thorn himself. Placing immense importance on the Maoist practice of the *enquête*, Thorn, through his engagement with *établissement*, had undertaken a nearly decade-long investigation. The results of the complicity between him and those workers on strike are entirely evident in *Le dos au mur*. Perron writes, "to this crepuscular film about a failed strike flocked the last collectives of the post-'68 period – where many felt the coming defeat, without wanting to renounce all of their utopias".[154] Besides Bruno Muel, those who worked on *Le dos au mur* included Alain Nahum, Eric Pittard, Richard Copans, Guy-Patrick Sainderichin, and others from Cinélutte, as well as Théo Robichet, also from Le groupe Medvedkine de Sochaux. Interestingly, both of these collectives (Les groupes Medvedkine and Cinélutte) worked extensively on films about "ends". Muel's *Avec le sang des autres* and Cinélutte's *Á pas lentes* were expressions not only of the end of the collective but also of the end of the Lip factory movement. The participation of the above figures in *Le dos au mur* meant that although the film was attributed to Jean-Pierre Thorn, it was also clearly a collective project. This was true both in the sense of its being collectively made, but also in the sense that it is about a collective, as the factory itself takes on the importance of collectivity, showing on the one hand its utopian possibilities and on the other its hellish realities.[155]

Thorn has said that *Le dos* owes much to Barbara Koppel's *Harlan County, USA*. Openly inspired by direct cinema, the film is in debt more to American traditions of documentary than to the formalist work of Soviet filmmakers. Thorn wanted to capture the events of the strike without trying to manipulate it, to show the complexity of the contradictions within the strike without violating its reality.[156] When comparing *Le dos* with earlier films, especially *Oser lutter*, we can see that one of the biggest shifts is that, while both films are replete with the spoken word, and the use of text suggests the distinction cited above, *Oser* speaks while *Le dos* listens. In *Oser lutter*, the written word – not just in the banners brandished by the strikers, but in the massive and furious use of intertitles – overwhelms the viewer. This results in a filmolinguistic Kalashnikov firing its Marxist–Leninist message at the audience. In contrast, *Le dos*, while including the strikers' banners, tends more towards letting the audience listen to those speaking. The example of this tendency *par excellence* is the interview with the three non-union workers.

Responding to this approach was one of the film's critics, Guy-Patrick Sainderichin, a former member of Cinélutte who had participated in the production of *Le dos au mur*. In a critique of *Le dos au mur* for *Cahiers du cinéma*,[157] Sainderichin began by discussing *Margoline*, suggesting that it was not a propaganda film but, on the contrary, an agitation film. His position was that people begin to be "seduced" when they are simply confronted with the existence of the workers, and that *Le dos au mur* benefits from this effect. He concluded that, as a militant film, it was not militating *for* anything, and he could no longer detect the reasons for its engagement. That is, it had all the elements of a militant film except for its "political programme, which let's admit is its most tedious aspect".[158] In closing, his full position is laid bare: "perhaps this is a film of *transition*, a way of saying goodbye to the proletariat who would hold onto the style of the visit we had with them (admittedly a long one in Thorn's case), out of a sort of courtesy".[159]

While Sainderichin's critique points out these failures, it can be countered that those areas of confusion or uncertainty are precisely what raises the political and aesthetic stakes in *Le dos*. And further, it is in those apparent hesitations that the film reveals its capacity to listen. Contrary to the detracting remarks made by Sainderichin, Perron described *Le dos au mur* as "the end of the ephemeral blaze of the Maoist ideology in France, without falling prey to the problems of the Union de la gauche [the PCF-PC alliance had just undergone its first rupture], and without resigning itself to the probable election of the socialist candidate [François Mitterrand], about whom a number of militants didn't have any illusions".[160] It is a documentary about the end of the 1970s.

For the production of the film, Thorn went to ISKRA, where Chris Marker offered his assistance, participating to some degree during the shoot.[161] However, Thorn had some legal problems with the film upon its completion, as Alstom did not want the film distributed. There were equally critical issues regarding the response from members of the CGT and CFDT, who accused Thorn of speaking for the workers and signing his own name to a collectively made film. These issues had an impact on the screening of the film, given that Saint-Ouen was communist, and the mayor of the department wasn't going to allow Thorn to screen his film for the workers. Here is what Thorn had to say:

> [B]efore the official release of the film in Paris at Saint-Séverin, we had set up a meeting with the workers for a screening at the public hall in Saint-Ouen, where I had filmed the big general assemblies where the workers voted on whether or not to go back to work. For almost six months, a petition circulated on the various shop floors, saying that as a former employee of the factory I had a right to present my vision of the strike. The strike committee gathered more than 260 signatures. The CGT gave up and I was given the hall at Saint-Ouen, and it was by far my favourite screening. The place was full, Chris Marker showed up, and the people would see themselves on the screen and be talking over the images and trying to resolve the contradictions that they were seeing.[162]

The film was released during the electoral campaign of 1981.

2.8 Georgette Vacher

For nearly 20 years, Georgette Vacher had been a delegate for the CGT and a member of the Commission feminine de l'Union départementale CGT Rhône. In the mid-1970s, Vacher began to question the structure of the CGT itself, and this, perhaps along with her writing for *Antoinette*,[163] prompted the departmental union to relieve her of her union responsibilities on 28 September 1981. On 20 October, at the age of 52, Georgette Vacher committed suicide. In the note she left behind, she wrote: "Je suis le dos au mur. C'est la fin d'une grande histoire d'amour avec la classe ouvrière" (My back's against the wall. It's the end of a great love story with the working class).

Thorn came across this remark and was convinced the woman had seen the film. So he travelled to Lyon to try to get in touch with those who were close to her in the CGT Rhône. There he discovered a collection of audiocassettes that contained recordings she had made every night, and while playing one of the tapes he stumbled upon her criticism of *Le dos au mur*. In her critique, she focused on the three non-union workers, saying that she wished every worker would see this film in order to interrogate themselves on similar questions. The thrust of her argument was that the compromises had to stop in order to save the ideas of communism and those of the left. This was 1981, and she was not as elated as some about the arrival to power of

Mitterrand's left-wing government. She wrote, "What good does this victory serve, given that the spirit of the working class itself has already been broken?"

Le dos au mur has been called a kind of "end of militant cinema".[164] It was also the last film Thorn made before embarking on his first feature-length fiction film, *Je t'ai dans la peau*, based loosely on the life of Vacher and a *prêtre ouvrier*. Thorn has described the circumstances that impelled him to make the feature, such as the interview in *Le dos* with the three workers who do not belong to any union. The question that emerged from the critique of that sequence was, for Thorn, not so much one that would challenge him in terms of his political position on union membership (although he has stated that he filmed these three because they were friends of his, and he was trying to understand what drove their non-adherence). Rather, it was a specifically cinematic question — one of form and the desire to create a film more individually. As he has said, film is a collective art, but the work of creation is by definition solitary. But while Thorn has insisted that he remained cautious about the myth of the collective, he was equally suspicious of the individual, authoritarian director.[165]

Chapter 3
Cinélutte: "Tout ce qui bouge est rouge"

3.1 Cinélutte beginnings

Our analytical methods and our practice have as their foundation Marxism–Leninism. Nonetheless our unification and the debates that we set off rest upon the specificity of our practice and not generalities.[1]

Cinélutte was officially founded in 1973, but a number of its members had already been active in other militant and filmic capacities. Cinélutte members Mireille Abramovici and Jean-Denis Bonan were both active in Atelier de recherche cinématographique. After filming a demonstration in Berlin in support of the Vietnamese revolution, they filmed with Rudi Dutschke and Students for a Democratic Society (SDS) in February 1968, and the footage they shot was subsequently bought by television. This group's approach to film production participated to some degree in the tradition of spontaneous documentaries about the events of May 1968. Often, the material shot by members of ARC was shared by Les états généraux du cinéma and other militant film groups participating in the events. Joining forces in this way created a kind of "arbitrary image gathering",[2] an attempt to amass a profound documentation and corroboration of the events. Following the breakup of ARC, certain members (for example, Bonan, Abramovici) joined Ligne rouge,[3]

Figure 3.1 Cinélutte catalogue, 1979

others the GP (Kébadian), and, finally, others like Michel Andrieu (who had remained anti-Stalinist for the whole of his political engagement) rested within the political framework of Socialisme ou barbarie.

With the dissolution of Les états généraux du cinéma came a new break between those who were in accord with the PCF and those who were now thinking otherwise. In the fall of '68, the CGT meetings were, according to Bonan, overflowing with all sorts of new progressive political tendencies for the first time:

> We began to hear "We're going to force the government to finance huge super productions that will give the most work to the most people". That's when a number of people began to leave, not particularly excited by the idea of participating in super-productions à la "de Funès".[4] Here's where you see this aspect of the P"C"F that doesn't really care about the content of the films but rather maintains a line that insists on preserving the aristocracy of the film production technicians.[5]

From Bonan's point of view, Ligne rouge recognised the importance of cinema as a means of propaganda and political agitation. As we saw in Chapter 2, section 2.3, the overarching aim of Ligne rouge's theoretical and political project was to group together the most advanced or avant-garde workers. These workers already understood the importance of the questions of (1) the dictatorship of the proletariat and (2) the struggle against revisionism.[6] Yet the group was never capable of establishing the kind of contact with the workers that it strove for. This lack of connection created the kind of impasse that ultimately led to a scission and mutation that resulted in the formation of a group called Drapeau rouge, which nonetheless disappeared shortly after its establishment. As a result of this fracturing, a number of militant filmmakers were not attached to any party. They were left without any structure within which they could reflect upon and formulate their political positions. Faced with this seeming aporia, some militant filmmakers became *établis*,[7] while Bonan and Mireille continued to believe that film remained an important means of political action that should not be entirely handed over to the "modern bourgeois revisionists".[8]

Apart from his brief encounter with *établissement*, which followed his work with ARC, Bonan continued to make militant films individually, sometimes in tandem with Kébadian.[9] He had also worked with Newsreel in the United States.[10] However, of all the work that Bonan created between his time with ARC and the eventual founding of Cinélutte, the most widely seen was a film he collaborated on with Abramovici and Caroline (Biri) Swetland,[11] entitled *Kimbe red, pa moli* (*Tiens bon, ne faiblis pas* [Stay strong, don't give in], 1971, 17 min.). Swetland was a writer who was interested in making a film about the Groupe d'organisation nationale de la Guadeloupe (GONG), a national liberation movement in Guadeloupe, islands in the French West Indies.[12] Given that she wasn't a filmmaker, Swetland ultimately contacted Bonan and Abramovici to assist her with production. The goal of the project was to create an agitprop film about a sugar cane workers' strike, but Bonan didn't have the money to go to Guadeloupe. Instead, he proposed (as he had been working with ceramics) to create an animated project using modelling clay. The film was shot in Super 8 and edited on a film projector.[13]

Kimbe red, pa moli is in colour with French and Creole voiceover. Along with modelling clay, the film employs still photographs, opening with a rapid account of the colonisation of Guadeloupe and arriving quickly at a strike by sugar cane workers in 1971. The film, in striking fidelity to reportage style, shoots a sequence comprising an interview in Creole with a peasant couple made of clay, who recount the living conditions their factory has imposed upon them. The narrative of this short film ultimately recounts the story of the creation of a new agricultural union. And it is from this specific history that one of the most magnificent moments in the film emerges. Its magnificence lies in the absolute fidelity to a politics largely formed by the French Marxist–Leninist experience. Even in this short film about Guadeloupe, the filmmakers conduct an assault on the PCF(G), the CGT(G) and even to some degree the CFDT. While we have seen Bonan as an engaged filmmaker in many incarnations, here we get the truly nascent utterance of Cinélutte's project. And while this is perhaps too speculative, it is worth noting the way these little clay figurines take on a symbolic form: the CGT and PCF are represented as little clay snakes "spreading their venom wherever they go".

Although *Kimbe red, pa moli* was a seemingly minor creation in Bonan's filmic output between ARC and Cinélutte, an anecdote recounted by Bonan offers a perspective on the impact the film may have had. A few years after its production and distribution, Bonan went to Guadeloupe, where he met a psychiatrist. The two were talking, and eventually Bonan said that he had worked on a film about a sugar cane strike. The psychiatrist immediately asked whether he was referring to *Kimbe red, pa moli*. She went on to explain that she had four copies of the film and insisted that the film had been seen quite widely throughout the islands. One aspect that aided the popularity of the film was that the Guadeloupian population was, to some extent, cut off from the world. And suddenly a film had appeared that not only was made by French filmmakers about a Guadeloupian subject, but, more importantly, had Creole dialogue.[14]

Figures 3.2–3.5 *Kimbe red, pa moli*

During this same period (between the events of May–June 1968 and fall 1973), Bonan was teaching, though not yet as a full hire, at both Censier and IDHEC. IDHEC, as we have seen, had been more than instrumental in the production and distribution of militant films during the events, maintaining ties with Les états généraux du cinéma as well as providing material assistance to filmmakers at ARC and other collectives. The results of the school's support of the movement did not end with the waning of the events, but instead carried over into the following decade, the early part of which found the school at its most politically radical.

After May '68, a young Richard Copans, who had been active in the student movement, was working part time at IDHEC and was particularly engaged in the student union. Copans, born to an American father and a French mother (both of whom were communists), began his political activity at the age of 14. Copans' older brother was close to Alain Krivine, an influential student activist who had split with the Communist Party at the beginning of the 1960s, towards the end of the Algerian War of Independence (1954–1962). Copans' political engagement, like that of many of his generation, had been inspired by the Algerian War, and in 1961 he became a member of the Jeunesse communiste révolutionnaire (JCR). From 1965 to 1968, Copans followed the JCR, and in 1968, at IDHEC, he joined Ligne rouge and eventually Drapeau rouge.[15]

In 1972, Copans made a radical shift and joined Révolution! (or Revo!), a militant organisation formed as a result of a split from the Ligue communiste révolutionnaire (LCR). The group was a hybrid of Maoist and Trotskyite tendencies that tried to fuse the Cultural Revolution with a permanent revolution.[16] Révolution! was detested by the Maoists, who thought its members were Trotskyites, and equally detested by the Trotskyites. Copans remained at Révolution! from 1972 to 1978. In 1976, Révolution! fused with Gauche ouvrière et paysanne, which had split from the Parti socialiste unifié (PSU), to become the Organisation communiste des travailleurs (OCT).[17] In 1978 these various fusions fell apart, and Copans ended his party-affiliated militant activity.[18]

At the beginning of fall 1968, Copans began to negotiate the possibility of reforming the entrance exam to IDHEC. By the end of September of that year, the CNC (Centre national du cinéma et de l'image animée), along with the SRF (Société des réalisateurs de films)[19] and the IDHEC students, agreed to undertake the project. They put the 21-year-old Copans in charge of restructuring the entrance exam. The reform sought to create a curriculum that would emphasise the entirety of film production, revising the pedagogical orientation to undo what was perceived as a rigid division between labour and education. It would move towards a more universal approach to filmmaking that would teach each student every aspect of the film production process. The entrance test, as it existed prior to the reform, consisted of about a dozen written exams covering subjects like general culture, history, literature and theatre. Copans has said that his intention was to develop a pedagogy that was based entirely on practice, but a practice that allowed one to move closer to theory and then return to practice; thus, it was at its core a quintessential Marxist reform.[20] The decision was made to create an exam in which audiovisual practices were foregrounded, including photographic montage, audio montage and writing a film proposal.

In January 1970, Copans was charged with finding candidates for a new director for IDHEC. He successfully convinced the search committee to hire Louis Daquin, a filmmaker well known for his association with the PCF. With this addition to the faculty, an implicit alliance between the communists and the far-left movement was forged at IDHEC. Along with Daquin, IDHEC hired two other professors at the same time. Copans hired Jean-Denis Bonan, whom he knew from Ligne rouge, Drapeau rouge, and so on, and Daquin hired Jean-André Fieschi, who was close to the PCF and had made films with Unicité, formerly Dynadia.[21]

Dynadia emerged from the movement of '68 and was, in some sense, an attempt to break with the CPDF (Coopérative de production et de distribution du film). One of their first projects was a slideshow entitled *Dix ans de gaullisme, ça suffit*. The collective was always somewhat confused about its approach to aesthetics and film form. For instance, in the fall of 1968, the group undertook a *Ciné-tracts*-style project about Vietnam, a film that was clearly under the formal sway of Godard. One of the issues that plagued this group was that the PCF seemed to have more respect for theatre than cinema, and this position meant Dynadia was often in conflict with its own party. Eventually, the group took the name Unicité (Uni/té Ci/néma Té/lévision Audio Visual). Jean-Patrick Lebel has said, in reflecting on the experience of Unicité, that there was never really any aesthetic reflection and that the group had largely considered cinema as merely an instrument of communication.

Figure 3.6 Unicité catalogue

This seeming conflict of interests among faculty managed to work for a period of time. Copans suggested that the fact that the extreme left wasn't hurling insults about revisionism at the faculty associated with the PCF was the result of a practical alliance, as well as the fact that Louis Daquin was particularly open to the younger generation.[22] Bonan remarked that, nevertheless, he and other *gauchistes* at IDHEC had conflicts with Fieschi because of his ardent fidelity to the PCF, and that these respective fidelities, though they seemed to coexist harmoniously, would eventually cause rifts within the programme.[23]

3.1.1 *Chaud! Chaud! Chaud!*

It was in this reformed atmosphere that, in the spring of 1973, a film project was developed out of a collaboration between students and professors (including Sainderichin, François Dupeyron, Copans, Bonan and Abramovici) at IDHEC. Paris VIII Vincennes (where, during the school year 1970–1971, a group of Maoists had created a "reflection group" on the question of cinéma[24]), Vaugirard and the film school at Censier all participated in documenting the Mouvement de jeunesse contre la loi Debré, demonstrating against the *loi Debré* and the DEUG (Diplôme d'études universitaires générales). The *loi Debré* was a law that overturned the stay of military service for students, and *lycéens* (high-school students) across France had gone on strike to protest it. In support of the *lycéens*, university and polytechnical institute students also joined the strike. However, in a way similar to the strike at Flins portrayed in *Oser lutter, oser vaincre*, divergences regarding the strike, the demonstrations and other methods of contestation became apparent between far-left student groups and the PCF's student organisation UNCAL (Union nationale des comités d'action lycéens).[25]

The project of filming the demonstrations was not conceived as an autonomous one, created outside of a university setting, but was rather conducted as part of the curriculum. The loose organisation of student and faculty filmmakers that developed was characterised by a structure similar to the multitude of participants who had filmed for Les états généraux. Under these circumstances, the production of the film fell squarely in line with much of what had been critiqued in Ligne rouge and Jean-Pierre Thorn's tract *Vive le cinéma, arme de propagande communiste*:[26] in short, it suffered from *spontaneity*.

The formal spontaneity of the film could easily be attributed to the manner in which the strike was approached and the film crews organised. On the one hand, that the project was undertaken in this manner would seem surprising, given that some of the project's participants (such as Bonan and Abramovici) had been members of ARC. Therefore, these were filmmakers with a history of militant production and, more importantly, an increasingly specific political orientation. On the other hand, the spontaneous tendency is less surprising given the framework in which the film was made: a student project undertaken by a relatively heterogeneous group (most of these students had been inspired to take on this work by their experiences in the Latin Quarter during the May events), among whom there was no specific political reflection or discussion.

The so-called spontaneity, however, was countered to some degree by the formation of a smaller, more politically distilled group of students and professors who undertook the editing and began to work out and articulate a specific political (if at times dogmatic) programme. For this reason, in a way that recalls Thorn's work on *Oser lutter*, the project was a film created during the editing phase of production. With Bonan, Copans and the other faculty and students from IDHEC, the group edited the footage into a 75-minute film entitled *Chaud! Chaud! Chaud!*, which ultimately resulted in the founding of the group Cinélutte.

In an assessment of *Chaud! Chaud! Chaud!* made at the end of 1974, Cinélutte considered the youthful energy of the film as being fresh and giving life to a sometimes-dreary militant tendency in engaged film. Further, they cited the fact that the film allowed for the interrogation of several fundamental political issues: the demonstration of a mass movement with no revolutionary proletarian party; the class composition of the youth movement; how the PCF manages to continually hijack and recuperate movements that are constituted outside the bounds of their organisation; and what precisely constitutes a class army, or an armed class. In the estimation of Cinélutte, this concrete political line and point of view is what separated *Chaud! Chaud! Chaud!* from other militant productions.[27]

As for the shortcomings of the film, Cinélutte attributed them largely to an unformed "cinematic" presentation of the film's political potentials. They cited the "almost magical appearance of the PCF during the struggle"[28] and the articulation of two classes in the film (the polytechnic students and the *lycéens*) without attributing specific ideological presuppositions to them.[29] But overall, the auto-critique portrayed the film as overgeneralising, and as seeming "to hesitate between the *description* of the movement and its *analysis*".[30]

It is interesting to note that this critique by *Cinélutte* announced that the problem with this film was partly the lack of a strict political line. And yet the popular press's critical reception of the film (by no means an overwhelming amount of critical response) was quite the opposite. *Le Monde*, for instance, pointed to the spontaneous elements of the film as being perhaps its most interesting aspect, from the point of view of the spectator. The appearance of whatever remnants of a political line may have been in the film, that is, the dogmatism or what *Le Monde* saw as the "wooden language", is where it believed the film faltered:

> The quality of the film begins to deteriorate once we leave the events captured on the fly and enter into the revolutionary "discourse". For instance, regarding the army, the spectator is subjected to a long and dull monologue while two soldiers get their hair cut. And regarding

the Communist Party and the CGT, the film goes on endlessly like some sort of grammatical rule that "the PCF doesn't want a revolution".[31]

Out of their reflection on *Chaud! Chaud! Chaud!*, Cinélutte began to form what would be, for a number of projects, their political line – particularly with reference to working as a collective. Perhaps more importantly, the group began to articulate their practical approach to filming – one that would remain more or less in place until the fracturing and reformation of the group. This practical approach sought first and foremost to "burn down *spontaneity*" with regard to the shoot.[32] It acknowledged the importance of the immediacy of a project like *Chaud! Chaud! Chaud!*, but conceded that to carry out a political project with a specific political line, the group could not rely on the old production methods of May (that is, arrive at a strike, demonstration or occupation and simply start shooting). This meant that reflecting on the subject and analysing it could not take place only after the shoot, that is, during montage. Rather, for Cinélutte, the reflection and analysis had to come before, during and after the shoot. In practical terms, such a concept meant that the production crew had to participate in the struggle, understand the struggle and, ultimately, transform the struggle.[33]

This last requirement – transformation of the struggle – could be understood in two ways, and further had twofold practical effects. First, the crew could transform the actual struggle during the time of the event (strike, occupation, and so on) by participating in and recording the event. This filmic addition would incite the participants of the events to act in ways they might not have otherwise done. They could be empowered by the presence of those filming, both because they would recognise that their struggle was important enough to be documented and because the film crew could exert (like the *établis*) its own political influence on the bosses, the PCF, the unions and other players. Second, this transformation took place at the formal level of the film; that is, the film as an historical document of an event could have a reasonably wide reception and become a description and historical account of the events. Owing to its wide reception, the event communicated in this form could become the dominant or popular understanding of the event, transforming it into something other than just a strike, demonstration, and so on – making it seem "larger than life". In some sense, this meant that despite their protestations to the contrary, Cinélutte still adhered, albeit formally and experimentally, to the notion of counter-information or counter-cinema. Cinélutte's approach in this regard would, in its mature form, take on the dynamism of which it was capable and become materially apparent in the films. However, their vision wouldn't come to fruition until the production of two projects discussed later on: *Petites têtes grandes surfaces* and *Un simple exemple*.

Cinélutte seemed to have somehow taken into account the critique cited above in *Le Monde*. After articulating the necessity of abandoning spontaneity during the production phase, they were also noting the necessity of doing away with dogmatism (something that would have to be differentiated from their political line) during the montage stage.[34] Regarding *Chaud! Chaud! Chaud!*, the group attributed the faults of dogmatism and the seemingly forced, a posteriori discourse to a number of errors. First, there was the spontaneity of the shoot, but equally there was the fact that the group who shot and the group who edited were not the same; thus, there was a breakdown within the stages of production. Second, Cinélutte suggested that the errors came from not having in place the production criteria of participation, comprehension and transformation. And third, they illustrated the need to conceive of montage at each stage of the film. That is, an a priori approach to montage can, if not dictate the shoot, at least steer it towards certain political ends.[35]

In developing a practice that would work for a film collective, Cinélutte saw the work they were preparing to undertake as "a constant back and forth between those who film and those who struggle, those who film those who struggle by struggling with them, and those who struggle by filming their struggle alongside those who film".[36] Within this framework, a film is "the product of a long collaboration – discussions, common struggles, critique – between struggling workers and a film crew".[37] Given that they considered every film project to be a political one, the group articulated the need for "working groups".[38] These working groups were meant to differ from other film crews, given that film as an art was (without any conscious political reflection) already a collective art form. To counter traditional film practice, wherein the apparent collectivity is ultimately the sum of its individual participants, Cinélutte suggested early on that a division of labour was essential. Even naming a director for a project would be necessary. However, the reflection process and the ability of each member of the group to offer a critique were at the heart of their collective approach.

According to Bonan, the collective was not merely a group of individuals working in the exact same manner. Rather, each member worked to some degree on every aspect of a film – distribution, filming, sound recording, and so on – much as students would work under Copans' reformed IDHEC curriculum. Yet while this practice sought to do away with specialisation, it did call on industry professionals or specialists sympathetic to the collective's projects and political line to assist on the shoots. These specialists were usually pulled from the professionals assigned to (or chosen by) IDHEC students for their school projects. Names such as Henri Alekan, the Argentine cinematographer Ricardo Aranovich and Vincent Blanchet, as well as more militant filmmakers like Bruno Muel and Yann Le Masson, were brought on board. The idea of calling on professionals, which may at first seem counter to the popular political approach at the core of most militant cinematic undertakings, fell within Cinélutte's political programme. The group suggested that if one were trying to convey a political viewpoint through cinematic technique and, for instance, a tracking shot were out of focus and shaky, the politics would risk being overshadowed by aesthetic poverty.

Apart from specialisation and the issue of collective organisation, the group had another inaugural preoccupation. Would they remain independent, or would they attach themselves to a party, union or other group? Although actively a Marxist–Leninist group, they ultimately decided to remain independent of any specific organisation. Instead, the foundation of their cinematographic enterprise would remain faithful to the workers' cause, as later articulated in *Révolution!* (the collective's eponymous journal):

> There is no possible film without political liaisons with the workers. We are not just film-makers; we are revolutionary filmmakers, which means that we have a point of view that comes from the struggling masses, a class point of view.[39]

Cinélutte was highly critical of the possibility asserted by one of its contemporaries that a group/party could claim the *true* "proletarian" title. They held that there wasn't even a group that constituted an embryo of a future revolutionary party:

> This conviction doesn't just spring from our ideas but is the fruit of the massive distribution that we have done here and there. We believe that there are members of the working class who, without necessarily defining themselves as such, could be considered as de facto partisans of the dictatorship of the proletariat, who manifest concretely in their struggles

that they are for working-class power in one way or another. They are anti-reformists and anti-revisionists, even if they don't use these terms. This left-wing working class isn't yet Marxist–Leninist, nor is it ready to organise the taking of power, but we're convinced that from these elements will be born a Marxist–Leninist proletarian organisation.[40]

In their own way, Cinélutte addressed the appearance of the so-called micro-struggles. They argued that, while revolutionary struggles were clearly present throughout France, they rarely attacked the bourgeois state. In their opinion, the Lip factory, immigrant workers, bankers, and so on, while being the eventual fodder for Cinélutte films, could not undertake a revolutionary political programme without the aid of a central revolutionary organisation, and that organisation did not exist: "The proletarian party won't exist until the working class becomes conscious of its necessity."[41]

Even so, as we will see, Cinélutte did not remain neutral on these micro-struggles but in fact turned to them for the subject of their films. Given that the central party they posited did not exist, they were not about to align themselves with another party. The idea was therefore to take these seemingly disparate subjects and to present them in film form as consciousness-raising tools. They believed this would lead to the eventual formation of the centralised party they saw to be lacking, which would "Popularise, educate, and excite all the sectors towards the revolution, for the revolution".[42]

This meant that what unified Cinélutte politically was not only the question of Marxism–Leninism, but equally the belief that the films had to address the largest population possible. They envisioned a militant cinema for the masses, as opposed to politically avant-garde films addressing a politically avant-garde audience.[43] From this position emerged an idea that "tout ce qui bouge est rouge" (all that moves ahead is red). Filmmakers such as Yann Le Masson and the Cinéthique collective were vociferous critics of this position, but Cinélutte responded by saying that it was necessary to know at what stage they were in with regard to the construction of a party:

> To repeat: for us it is from the revolutionary left that [the party] will be born, from the working-class left, who have revolutionary ideas, from this working-class left who direct their anti-reformist battles apropos of the democratic character of the struggles or the democratic union that attempts to forge the working-class unity, who take initiatives to popularise or centralise the struggles. Our role is to favour a unification based on precise objectives by introducing debates that advance the unity of this working-class left. We don't defend just any objective.[44]

Further, remaining unattached to a specific party gave Cinélutte the freedom to frequent and represent groups without appearing overly sectarian. They could make themselves welcome in more circles than if they had been the filmmaking wing of the PCR, PCMLF or Révo!. In general, their programme was that of cultural workers in the service of the struggling working class – or what they often referred to as the "advanced workers". Examples of those whom they considered to be advanced workers became the subjects of a number of their films – from those who featured in *Jusqu'au bout* to the printers at Darboy, and finally to the women workers at Lip.

Yet Cinélutte's political-cinematic ambitions were not to be realised solely through film production. The group would, over the course of their development, also articulate and concretise a politics of distribution. Ultimately, in their public proclamations (interviews, cultural interventions, and so on), Cinélutte placed perhaps even more emphasis on their role as distributors than on their role as filmmakers. As we have seen in Chapter 2 (section 2.4), Cinélutte criticised the distribution policies of groups like Cinéma Libre. Cinélutte differentiated themselves from the *boîte aux lettres* or generalist position by having recourse to the idea that production was always in the service of distribution; also, they held that distribution included more than just the dissemination of their own titles.[45] For Cinélutte, a "film only exists by the effect it can produce on its spectators".[46]

Considering the primacy they placed on distribution, we begin to see a point of view that is even more long-term or far-seeing than, for instance, Jean-Pierre Thorn's insistence on the necessity of thinking through montage prior to shooting. As a result of their reflection on film production, Cinélutte were ardent supporters of addressing strategies of montage prior to shooting; however, their thinking moved past mere production and post-production. In fact, they were already considering distribution before creating a film. Their desire was to hold screenings in the spaces where the respective struggles took place. Cinélutte touted the idea that "distribution is the logical prolongation of our political work; its meaning is communicated only in so far as the film is debated, rewatched and used".[47]

> The political line of our films is equally and above all their militant distribution/projection and their capacity to be inscribed in the working class and popular left-wing debates. We refuse to simply tack on prefabricated analyses and bludgeon the masses with dogmatic truth at the untiring rate of 24 articles of faith per second. For us *production is in the service of distribution* [author's emphasis] [...] distribution makes up part of the extension of our work.[48]

For Cinélutte, addressing the question of distribution permitted the group to deepen its reflection on the questions concerning film form. *Oser lutter, oser vaincre* always served as a model film for Cinélutte. Even so, it was problematic, given that the film was a kind of "pedagogical film about the PC, the CGT and revisionism; thus it couldn't be screened for just any group of workers".[49] The film was a workable model for *Chaud! Chaud! Chaud!*, but that film was rarely distributed. For Cinélutte at that moment, "Four screenings of a film based on a Communist pedagogy were worth more than the 200,000 spectators in one week for *Jaws*."[50] To think about film as a mass art meant that one needed to take into consideration to whom the film was addressed. Reflecting in this way opened up the possibility of confronting the increasingly prevalent dictum *cinéma militant, cinéma chiant*. For whom is this militant cinema *chiant* (dull)? For which audience? Formulated this way, the expression's relativity is revealed. Much later on Copans remarked that it had no real critical basis; the expression was, in his words, a kind of "reflux" or ebb. He rightly posed the question: is the film *chiant* for the workers at Margoline or for the workers at the Chausson factory?[51]

Much later in the history of Cinélutte, the group took up the task of defining their concept of a revolutionary film and synthesising the matters of production, party and distribution:

> A) What is a revolutionary film?
>
> A cultural product is not eternally revolutionary; its impact depends on the political situation in which it acts.
>
> 1. This depends on the political period in which it intervenes
> 2. This depends on those who direct the product, *the distribution of the cultural product* [...][52]

If Cinélutte is unable to present the problem of the dictatorship of the bourgeoisie and the necessity of the dictatorship of the proletariat correctly, we can at least emphasise:

1. The workers can overthrow the bosses;
2. The workers can manage themselves;
3. The workers can be in charge.

These three axioms must remain the backbone of our productions.[53]

The group stressed that their method was to start with reality in order to develop concepts, not the other way around. For Cinélutte, this approach was enhanced by their concept of distribution; that is, starting from the reality of the debates about and responses to the films they made, they could continue their work of social integration with the working class. Cinélutte believed it was primarily through screenings that they were able to test the veracity of their ideas; by debating with left-wing workers and engaging with their concrete struggles, Cinélutte were able to develop their ideas.[54]

Cinélutte articulated two objectives of their politics of distribution: (1) to take the offensive with regard to screenings for the working class and distribution, that is, organise screenings during workers' struggles to popularise and animate debates; and (2) to more systematically create relationships with, and screenings for, organisations like Culture loisirs animation jeunesse, Culture et liberté and other groups that sought to expand the political work of the working class.[55]

Apart from this focus on distribution, Cinélutte took a position on one of the primary debates of the period within the domain of *cinéma militant*: that regarding putting the camera into the hands of the workers. In a roundtable discussion on *cinéma militant*, Cinélutte member Eric Pittard challenged René Vautier, who supported the idea of giving the camera to the workers. Vautier's defence of the practice rested in large part on the idea that as a result of giving the workers a new means with which to express themselves, new images would emerge.[56] Pittard took issue with this assumption, saying (as most in Cinélutte had said) that the filmmaker is fulfilling his or her work as a filmmaker and therefore has the training and means with which to undertake a cinematic project. These means are not just the simple technical apparatus but also the "practice" of filmmaking, the experience.

While this opposition to giving the camera to the workers in order to film their own struggle was largely an idea that came from Ligne rouge, the controversy emerged at the time of Les états généraux du cinéma. Within Les états généraux, two tendencies coexisted. On the one hand, some filmmakers believed that their real role was to turn over the cameras to the workers and ultimately to self-efface. On the other, some argued that their work as intellectuals was to put themselves in the service of the workers but to continue their work as Marxist–Leninists; this meant to oppose the spontaneous tendency in militant filmmaking. Cinélutte remained within this latter category, being in the same theoretical lineage as Ligne rouge, and thus were opposed to merely turning over the camera to the workers. In general, Cinélutte thought that simply handing over the technical apparatus of cinema was a *spontaniste* shortcut that sidestepped the real problem of representing the experience of the working class; that is, this approach seemed to suggest that if one put the camera in the hands of the workers, then everything would be resolved. But for Cinélutte, that wasn't the case. Groups that did experiment with this technique included Cinéma Libre and, as we will see in Chapter 4, SLON and Les groupes Medvedkine project.[57]

The idea of Chris Marker and Les groupes Medvedkine was that the cameras needed to be handed to the workers so that they could create something resembling authentic self-representation on film. For Alain Nahum of Cinélutte, the result of such a project would be a film by someone who is in the process of discovery. His understanding was that the worker who undertakes a film project is undertaking a multidirectional apprenticeship: exploring and interrogating his or her own culture, sensibilities and manner of seeing the world, and in the process reflecting on his or her own problems. Such a project can produce, according to Nahum, "some very beautiful things, but equally some undeveloped, poorly represented ideas".[58]

This practice of turning the camera over to a population of non-filmmakers was applicable to other groups besides workers. In this way, Cinélutte managed to basically escape the charge of classism and elitism in their choice of filmmakers by decrying the proverbial practice of turning over the camera to the theoreticians. At the time, *cinéma militant* was producing its fair share of austere works, but one aspect of particular importance to Cinélutte regarding the filmmaker was cultural practice based on a relationship with people working collectively, or, quite simply, filming people as objects of a given project. This meant for Cinélutte that social reflection was at the root of what they were doing. As we will see, there is a very clear socio-aesthetic change moving from *Chaud! Chaud! Chaud!* to *À pas lentes* that corroborates this notion. Cinélutte's early films stress their political line, but little by little that was changing. Nahum has stressed that if they managed to remain a collective it was because they were a film collective *before* they were a political collective. Cinélutte was political in order to make films: they were not a cinema of propaganda. Theirs was a cinema that wanted to show the world, recount certain stories and get things moving politically and socially. This is where Cinélutte saw itself as differing from the theorists, particularly a group like Cinéthique.

For Cinélutte, the kind of films being produced by Cinéthique were works that used celluloid to do something that could have been done in another manner or form. Cinélutte, while never formally engaging in the theoretical debates between the PCF's Jean-Patrick Lebel and the writers at *Tel Quel*, *Cinéthique* and *Cahiers du cinéma*, nevertheless connected this idea to the essays on the cinematographic apparatus that were published in *Cinéthique*.[59] Cinélutte believed, in opposition to the apparatus theory, that some people use the apparatus in completely different ways, and, following the way in which it is used, manage to work with or create a different ideology. Cinélutte continued to stress that the group's method was *social*, and that in developing their relationship to the people they filmed, they were able to dodge the bullet of an historically and ideologically conditioned apparatus:

> People had applied theoretical ideas, but not to the functioning of reality itself, because reality is more complex than just a given idea. It's as if you say perspective in painting is as such, but that's wrong, or rather it's true but only when you use it that way. When Orson Welles uses deep focus we can't say he is being more ideological – on the contrary.[60]

For Cinélutte, the problem needed to be posed in another manner: what kind of relationship does one maintain with the world, with the spectator, with the people filmed? Why does one film? How does one film? What is it that one wants to show? Clearly, the collective acknowledged that the debate about the ideological status of cinema and its technology was relevant and even productive. But their response to the elaborate formulations on all sides of the debate did not attempt to add to, resolve or detract from it. Instead, they returned to the fact that they saw themselves as filmmakers, and that if their collective had survived for as long as it had, it was because they were first a filmmaking collective before they were a political collective.

3.2 *Jusqu'au bout* (1973, B/W, 40 min.)

Shortly after assessing *Chaud! Chaud! Chaud!* and formulating their preliminary theories about creating a film collectively, Cinélutte began work on their first project bearing the name Cinélutte.[61] *Jusqu'au bout* was created during the same period as Thorn's *Margoline* (which, as noted before, benefited from the aid of Cinélutte). Given the similarity in theme (both films deal with the issue of immigrant workers and the Fontanet–Marcellin memorandum), the two films were distributed together. *Jusqu'au bout* was the first practical manifestation of Cinélutte's creative programme, and in a later reflection on the film, the group felt sure that their new methodological approach was apparent:

> From the beginning [...] we can see that these films [*Margoline* and *Jusqu'au bout*] are not content to simply be the account of a struggle created by "exterior elements", but rather are truly co-produced by the workers, even produced by the workers themselves with the aid and intermediation of militant filmmakers. Further, the latter are not satisfied by merely implicating themselves a little bit more than any common filmmaker would (but would the common filmmaker venture into a factory in the middle of a struggle?), but rather entirely take up the workers' struggle, occupy the factory with them, eat with them and integrate themselves as much as possible into the striking workers. This obviously allows us to speak about the struggle without betraying it, and to represent it in the most sensitive and "true" manner.[62]

In looking at *Jusqu'au bout*, certain elements of this analysis ring true, while others appear less developed than the group had perhaps hoped at the time. One thing that is evident in this film, however, is the concretisation of Cinélutte's political line, based on the Marxist–Leninist film production (as well as theory and distribution) that was being formulated, as we have seen, beginning with the montage of *Chaud! Chaud! Chaud!*.

Jusqu'au bout documents a hunger strike by 56 Tunisian workers at the Ménilmontant Catholic church in Paris, directed against the Fontanet–Marcellin memorandum, which was the central focus of Thorn's *Margoline*. The strike addressed issues raised in *Margoline* (for instance, obtaining work permits), but it also addressed the immigrant workers' need for freedom of expression, and it attacked racism (as in *Margoline*, there are images from the racist group Ordre nouveau's meeting on immigration) and the

Figures 3.7–3.8

increasing number of hate crimes during the time of the memorandum. The strike lasted more than a month and brought about certain gains, like those described in *Margoline*. Cinélutte has said that *Jusqu'au bout* was ultimately a film that sought to unify French and immigrant workers; specifically, it was directed at the French worker in order to offer insight into the difficulties the immigrant worker faced.[63] Paradoxically, one of the issues that arose during distribution was that *Jusqu'au bout* was seen mostly by immigrant workers.[64]

Figure 3.9

Structurally and formally, *Jusqu'au bout* resembles *Margoline*. The film begins outside the domain of the event; and there is the use of diegetic text, stills, voiceover and credits written in both French and Arabic. *Jusqu'au bout* opens with a direct shot of a striker who rattles off, like a machine gun, details of the politics of recruitment in Tunisia of employers looking to hire. This shot cuts away to the film's credits, with a Tunisian song accompanying the text; this view eventually gives way to a highly composed shot of the singer, a Tunisian man, arm in arm with two French women (Figure 3.9). The trio sits in a desert, and after panning over this landscape, Cinélutte matches the pan on a sea of Tunisian men who are waiting in front of a recruitment centre.

At this first stage of the film, Cinélutte is able to permit itself what could otherwise have been written off within their own political terms (and Thorn's) as a naturalist caprice. In a sequence of pure, direct cinema, we attend the interview process of a French recruiter (apparently working for a Dutch company) vetting potential Tunisian recruits. The sequence is shot primarily in close-up and is replete with confusion on the parts of the French recruiter and the Tunisians struggling to understand him. The filmmakers adeptly capture a sinister and condescending aspect of the recruiter's expressions, which border on the comedic. The sequence shows the recruits taking a test of manual competence and then moves to the recruiter describing the contract.

Formally, in this sequence, Cinélutte made use of a technique that would be eliminated in subsequent projects and that had direct social implication for the group: the zoom. In this sequence, the reliance on the zoom (albeit practical) implied within the continuing formulation of Cinélutte's political line that they were not entirely implicated in the event being filmed. Rather, the zoom permitted them a distance that suggested them to be somewhat objective or outside observers. The use of the zoom implied, to some degree, that an error had occurred at the level of social relations: an ideology of proximity via the image is maintained at the expense of an enunciation of the apparatus. The pedagogic aspect of the film supposedly consists of capturing the reality of the event, yet accomplishing this by means of the apparatus entails revealing what is hidden, that is, the specificity of cinema as the agent of mediation.

This sort of approach might seem dangerously close to the reviled naturalism, but what permits Cinélutte to maintain the dignity of their political line is the context they provide with just the very short clips preceding this sequence, as well as what follows. This articulation of a given historical, social or political context through moderately didactic means points to the difference between a film by Cinélutte and someone in the direct tradition, such as Frederick

Wiseman. It is easy to imagine the difference between these two hypothetical approaches, even forgetting that what has been described thus far in *Jusqu'au bout* is merely the first ten minutes of a film that is going to completely shift its terrain.

A filmmaker such as Wiseman would give us the exterior shot of Tunisia and then throw us into the interview with the recruiter. The result would not be entirely apolitical, or even without its radical elements, but it certainly would not express a concrete political line or enter the domain of historical specificity. The Wiseman-esque film (representing the traditional direct approach) would bear down with its cinematographic microscope over a power relation whose class history may be subsumed by the formal self-effacement that appears to give access to the truth of the situation filmed. In contrast, Cinélutte, by opening with the striker at Ménilmontant and the highly composed tableau of the singer before taking us into the recruiting scene, gestures towards a concrete political line and analysis.

This issue of direct cinema was not something that Cinélutte tried to escape without reflection; it was an integral part of their practical approach and had been the subject of long reflection. If, at the public level, the group professed no interest in the direct form, their internal discussions, their individual personal experiences and, above all, their films pointed to this film style as a constant concern. They diverged from direct cinema because they were uninterested in creating ethnographic documents that simply recorded the words of their subjects. Rather, the group insisted that filmmakers had to locate a point of entry into the subject. This method of intervening would yield what perhaps was missing in direct cinema: a point of view or, more specifically, a "class point of view".[65] We have already seen some examples of formal elements that create such a point of view in practice, particularly in Thorn's films, whether a voiceover or the mobilisation of text through a multitude of platforms.[66]

Yet when faced with the question of how to oppose the direct tendency in *cinéma militant*, as much as Cinélutte attacked the process of passive recording, they equally criticised those who relied too heavily on text as a strategy to break with false objectivity and the illusion of verisimilitude. Cinélutte pointed to the films of Cinéthique as being almost a caricature of this tendency to abuse intertitles. Cinélutte saw the problem with Cinéthique's approach as their belief that once the political questions had been posed, the aesthetic solutions should quite naturally follow. For Cinélutte, it was entirely possible that a very clear political idea might be absolutely unfilmable. They said they had the twin tasks of filming the revolution and revolutionising film. Formally, one strategy that Cinélutte relied on was constructing a narrative chronology that replaced the actual historical time of the event's development. The example Bonan used is the way in which Darboy was edited out of order to form a cohesive narrative, when, historically, it unfolded differently.[67]

For Cinélutte, artistic work had to synthesise and condense the ideas of the masses. One criterion for testing this, Nahum suggested, is whether the subjects of the film recognise themselves in the film beyond the rushes; the real challenge of recognition would come after the montage.[68]

In a concise statement on direct cinema, Bonan said:

> If we participate in direct cinema it is for three reasons: (1) We are politically unorganised individuals not without contradictions. What unifies us is not the discussion amongst us, but the confrontation with a concrete reality during an event of class struggle; (2) Given that almost none of us at Cinélutte has a militant practice elsewhere, our link to the masses is by screenings and our participation in conflicts during a shoot; it is equally from there that we

get our ideas; (3) Even if we can't say "reportage is credible and fiction untrue", it remains true that it is harder to dispute the authenticity of a scene shot in the direct style.[69]

Cinélutte continued, in another interview:

> We have come up with a very clear idea that you have to begin with the lived experience of the people in order to move up to rational knowledge. In a militant film you have to approach the everyday existence and problems of the people in a concrete manner. Then you must show in a very living, lively way how contradictions emerge from amongst the people or between the people and their enemies. You also have to know from what vantage point one should position [them]. It's about organising a series of elements that will inspire debate. These are a few of the elements that we have been able to develop by our militant filmmaking practice in order to bring to light a new aesthetic.[70]

Ultimately, the approach is one of putting filmmakers into the event and then fictionalising that direct approach. The filmmakers must also establish authentic relationships with the people filmed. Again, a kind of co-conspiracy takes place: when those being filmed are conscious of the cinematic project, they begin to collude with the filmmakers. They incite events to allegorise the ideas of the film – to offer the spectacular world of the fictive while "really" creating an event.

As Cinélutte continued their work, they began to employ staging as a methodological intervention. This is perhaps one of the most significant elements allowing us to reframe Cinélutte and see them not as a group creating propaganda films but as a group wholly engaged in filmmaking. While this method developed as their work progressed, Sainderichin has said that already in *Jusqu'au bout* certain scenes in the church were staged.[71] From the boarding of the airplane taking the Tunisian workers to Holland, the film moves to the striking immigrants at Ménilmontant. As in *Margoline*, the spectator is confronted with title cards, voiceover, multiple forms of text and a musical performance, ultimately leading to what the strikers called a first victory and the end of the hunger strike.

With *Jusqu'au bout*, we are in some sense not that far from *Chaud! Chaud! Chaud!*. Going back to the critique in *Le Monde*, we can perceive some of the same errors being made in this film. The opening sequence, shot in a quasi-direct-cinema style, is wholly captivating: it is situated in the territory of cinema, outside the realm of pure didacticism and pure propaganda. The strike footage, however, while engaging, is not able to free itself from the constraints of its avowed mission and formally remains caught in the aesthetic tendencies of Thorn. What is not yet apparent in the film is the way in which the group (and its political line) is implicated, and how it understands and transforms the events it depicts.[72] We can attribute this lack of clarity to the fact that the film was made very shortly after the completion of *Chaud! Chaud! Chaud!*, and so the group were still in the process of digesting and understanding the approach they had articulated at the level of theory. And it would be precisely the next Cinélutte film, *Petites têtes, grandes surfaces*, which would give the first mature articulation of their practical methodology.[73]

3.3 *Petites têtes, grandes surfaces – anatomie d'un supermarché* (1974, B/W, 36 min.)

> It is correct what Mao said when he said we can't taste a pear without transforming it.
> – Alain Nahum[74]

Petites têtes, grandes surfaces – anatomie d'un supermarché is an historic turning point in Cinélutte's trajectory. This film was also the first concrete demonstration of what Cinélutte had articulated as its political line and method of intervention. What separates it from the first two films is that it is not an intervention during a strike, an occupation or even a demonstration. It is a documentary made within the framework of a *film de promotion* (a film made by students in order to be able to advance to the next stage of the academic programme) at IDHEC and explores the exploitation of cashiers at a Carrefour supermarket. Rather than entering into an explosive political situation, the filmmakers address a more perennial, quotidian issue of exploitation in a work environment without union representation. The subject of the film does not have the chaotic urgency of a demonstration or the precarious nature of an occupation, so it gave Cinélutte a subject with which the filmmakers could calmly and methodically carry out their cinematic political agenda. The film dramatically benefits from this lack of urgency, which keeps it from falling into the trap of *spontanisme*.

Petites têtes was primarily Guy-Patrick Sainderichin and François Dupeyron's film. The two students decided to create their IDHEC *film de promotion* under the auspices of Cinélutte and the supervision of documentary filmmaker Vincent Blanchet.[75] The two were in the editing division of the programme, and in order to have the material to edit, they had to shoot something. They wanted to shoot a subject that was stylistically in the domain of *cinéma direct* but that was also an investigative report.[76] The students and others at Cinélutte discussed collectively what to shoot and decided on the idea of going to a supermarket. The idea came during a period that saw a renewed interest in, even obsession with, "things", one of the most prominent examples being Jean Baudrillard's *The System of Objects*. The filmmakers at Cinélutte wanted to demonstrate that, for them, the importance was not in things themselves but in the social relations within the company.

The film's strengths lie largely in the complicity developed between the filmmakers and the supermarket employees. The filmmakers needed to transmit this complicity – not only within the emerging narrative of the film but also by means of a cinematic form. Formally, the filmmakers followed Vincent Blanchet's dictum that the zoom must never be used, favouring instead a fixed 12 mm lens. This practice obliged the filmmaker to move physically closer to the subject, encouraging more direct participation as well as the possibility of establishing a social–cinematic relationship. Hence, the practice was referred to as the "biological zoom".[77]

Petites têtes opens with a long tracking shot passing by the cash registers at Carrefour as customers purchase their groceries, accompanied by a voiceover of shoppers describing the experience of shopping at the supermarket. Sainderichin shot everything in the film apart from this opening tracking shot (taken by Blanchet while perched inside a shopping cart). He said that this shot – very similar to a tracking shot in Godard's Groupe Dziga Vertov film *Tout va bien* – was an attempt to establish a non-social relationship. This non-social relationship was filmed from a point of view distant from the subjects, with the emphasis on the things, the products, in the supermarket. It included a voiceover largely describing the abundance of products the supermarket offers and the ease with which they can be purchased.[78] In this sense, the shot was created, according to Sainderichin, precisely to hint at the film they were *not* about to make. In the subsequent reversal, the film switches from a fascination with things to a devotion to establishing the political nature of the social relations and hierarchies in the supermarket. This change is evident in a new film style, as the following shots are dedicated almost entirely to interviews with the employees of Carrefour. There is also a change in the subject of the voiceover, in that the final speaker of this sequence begins to address the difficulties the cashiers experience, saying that the store is a "real factory".

After the tracking shot, the film turns to interviews with the management at Carrefour and stresses the organisation of management throughout the various departments. In fact, Copans has pointed out that one of the less commented upon, but no less interesting, aspects of the film is the way it demonstrated the remarkable way in which the Carrefour management was organised.[79] The interviews with management personnel (portrayed in the film as being composed entirely of men) become increasingly revelatory about their treatment of, and feelings regarding, the female cashiers. This ability of the filmmakers to gain the confidence of management will raise *Petites têtes* from mere reportage to a film that works to transform the actual situation within the store, as well as transform itself into a work of dramatic form.

The filmmakers present shots of managers training personnel for various tasks. They then begin to reveal that, when there are too many cashiers and not enough need to have all the registers open, the women are sent to various department warehouses to undertake other jobs. The filmmakers here introduce one of the principal cashiers, who has been taken off her register to price books. After she explains how each day she is taken off a register (the job for which she is trained and paid) and put on some other duty, the film shows something similar to that shown in the opening tracking shot. Whereas the opening shot faced the registers from the point of view of the store exterior (revealing the lines and the massive amounts of products), this second shot, handheld, reveals the cashiers and the registers from inside the store looking out. This changed perspective, along with the introduction to the exploitation (not yet fully developed, but at least announced), opens up the sociopolitical territory Cinélutte seeks to explore.

Nahum, in reflecting on this use of tracking shots, was not entirely convinced that the young filmmakers were not merely trying to replicate the tracking shot in *Tout va bien*. He went on to say that to depict the reality of the supermarket, the group needed to show it in its temporality, and the tracking shots permitted this:

> If you make a film about a supermarket, about the girls who work on the cash registers, there's no film, and to some degree if there weren't those tracking shots in the film, the film wouldn't really exist. It is precisely because of those tracking shots that they can then go in and do the close-ups; if they weren't there we'd just say that we're simply doing television work. These shots announce the fact that the filmmakers are engaged in making cinema; by doing a tracking shot that is longer than normally seen, for instance, on TV or in a news report, there is a kind of revelation of the filmmaking process. If it didn't have that shot, with the cashiers running back and forth, well it is precisely that which then allows them to go in and use the other shots, which are seen, thanks to the tracking shot, in another light.[80]

At this point in the film, two of the three primary tactics of Cinélutte's programme have been put into motion: the filmmakers are clearly participating in and coming to understand the situation they are filming. The understanding will need to become clearer, and some sort of transformation will have to take place.

After the second tracking shot, the film, through interviews with the various department managers, describes the process of promotion for those on the managerial track, moving upwards from intern. To illustrate this ladder, the filmmakers shoot an interview with a former intern who was eventually promoted to full-time employee. The interview is proposed by one of the managers we have been following, and he suggests that this former intern might best be able to describe the Carrefour "experience". The interview concretises what has already been alluded to – namely, that those on the managerial track have a substantial amount of mobility within the ranks of the hierarchy. What begins to articulate the needed transformation is that, while the manager and the former intern both figure in the frame during the interview, so does the woman pricing the books. She is almost lost in the piles of

Figure 3.10

books, but she smiles ironically at the camera from her position in the background, as the former intern describes his sense of freedom at Carrefour (Figure 3.10).

This shot is a clear instantiation of the integration and complicity with their subjects that Cinélutte managed to accomplish. While gaining the confidence of managerial staff, they have also nurtured an alliance with the cashier. In this nascent alliance, we also witness another key element of the Cinélutte programme: a point of view. Up until this point, the interviews with the management staff have been more or less neutral and practical, slowly tending towards a description of the exploitation the female cashiers are undergoing. The film shows cashiers running from register to register, intercutting this chaotic work environment with the increasingly cynical yet calm managers describing the near total promotional immobility of the cashiers. One manager cynically responds to the question "What happens to the cashiers after hire?" by saying "Well, once a cashier, always a cashier." Another says that one of the store's primary economic principles is to have the minimum number of cashiers and the maximum number of registers, while yet another remarks that the only sector of the store that has "social problems" is the cashiers. Finally, in discussing the petty calculation errors a cashier might make on a given day, one of the managers says, "Sometimes they get out of line, start complaining, and that's when you gotta come down hard on them; I mean they're women, you have to keep them in line." It is precisely the candour of these managers that is a testament to Cinélutte's method.

The transformation hinted at thus far, in terms of both drama and the sociopolitical situation, comes as a member of the management discusses the fact that there is no union representation at the store, and that helps keep the women from causing any substantial problems. At the end of this voiceover, the film cuts to a group of cashiers listening to the audio recording of the manager's speech (Figure 3.11). The film continues with the women listening to the various examples of the managers describing the ways they exploit and control the cashiers, along with the women's response. The women describe the ways they experience this exploitation without representation and the way that the management pits one cashier against another. And while they agree that union representation is what is needed, there is no resolution at the end of the film.

Although the question of representation at the supermarket remained unanswered in the film, Cinélutte did accomplish its tripartite approach with some success for the first time. Bonan and Abramovici edited the film, but because of the established production method, it could not be considered a film created solely in montage. The intellectual trajectory of the film was already bound up in the temporality of the production: the crew went into the store and made their way to the heart of the method of exploiting the cashiers. The managerial staff

provided all the necessary points of departure (for example, announcing that there is
no possible promotion for the cashiers and
that they need to be kept in line). Because
of this almost naturally occurring narrative, the filmmakers at Cinélutte were able
to create a militant film that did not need
an a posteriori Marxist–Leninist discourse
overlaying it through texts or dogmatic
voiceover. While this can be considered
real progress in terms of Cinélutte's work
within the domain of *cinéma militant*, the
group nevertheless had concerns about
how the film would be received.

Figure 3.11

Following the completion of *Petites têtes*, the group began to question the possibility of
distributing it. One of the difficulties that arose was its lack of voiceover or dogmatic political
programme (this difficulty, ironically, also indicated that the group was developing a concrete
and specifically Cinélutte-style political cinema). One of the potential problems the group saw
with the lack of a didactic political (Marxist–Leninist) presentation was that this opened up
the film to recuperation by the PCF and other "revisionists".[81] This aporia might pose certain
incidental political difficulties, but it clearly resulted from an experimental new approach to
political cinema. It would move the group closer to the sort of staging (transformation of situations) that it would increasingly employ.

After some reflection, Cinélutte went ahead and distributed *Petites têtes*, which enabled the
group to more empirically assess the film and its political effects on the spectators:

> We came to see that the workers who saw the film were of a divided opinion on the ques-
> tions the film posed. On the one hand, those who were influenced by the P"C"F saw the
> higher-level workers as the privileged allies of the working class, while others thought that if
> that was the case the alliance could only be based solely on the positions of the working class
> itself [...] Ultimately the revisionists are afraid of such a film; they think that the upper-level
> workers are their allies and that they are allied not on the basis of proletarian ideas, but on
> those ideas of the upper-level workers themselves.[82]

The completion of this film coincided with a sea change for Cinélutte. After *Petites têtes* there
occurred what Cinélutte perceived to be as a "revisionist" putsch at IDHEC, primarily consisting
of the PCF-loyal faculty and filmmakers strengthening their "bourgeois line".[83] The tensions
between the political rivals that had somehow been smoothed over for a period of time finally
came to a head as Louis Daquin and Jean-André Fieschi, both members of the PCF, fired Copans
and Bonan. The result was not just the scission of political and practical affiliations, but, more
important for Cinélutte as a filmmaking collective, the withdrawal of the practical, material
base they needed in order to continue making their films.[84] This rupture with IDHEC pushed
Cinélutte to make new alliances. It was under these circumstances that they began to work with
students and professors at the experimental university at Vincennes. Two figures that would play
a particularly important role in the coming Cinélutte project were Serge Le Péron and former
Godard/Groupe Dziga Vertov collaborator Jean-Henri Roger.

Starting in 1970, Vincennes underwent a restructuring of the film department similar to what occurred at IDHEC, in which militant film production became a mainstay of the programme.[85] The restructuring was intended to leave behind the literary and semiological analytic framework that had been the foundation of the programme. It sought to move the department towards a pedagogy based first on production/practice and second, in terms of analysis, on the new orientation towards methods that demonstrated how

Figure 3.12 *Soyons tout*

cinema could best serve the people's struggles. A number of films associated with individuals and collectives emerged from this period. These included work that would eventually go on to form part of the catalogue of the militant collective Front Paysan and Serge Le Péron's collectively made *Attention aux provocateurs* (1972) and *Soyons tout* (1971).

Soyons tout is particularly interesting in terms of how it represents a strike, given that it was a low-budget, black-and-white militant production, but, more importantly, also a fiction film. Within the dominant militant filmmaking tendencies that had reigned up to this point, documentary production was the preferred, or at least the most commonly chosen, form. Notable exceptions were larger-budget films, like those of Godard's collective and Marin Karmitz's polemic-inducing *Coup pour coup*. The political motivation for creating *Soyons tout* came from assessing the majority of *cinéma militant*. Up until 1971, it had been dealing with interventions (such as strikes) that occurred, if not randomly, then at least, in the eyes of the Groupe cinéma de Vincennes, "intermittently".[86] This lack of consistency prevented the movement from creating a film that was able to describe the whole of what Le Péron referred to as "la gauche ouvrière".[87]

While the political aspirations of this project are intriguing, it is the formal aspects of *Soyons tout* that constitute its originality among much of contemporary militant film work. Of course, the formal decision to create a fiction film cannot be separated entirely from its political motives. It is further this formal reflection that, two years before the founding of Cinélutte, was already investigating new methods for avoiding the trap of wildcat, undirected shooting. The choice of working in fiction instead of documenting a specific political event allowed the filmmakers the time and space to reflect deeply on a given political problem. In Cinélutte's terms, fiction offered the real possibility to "participate, understand and transform". And ultimately, for Le Péron, fiction was, "for the workers who would see the film, a much more approachable, understandable and even enjoyable form".[88]

The other film that Le Péron and the group created was *Attention aux provocateurs*.[89] *Attention* was created from staged scenes along with archival footage. Like much *cinéma militant* of the far left, it dealt with the revisionism of the PCF, or, more precisely, the role of the PCF in the Algerian War. The film investigates the period between 1936 and 1962, looking at the liberation struggles of the Algerian people against their French colonisers:

> The film takes the point of view of the liberation struggle and analyses the various instances of the PCF usurping power: the dissolution of the North African Star in 1936, Setif in 1945,

November first 1954 [...] The principal aspect of this film is the fact that it sheds new light on this period [...] The reality is that once again, this time during the Algerian war, the PCF has reached new, ridiculous, even odious heights.[90]

Figure 3.13 Marxist folk singer Dominique Grange performs in *Soyons tout*

It was their common themes and reflections on cinematic practice that allowed the two groups to work together under the auspices of Cinélutte. Together, the filmmakers of these two collectives came up with an idea to make a film about the "electoral illusion".[91] Although this film was attempted, it was never realised; instead, three short- to medium-length films emerged that were distributed together under the title *Bonne chance la France*: *L'autre façon d'être une banque* (1974, B/W, 40 min.), *Portrait* or *Comité Giscard* (1974, B/W, 20 min.) and *Darboy* or *Un simple exemple* (1974, B/W, 45 min.).

3.4 *Bonne chance la France*

3.4.1 *L'autre façon d'être une banque*

Figure 3.14 *Soyons tout*

The short subject *L'autre façon d'être une banque* is the account of a strike at the bank Crédit Lyonnais. This strike was directed not only at the management of the bank, but at the CGT, who, once again, in the eyes of the filmmakers, had failed to support the striking workers.

The core of the narrative of *L'autre façon* deals with the development of strike committees and the participation of the unions. For instance, the CFDT's role in the strike regarding the formation of strike committees is at first unclear, but later it forms an alliance with the Trotskyite Force ouvrière.[92] However, as in many of the films examined so far, the corrosive syndicalist element of the strike is the CGT. The clearest illustration of CGT's nature comes when the question of the return to work is dealt with: two assemblies were organised, one consisting of 1,500 participants from the strike committees (composed of many different unions) and another composed of 91 participants (all members of the CGT). The 91 participants of the CGT assembly vote to return to work, while the 1,500 from the strike committees vote to continue the strike.[93]

The film has two sequences that are difficult to read passively. While the film clearly takes the side of the strike committees, who oppose the return to work and perceive the failure of the CGT to act effectively, at moments the film makes it difficult to sympathise with the strike committee. These moments are directly linked to the history of the far left during this period. While France never degenerated into the violence of other Western European countries during the same period (for example, the Angry Brigade in England, the German Red Army Fraction and the Italian Red Brigades and Autonomists), it did go through a period when the use of violence as a political tactic was increasingly becoming an option. The Nogrette Affair was a widely publicised example of this tendency.[94] The various violent actions effectively weakened a number of far-left organisations, as many people left when the groups turned to these more violent means.

Yet if this violence became notorious as a result of actions like the Nogrette Affair, it was already a part of the strikes that rocked this period. Two overly debated films that dealt with this subject were *Coup pour coup* and *Tout va bien*, which both raised the issue of the sequestration of the management, bosses, owners and shop-floor clerks. In a sequence in *L'autre façon*, one Monsieur Carrier, an upper-level worker who not only did not support the strike but also supposedly worked against it, is singled out while eating in the office canteen. The striking workers begin to call him out and even start throwing food and garbage at him, all with broad smiles on their faces. Further, they follow Carrier out onto the street and heckle him. In a rather derogatory reflection on this sequence, and on the film more generally, Sainderichin has said:

> The Credit Lyonnais film has no characters, and there is this absolutely atrocious scene where the workers follow the guy from the management in the street, and he's a guy who has absolutely no real importance relative to the situation [...] he's a little boss of nothing. That scene really upsets me because I feel like I see the Cultural Revolution before my eyes, that eventually we were going to end up hanging a placard around this guy's neck that said he was a bourgeois.[95]

A similar sequence shows the CGT workers returning to work. Members of the other committee enter the workplace and harangue these workers for having betrayed their co-workers. Although similar sequences have appeared elsewhere in the film without the underlying violence, this sequence is particularly unsettling, largely because of the way the events are depicted. For example, we see young workers vehemently harass an elderly woman (but with apparent jouissance, betrayed by their facial expressions).

The film ends with an acceptance of the return to work after a number of demands were accepted.

3.4.2 *Portrait* or *Comité Giscard*

Portrait or *Comité Giscard* is a film unlike any other Cinélutte project. It did not take as its point of departure the struggle, either quotidian or during a *temps chaud* (for example, a strike, occupation or demonstration), of those with whom the group sympathised. *Comité Giscard* instead documented an election committee for Giscard D'Estaing situated in the 17th arrondissement of Paris. The film is the shortest of all the Cinélutte projects (20 minutes) and was shot clandestinely (the group professed to be supporters of D'Estaing in order to gain access to the various committee "militants"). The film's subject suggests that it could be one of the most important films in the Cinélutte catalogue – a film that confronts the "enemy" outside of the historical and immediate situation of being the opposing camp in a struggle. Unfortunately, it is unable, perhaps owing to the conditions under which it was filmed, to offer much more than a sometimes frightening, satirical glimpse into the world of the bourgeois right wing.

Comité Giscard is filmed in a direct style and uses very little additional textual commentary. It employs music in the opening and closing (nondiegetic in the opening, diegetic in the closing). And during one interview, a brief voiceover announces that the man being interviewed, a Giscardian, is suspected of being a member of the SAC (Service d'action civique).[96] The film is constructed primarily from a series of interviews and closes with a large rally of D'Estaing supporters. The interviews provide insight into the anti-communism of the election committee and D'Estaing. When confronted with the question of immigration, the interviewees even admit that refugees from Yugoslavia and Hungary (that is, those who escaped the ravages of communism) are working on the campaign. However, we also gain a strange insight into the committee's understanding of communism. The subjects suggest that the committee would like to employ the same methods as the Communist Party for increasing their votes, and one supporter even refers to himself as a "Giscard-*Spontex*".[97]

3.4.3 *Darboy* or *Un simple exemple*

By 1973, the Darboy print shop had been running for 44 years; it was founded by "a Dufour, and currently directed by a Dufour".[98] In January 1974, the print shop had 93 employees, and since 1972, the director of Darboy had made a number of large investments, including leasing two four-colour offset printers and a paper cutter.[99] By the time the workers occupied Darboy, these investments still hadn't been paid for.[100] The majority of the workers at Darboy were members of the CGT.

The crisis that led to the occupation began in January 1974, when an executive was called before the banks. On 1 February of that year, the same executive announced that, that week, the workers would receive only 30 percent of their usual salary. The following week saw the same situation repeated. On 28 February, the workers received a letter of termination, and were let go without severance pay (their wages due up to that point being paid).[101] The liquidation of the factory occurred rapidly, largely because of a law created in December 1973 as a result of the efforts of workers at the Lip factory. Under the terms of this law, in the event of bankruptcy, "the workers would become the primary creditors (thus, the first paid) without waiting for the company to be put on the market".[102] This law was to go into effect on 1 March; the company filed for bankruptcy on 18 February.

The decision to occupy the factory came from a number of roundtable discussions and was eventually made with the support of the CGT Syndicat du Livre Parisien (Book Union of Paris). *Darboy* recounts the occupation of the print shop in Montreuil during the spring of 1974. The strike was directed against the firing of 90 employees owing to the current economic crisis. Like the first film in this triptych, *L'autre façon d'être une banque*, *Darboy* highlighted the ludic and sometimes carnivalesque aspects of a strike. The film also marked another turning point in the history of Cinélutte and was the last project on which many of the first generation of Cinélutte members would work.

The film opens with a brief text that states, "On 16 April 1974 at the Darboy print shop, the workers in the book

Figure 3.15

industry dare to restart their presses, they dare to struggle, dare to win [*ils osent lutter, osent vaincre*]." This text is followed by a list of those that the workers wish to thank for supporting their strike, among which are the striking banks, MLAC (Le mouvement pour la liberté de l'avortement et de la contraception) and the workers at Lip. The similarity between the strike at Darboy and what was transpiring at Lip would take on another dimension with the next and final film by the Cinélutte collective: *À pas lentes*. The list of thanks also included the CFDT and the local CGT, the latter being something of a surprise, given that the role of the CGT during the strike would be questioned in this film.

Darboy opens on a festive note with a marching band and Rémy (one of the principal actors of this occupation and film) explaining the strike to onlookers, and ultimately to the film's eventual audience (Figure 3.16). Some of what emerges from this brief introduction hints at the overall strategy of the film. Rémy reveals that we are entering the film on the 74th day of the occupation of Darboy and that not only have the workers succeeded in getting their severance pay, but the shop has also found a new owner. Thus, we are entering the film at the end – the workers' occupation and self-management have succeeded, and only "good things" (as one woman puts it during the opening) have happened. It plays something like a militant fairy tale.

The film offers a Marxist interpretation of the history of the economic crisis of '74, which resulted in, among other things, the firing without severance pay of the Darboy workers. The general history of the crisis is recounted in voiceover, and an accompanying montage of newspaper headlines describes the ravages of the crisis, featuring a shot of a woman cleaning off anti-capitalist graffiti from her shop window. Because of the crisis the print shop had to stop production. All the workers were let go without compensation, and following this the workers decided to occupy the premises and demand severance pay. The voiceover that recounts this history alternates between two different voices, both members of Cinélutte (Bonan and Copans).

The voiceover gives way to the striking workers, but their actions are still presented in a *recounting* mode, meaning that the entire film consists of a retrospective look back on the strike. This temporal gap between the voiceover and the images of the occupation is one way that the film does not fall prey to a naturalist, direct approach. At the same time, the Cinélutte voiceover manages to escape a wooden Marxist–Leninist discourse. Further, the first worker's voiceover describes how normally during a struggle, the workers are confronted with a boss, management or some sort of opposition, and yet here they are more or less unopposed. This aspect reinforces the notion that the struggle is not occurring in the whirlwind, or perhaps spontaneous, chaos of a typical strike. Therefore, the form as well as the subject of the film permit (and demonstrate) a certain methodical reflection on the events.

What is notable about the opening is that it does not immediately attack the hard political core of the occupation. Instead, it focusses on how the workers get food for their lunch, offering a detailed description of what they ate, and it further emphasises the fact that it was this social situation they created that allowed them (while eating outside) to attack issues of organisation. This "lunch" sequence, while

Figure 3.16

ludic in terms of presentation, is not without a pragmatic political context. For example, the food the workers receive comes from the municipal canteen in Montreuil.[103]

The occupation is portrayed via images of the workers sleeping and living together, accompanied by a song the workers wrote.[104] While one worker snores, another sketches him sleeping. Her voiceover explains that, although they had worked together for the last ten years, they never really knew each other or understood the hardships of the various workers' tasks. If this early film sequence has any militancy at all, it comes from an experience, not a hope; it is not a film about a desire to win but is presented as the narrative of a victory. Each step, thus far, has shown the pleasures of revolutionary activity, and even the pleasures of work. In fact, in *Darboy imprime Darboy* (Figure 3.17) it is explained that a big part of the reason for restarting the machines was a growing boredom with not working, the fatigue of "vegetating".[105]

One specific political question that emerges from the film is why the CGT did not support restarting the machines. After having heard the collective decision of the workers to occupy Darboy, the union (which one of the workers describes as the best possible) followed them and supported their action. However, the decision to undertake restarting the presses was not supported, which felt like a betrayal to many of the loyal *cégétistes*.[106] One worker, an older woman, describes the pleasure of hearing the presses start up – the beating of her heart out of fear, but also out of pride and excitement.

The film equally captures an incredible sense of pride when the first tracts come off the presses. It shows the development of the workday – how they would maintain the same number of hours per week, with the added element that the workers could stop at 6 p.m. or continue until 2 a.m. if they chose to.[107] One worker said that part of what felt good was not only the fact that they were undertaking self-management, but also that there was pride in the projects they undertook. They were

Figure 3.17

producing work that was helpful to other workers on strike, creating a unity among different sectors of struggling workers. They weren't just printing advertising.

The workers also demonstrated, for those who had never seen how the presses function, the processes of image stripping, assembling the plates, inking the rollers, and so on. This sharing of their quotidian experiences again highlighted the social and festive aspect of this strike. *Darboy* is a film that, so far, shows no real downside to the strike: it is largely a positive experience with no apparent negative consequences. While the CGT is criticised for its lack of participation, we are not faced with (as in so many other films about occupations) police knocking down the doors and using tear gas, or any of the now standard responses from the factory management and ownership.

The workers decide to print the history of their strike on a poster entitled *Darboy imprime Darboy* (Darboy Prints Darboy), and there is a Radio Inter interview with the workers at Darboy, in which they explain that they are looking for a new owner to buy the factory. A title card explains that on Thursday, 18 April, a former higher-up (Mr. Lebourg) in the factory offered to co-own the factory. The conditions were that Lebourg would buy the factory, that he would be a 50 per cent holder, and that the workers would pay him up to the point that they themselves would become 50 per cent holders as well.

The way the workers conduct themselves in the film presents an object lesson in remaining organised and constantly working towards the betterment of one's conditions and relations with the wider world. We see them sell lilies for 1 May (donated by a former Darboy employer) and visit the Lip factory. Such elements contribute to the apparent ludic aspect of this strike; they contribute to the portrait of then contemporary workers addressing the evolution of the forms of struggle, for instance, self-managed collectives versus rigid union structures. It is this sort of sequence that provides an historical image of the political left narrative arc of 1970s France.

The film returns to the Giscard campaigners ("Giscard à la barre!") from *Comité Giscard*. The film announces a return to Montreuil on 5 May for the first round of elections. There is a kind of carnival and an open house at Darboy. Rémy's voiceover becomes ever more dominant. We see shots from the opening sequence in which he recounts how the Darboy strike unfolded. In this way, the film becomes temporally experimental: it employs a retroactive voiceover and shot sequencing that have no fidelity to chronology; it is a film created by montage, one that begins with a very specific literary chronological form (the chapter headings) that fades away as the organisation of the film starts to mirror the autonomous organisation of the workers at Darboy. Towards the end, intertitles with dates

Figures 3.18–3.20 *Un simple exemple*

become more frequent. After the announcement of the presidential vote, a title card announces, "Monday, 6 May 1974", and this card is followed by another on ruled paper explaining that the workers have won both their severance pay and their employment under a new boss.

The voiceovers discuss the fact that they have been paid, that they have won and that this is what counts. And yet they are not convinced that the return to the former division of labour – leaving the factory and the community established during the occupation – entirely coincides with victory. The workers sing the Darboy song at the end, led by Rémy. As the song dies out, the film returns to a final voiceover and a shot of the presses rolling under occupied management unfolds. The voiceover recounts the ways they worked and the success of being self-managed. Nahum has remarked that

> [W]e used to think when a struggle was won that [...] they got a new boss, they were paid. Suddenly they have nostalgia for the new relations they invented, the new way in which they expressed themselves, looked at themselves; quickly they became very close, much more so than during all the years of work prior. Suddenly we have the feeling that rather than filming a struggle/strike from the point of view that it wins or loses, it's a desire for another type of relationship that should be recognised, and that, in spite of everything, is what that film tried to accomplish.[108]

The film manages to recount all that transpired – which is precisely its strength.

Cinélutte considered *Darboy* or *Un simple example* to be a rebuttal to the critique of those who referred to Cinélutte as "progressives" rather than "revolutionaries". With *Darboy*, the group could have created a highly didactic film on the nature of revisionism and the necessity of a revolutionary workers' party. For Cinélutte, to refuse to make such a film was to maintain the idea that their films must address a large audience in order to avoid cutting themselves off from the masses.[109]

Further, the issue of the voiceover and its similarity to the discourse of Cinélutte is raised by the hidden fact that at Darboy, Rémy (who led much of the strike and who often functioned as a spokesperson) was an *établi*, and originally a student from Vincennes.[110] The question this provokes is, to what extent is the representation of the occupation and self-management the result of everyday workers (both union members and not) deciding autonomously, as opposed to being provoked by a far-left intellectual provocateur? In a much later reflection on the film, Sainderichin said that, while the film clearly has its cinematic merits (but not political or historical ones), there is a dirty underside: the fact that the discourse, though largely refraining from overly dogmatic speeches, intertitles, and so on, is not simply the speech of the un-coerced worker, of the worker who has come to a kind of class consciousness in front of the camera. Rather, it is specifically Cinélutte's discourse. The fact that an *établi* serves as a kind of leader and spokesperson for the workers and that they didn't know he was an *établi* – nor is it revealed over the course of the film – compromises the integrity of the portrayal of the Darboy occupation.[111]

Others in Cinélutte, reflecting on the issue of Rémy in the film, have come to different conclusions. For instance, Serge Le Péron has remarked that the printers had an historically distinguished place among the French proletariat, and that they were in some ways advanced because of their long tradition of anarcho-syndicalism.[112] Jean-Denis Bonan suggests that while Sainderichin is right to say that the commentary is Cinélutte's, this does not mean, as Sainderichin suggests, that the

Figure 3.21 The workers of Darboy

intention was to manipulate people or to forcefully create an image of an actualised workers' movement when there was none:

> We had absolutely no intention of manipulating anybody, but it's also true that once the camera is in someone's hands, a perspective emerges. And frankly, it's worse when we try to pretend we're not manipulating. In this film we're honest – there are the intertitles, the citation. And as for the *établi*, we didn't even talk about it, that's just the way it was, it wasn't a concern for us. The question is posed a posteriori; it wasn't something that even the folks at Darboy were asking. I agree that there is something fishy about it, but it is a question that arises later and not at the moment of making the film. Guy-Patrick didn't pose the question back then. We didn't see things like that; obviously the political situation was not the same. At that time there was no question; the person who decided to become an *établi* was a worker, period. Not necessarily what I think today, but at the time, yes. If I wanted to be an *établi*, it was because I wanted to be a worker, not because I wanted to teach something to the working class.[113]

Alain Nahum also addressed the issue from another perspective. He suggested that, upon reflection, what Cinélutte managed to demonstrate with the figure of Rémy and his role in the occupation was that an *établi* can have a very real relationship with the workers.[114] *Un simple exemple* shows not that an *établi* is systematically and continually struggling alongside the working class to impose a particular discourse, but rather that discourse can be something that is shared or created collectively. There is a kind of osmosis that occurs, and one gets the sense that the partitioning of classes has not entirely closed them off to each other. The film shows that people can come to Darboy and make speeches, and that afterward the people are going to do what they want. As we will see, the experience for Cinélutte at Lip was similar: they went to talk to people independently of the film, discovering that the interventions on the part of the left were extremely important to the workers at Lip.

Bonan considered *Un simple exemple* (even *Bonne chance la France* in general) to be a foundational film and described the shoot in terms that might have infuriated the authors of *Vive le cinéma, arme de propagande communiste*, insisting that they had shot *everything*.[115] The process of corralling so much into the complete film began with disappointment with the rushes and apparently involved endless debates in the editing stage. Bonan remarked that the approach ultimately became one of treating the rushes as though the filmmakers were archaeologists who had stumbled upon these images and were charged with piecing them together to form a coherent narrative. Abramovici and Bonan undertook the editing of the film with some assistance from Sainderichin and Dupeyron.[116]

The first step of the montage process for this seemingly unwieldy mass of rushes was to remove all the sound and pay attention only to the images. Bonan then went back and interviewed the workers at Darboy individually, starting with questions like, what did the strike change in your private life? Is your marriage the same as before? Ultimately, these were questions that had not really been addressed during the shoot. In this way, the audio became contrapuntal and individualising. Bonan has suggested that, during the editing, he started believing that this methodological approach was the only way to enter into an understanding of a collective – that is, one had to examine the interior and not the surface.

It is not just by showing a collective where everyone speaks at the same time that we understand the collective, so how can we not see those who speak, the people in the voiceover?
These voices become unanimous; they become *the* voice of the workers of Darboy.[117]

This assertion about the production of *Un simple exemple* points out parallels between the narrative of Darboy's strike and Cinélutte's practicoformal method of *realising* the film. From start to
finish, an entirely dialectical relationship was at play between the individual participation and
the development of a collective project.

Bonan described some of the personal caprices that got him into trouble with others in
the group. For instance, for most of the film, Cinélutte managed to avoid an overtly Marxist–
Leninist discourse. Even so, Bonan ended the film with a citation from the *Communist Manifesto*: "But not only has the bourgeoisie forged the weapons that bring death to itself; it has also
called into existence the men who are to wield those weapons – the modern working class – the
proletarians."[118] Bonan asserted that, in the end, it "was a work that was on the one hand individual on my part, and yet, on the other hand, today the rest of the collective clearly claims the
project as a Cinélutte film".[119]

After *Un simple exemple*, Sainderichin and François Dupeyron began a final "thesis" project,
again under the auspices of Cinélutte. *Petites têtes* had worked very well with female audi-
ences, particularly during a strike at the Comptes chèques postaux. During that strike, the
group projected the film to an audience of more than 300 women, who, according to Sainderichin, were enthusiastically engaging with the narrative while watching it.[120] As a result of
this screening, they decided to make a film about the strike at Comptes chèques postaux. In
the Cinélutte catalogue from 1979, this film is given the title *Fortes têtes* and is described as
follows: "Four women working at Chèques postaux in Paris speak, and across the trajectory of
their discourse images of their oppression materialise: from the fear of returning alone to the
foyer late at night, to the boss's paternalism."[121] The film is dated 1976 and listed as having a
running time of 20 minutes. Today this film is considered lost. It was a project created out of
the rushes shot by Sainderichin and Dupeyron. The film is cited by certain catalogues as being
part of the Cinélutte filmography but is no longer available and has been forgotten by some of
its members. During this period, Sainderichin began to move away from the group, so it was
François Dupeyron who finished *Fortes têtes*.[122]

After *Bonne chance*, a number of serious changes occurred within Cinélutte, the first of
which was the dissolving of ties with the group from Vincennes. Bonan wrote that this breakup
made it difficult for the collective to rediscover its cohesion and unity:

> The political and scientific inequality amongst the comrades became very clear. The unbal-
> anced investment amongst the comrades was accentuated. It was from a common accord – to
> try to build upon the positive aspects of each comrade to combat the negative in order to
> avoid sabotaging our political work, which there was more and more expectation around –
> that we decided to end the sclerosis that was threatening us by opening the group to new
> members who could help consolidate the group and through a fresh critique bring about a
> tighter UNITY.[123]

This period also saw the departure of Sainderichin and Dupeyron. For Dupeyron, his leaving
was less political and more a case of his feeling less affiliation with collective filmmaking
in general. But for Sainderichin, the departure was specifically political: the revelations of

Cambodia, Aleksandr Solzhenitsyn and the work of André Glucksmann and other *nouveaux philosophes* were eating away at his understanding of Marxism–Leninism. In reflecting on the change, Sainderichin remarked:

> I went to visit Maroun Bagdadi,[124] who was in Lebanon before the civil war – even though we could tell something was coming, because there was the problem of the armed Palestinian army – and he explained to me that the problem is that one night a friend from school shows up at your door and shoots you. He said that was the civil war in Lebanon – the people who you went to the fair with, chased girls with, went on vacation with, one day they ring your doorbell and shoot you. I feel like that is sort of what happened with Cinélutte. I am ashamed of this political period, meaning, like everyone from my generation, I read one day on the front page of *Le Monde*, "Phnom Penh Liberated", and I was happy. I am ashamed of that. It feels like I was applauding at the massacre, that I was happy when they killed people.[125]

And further on:

> Look at this moment – there were still Trotskyites and maybe a few Maoists, but the Maoist moment was over, Prolétaire ligne rouge was still around, so that was kind of the end of leftism. I mean people left at different times, like in the PC, those who left in '56 say that those who left in '74 weren't too smart, but others say those who left in '56 should have left in '49, and those who left in '49 should have left in '34, and that those who left then should have left in 1922. And it continues today with the Front de gauche,[126] the NPA,[127] ATTAC,[128] etc. In a way I think we can even say that Lip was sort of the beginning of the end.[129]

This line of thinking was clearly becoming more and more common for many involved in militant politics who had been pro-Chinese Maoists around the movement of May '68. The question brings up the challenges of the *nouveaux philosophes*, who were not so distant from this group. In an interview with the sociologist Marnix Dressen, the question of rethinking one's position at the time, and the influence the *nouveaux philosophes* had on that rethinking, was posed. He suggested that while, even to this day, the *nouveaux philosophes* remain, if not anathema, at least something of a joke, their thought did begin to eat away "like an acid on one's political resolve".[130] Alain Nahum admitted that he was a Maoist and yet was quick to add that he never sanctioned the Chinese regime. Rather, he said – in what could be the slogan *par excellence* of Cinélutte as a whole – he sanctioned culture:

> At the time of the Long March, Mao was not "Nazi" in any way. What he was doing was extraordinary. So it's a way of avoiding looking at things historically, that's the first thing. We can't dump the discourse. If you do, then you are totally ignorant of a reality outside of your own. It's like saying, I don't understand this worker since he is incapable of reading Lacan. To read it you have to pass by Freud. When Joris Ivens goes to China, or when Godard makes *La Chinoise*, he doesn't now say that he's ashamed of it. When he makes *La Chinoise*, he doesn't make a film about Mao, he makes a film about France, the French, and how youthful idealism can interpret something that comes from far away. Obviously if these people had lived in Mao's China they would have seen that there was a lot of misery. By the time he took power, no one was Maoist. The only thing is that he said culture can bring

something new to the world; that's what it was to be pro-Chinese at the time. Through culture we can change the world. A utopia, but it's not the same thing as the Nazis. It bugs me that people speak that way. Look, it's not true that when Guy-Patrick was pro-Chinese he was for Mao. He didn't know him, nobody did really, we all just said: through cinema we can change the mentality. That's what being Maoist was for us; it wasn't linked to dictatorial politics whatsoever.[131]

While Nahum's account seems more flexible in its historical approach to what it meant to be a French Maoist, an internal document that was Bonan's attempt at an auto-critique of the collective reveals that each of the members was subjected to a critique. Sainderichin, in almost redundantly clichéd Maoist fashion, received the longest and most vituperative assessment of all:

When everything is going well for him he thinks everything is going well with Cinélutte: notably he contributed to the text defining our collective, he *can* have a correct style of intervening in the masses and he knew how to undertake certain aspects of Cinélutte productions. Alas, it's clear that today he refuses to participate with the others in Cinélutte and that he is ready – if he is not in agreement with the individuals or the positions of Cinélutte – to sabotage the whole of our work and to create a scission within the group on a non-political basis. His ultra-contemptuous and hyper-sectarian attitude leads to a general demoralisation. Guy-Patrick had shown his class position:

– going on vacation in the middle of a shoot
– going to concerts during the sound mix
– affirming that seeing the montage of [unreadable] doesn't interest him
– saying that going to Éclair pisses him off when he has all the time in the world [...] etc.

Guy-Patrick is well aware that he is putting the brakes on the [unreadable] of Cinélutte. By being in part responsible for creating a clan within Cinélutte (a clan which could in no case be accepted by the whole of the collective), Guy-Patrick cannot be unaware of the fact that he risks destroying Cinélutte.[132]

Given such an assessment, Sainderichin's departure from the collective is not difficult to grasp. However, a perhaps more dramatic personnel shift in the collective during this time was the departure of Bonan himself, along with his companion Mireille Abramovici. From the outset of the collective's development, differences had erupted regarding, if not the leadership role of the group (which would never be described as such), then at least the role of the spokesperson. The two perennial rivals for this position were Copans and Bonan, each of whom described this moment of deterioration differently.

According to Copans, in 1976 a television programme called *Le masque et la plume* was cancelled. The last show, hosted by *Nouvelle observateur* film critic Jean Louis Boris, was dedicated to cinema and politics, partially, according to Copans, out of provocation.[133] Boris invited Marin Karmitz and Costa-Gavras and asked for a member of Cinélutte. The invitation provoked the question as to who from Cinélutte was going to go on TV and represent the group. A discussion ensued about who was the best armed to articulate the collective's history and theory. Following a vote, Copans was chosen, not Bonan, and this incited the latter's departure, along with Abramovici.[134]

Bonan recounted the departure in slightly more political and aesthetic terms. His reflection on the subject was more in terms of the collective aspect of making a film with Cinélutte. At Cinélutte, films were made under the direction of an individual or, at most, a pair of directors; the others in the collective would then either agree or not to the proposed film. The group had, according to Bonan, the desire to cinematically represent their ideas and yet never quite managed to achieve that. Bonan cited this failure as being at the core of what he viewed as the myth of collective filmmaking. Cinélutte tried to create an idea of versatility (or polyvalence) informed by Copans' reformed IDHEC pedagogy. Within the collective, Bonan and Abramovici were largely in charge of editing during the first period of Cinélutte. For Bonan at Cinélutte, and even at ARC, the filmmakers had created a utopian myth about making a film collectively, which ended up causing conflicts. Bonan has described the conflict surrounding his departure, which is similar to that relating to his work on *Bonne chance la France*:

> It wasn't a political issue. It was more like "stop the tyrant", because I was considered a tyrant, because I had sort of taken the bull by the horns, and I admit I wasn't all that gracious about it. So in a sense these so-called collectives were at once very collective and yet not at all. We all thought similarly, especially with regard to politics, but at the level of making a film, it didn't work.[135]

This split in 1976 resulted in the creation of a second incarnation of Cinélutte. Whereas the first group had consisted primarily of Abramovici, Bonan, Sainderichin, Dupeyron and Copans, this second incarnation saw the arrival of Olivier Altman, Eric Pittard and Daniela Abadi. More important perhaps was the more active role that Alain Nahum began to play in the collective. Nahum was a peculiar case, as he was a year ahead of the others and had participated in making *Bonne chance la France* and *Jusqu'au bout*. But Nahum's most accomplished participation was to be the work he contributed to Cinélutte's final film, *À pas lentes*.

Nahum had been studying philosophy before entering IDHEC in 1969. He passed the *baccalauréat* exam (also known as *le bac*) in 1968 and was militant in the generational sense, but never belonged to any party. Close to the Maoists, he also followed the LCR. Like Copans, he came from communist parents. Nahum's father had left Egypt for France in 1945 and worked as John Berry's[136] assistant. Nahum recounts that he was under the influence of these people and their version of utopian communism. They lived together with Lee Gold.[137] His family was quite close to Americans who had been blacklisted and were living in France.

Before IDHEC, when studying philosophy at Nanterre, Nahum was an activist alongside Cohn-Bendit and aligned his political stance with that of the Situationists. He recalls that the work he was interested in wasn't just that of thought, but that which had the corporeal element of engagement.[138] Nahum was theoretically under the influence of Althusser and wrote for an Italian film magazine inspired by Della Volpe. Today, he stresses that if he was Maoist, or if the group was more generally Maoist, this was not necessarily inspired by Mao. Rather, the motivating force behind their adherence to Mao was the belief that cinema could change the world, that culture could change the world, and that Maoism was culture.[139] The group was interested in seeing what would happen if they put politics and film practice together, and how cinema or culture could be political and transform consciousness. A general belief that permeated the time was reiterated in Cinélutte: the idea that when they participated in making films, they were having an influence on people's consciousness and their way of seeing.

3.5 À pas lentes (1977–1979, 39 min.) [140]

> To make a film with no matter what group, to break with the traditional practice of a film crew that acts as an exterior element that comes and films two or three hours a day to try to capture a piece of the real, we think you have to live with the people, be with them at every moment of their everyday life.[141]

Originally entitled *Rien ne sera plus comme avant* (Nothing will be as before), *À pas lentes* took as its subject women workers at the self-managed Lip watch factory. The decision to make a film about Lip was a logical move for the group. After all, not only was documenting the Lip factory almost an obligatory rite of passage for left-wing militants in the mid-1970s, but Cinélutte's previous project (*Darboy* or *Un simple exemple*) had been about a self-managed print shop and had documented a trip to Lip. While still identifying themselves as a Marxist–Leninist film collective, Cinélutte wanted to create a film that was both open and affirmative: they sought to employ new methods to distance themselves from the well-worn yet increasingly ubiquitous slogan *cinéma militant, cinéma chiant*.

Cinélutte's Lip project was to be principally, though not exclusively, a film about women's experiences with work and politics. This focus on women's experiences in these two domains did not entirely break from the previous Cinélutte films, however. Already in *Petites têtes*, the subjects had been the female cashiers at Carrefour, and in *L'autre façon d'être une banque*, the leader of the strike was Arlette Laguiller. *Fortes têtes* was about striking women at the Centre de chèques postaux, and in *Darboy* there was an emphasis on the role women played in the occupation, particularly women who had never before been engaged in political action.

While *À pas lentes* widened its sociopolitical spectrum, it also signalled something of a formal mutation for Cinélutte, in that staging and re-enactment moved to the fore. The film at Darboy had already gestured towards this developing predilection by use of the voiceover, which recounted events of the past from the point of view of a changed present. A desire to construct something that resembled a coherent narrative began to take on an importance that had only been hinted at in the group's previous rejection of spontaneous filmmaking. Further, while *À pas lentes* included these elements of re-enactment and staging, it remained a documentary; and yet, the project had actually started out as a scripted fiction film.[142] Clearly the script, as we will see, was created from a long research process and included much of what the group had learned through interviews with those who would play roles in the film. This idea to turn towards a partially constructed narrative foregrounded the possibility of fully realising the methodological approach inaugurated in *Darboy/Un simple exemple* and *Petites têtes*.

With the idea of creating a fiction film, the new incarnation of Cinélutte – particularly as represented by Nahum and Copans – began research at Lip for a project that would allow women to speak for themselves. As Cinélutte emphasised, although the condition of working women was talked about, it was all too often talked about by sociologists and journalists, and not by the women themselves (at the time of the initial research into the project, according to Cinélutte, women made up 38 per cent of the labour force in France, totalling 8.5 million).[143] These women and their respective experiences had been approached as objects of study for presentation at roundtables or televised reports. Cinélutte wanted to undo this tendency by turning the *parole* over to the women themselves.[144]

After doing research in different regions and locations to decide on the particular subjects of the film, Cinélutte settled on Besançon and the Lip and Kelton factories, as well as a hospital.[145] Nahum has suggested that even if Cinélutte didn't always agree with the Lip workers or think they were right, the Lip workers did at least begin to interrogate themselves in a new political manner, and this changed their evolution:

> They [the workers] say happily we're no longer the same. It's not to say that they followed what we said, but without these exchanges […] I mean suddenly they're saying, "Why are all these people coming, what are they doing here?" Because they also want to change things. They want to change the ways of speaking, and so that got things moving.[146]

With this goal in mind, the group decided to work with those who weren't necessarily the most politically engaged. They chose the subjects largely due to the fact that the struggling militants had been the mainstay of their practice up to this point, as was evident with Rémy and the workers at Darboy or the militants in *Jusqu'au bout*. Now they were looking to capture a different kind of speech in what was to be a different kind of militant film.

After their initial visit to Lip, Cinélutte had to go back to defend their project to the workers at Lip, explaining, for instance, that they would not be filming the struggle or the unions, but rather would be focusing on the women workers. Their proposal was accepted, and the film-makers began working with two characters. Initially the film was going to include four primary participants: Fatima, Odette, Renée and Christiane. Of these women, two principal figures would remain for the final project; they chose two workers who were the daughters of cleaning women but were themselves not union militants: Renée and Christiane.

Cinélutte's approach to their subjects and the method of integration began with screenings at Lip of the videotape shot for the Chèques Postaux strike. It was an instructive and useful introduction to show what Cinélutte saw as the problems women encounter both at work and in political engagement: inequalities in salary, the sexual aggression they often have to undergo and the fact that the work they undertake is often considered "feminine". What was different in this context was the fact that they were presenting the work at Lip, and thus in an explicitly politicised work environment. That is, the women at Lip had themselves recently organised the formation of a collective and the production of a text, *Lip au féminin* (Figure 3.23).[147] Further, the film was to document a new period in the history of Lip, in some sense the second round, after the signing of the Dole accords.[148]

One of the results of the screenings, which were attended by both men and women, was that many of the male workers were able to interrogate their own positions vis-à-vis their female co-workers. Further, Cinélutte stressed, these projections pointed to ways in which the relationship of the viewer to the image/spectacle could be transformed.[149] Presenting the video within the context of an open house and in the factory itself allowed the spectators to distinguish the kind of work Cinélutte created from standard television reportage.

Figure 3.22 Renée and Christiane

This experience also opened up the possibility of socially integrating the filmmakers into the community, and in fact they were eventually invited into the homes of certain workers. Based on this integration, Cinélutte began writing the script for their film. One of the sequences they worked out with Christiane was scripted based on what she perceived as a foundational experience of the *rentrée* (the return to work) at Lip. This sequence found its way into the eventual documentary as a re-enactment. Cinélutte began to refer to this process as *cinéma vécu*,[150] given that those undertaking the dramatic fictionalisation were portraying themselves.

For Cinélutte, this move broke with the classic approach to fiction filmmaking and documentary. In particular, this *cinéma vécu* relied on and pushed to the fore the contradictions that were experienced not only in the workplace (for example, aspiring to the unity of workers while treating women differently) but equally in one's personal life:

Figure 3.23

> Our heroes live with their contradictions and their staging of them allows them to progress and transform the real. This staging of a lived collective allows us to move past the simple enunciation of a discourse through interviews, to represent our heroes in a tangible manner, precisely what will enable the spectators to identify with them, to recognise their own desires, anxieties and even failures.[151]

Cinélutte began the initial work of preparing the film by using ½" video.[152] The idea was that video, because of its capacity for instant playback, would allow the women to become familiar with their own filmed image. Video equally opened up the possibility of creating rough sketches of the staged scenes that could then be reworked through discussion with the filmmakers and the actors/subjects. Cinélutte envisioned this reworking as not only moving towards the perfection of certain formal hopes for the film, but also shifting power from the cineastes (as the creator/subject supposed to know) to the subjects, who could then take charge of their characters and their representation.

However, while the social and even interpersonal aspects of and approach to the film were emphasised, aesthetic concerns were certainly not abandoned. The project was initially proposed as a colour film, which would have been a first for the collective. The idea, as expressed by the group, was that they had a responsibility to the people they filmed "to work with extreme care on the image and sound, because they are their images and voices".[153] Further, they felt a responsibility to their audience:

We want to make a film about the situation of working women that transmits joy, pleasure and emotion. These sensitive relations with the workers, this staging mastered collectively and the game between everyday reality and fiction are the foundational stakes of our aesthetic.[154]

This is, in some sense, Cinélutte's least explicitly political film (keeping in mind the relativity of this statement, given that this is still a fundamentally Marxist–Leninist collective). Even so, it is much like *Classe de lutte* (see below) in its capacity to show that coming to an awareness (that is, class consciousness) has a profound effect on the participants of the film. One of the first to discuss this in the film is Alice, a worker from Lip. Cinélutte uses an intertitle citing *Lip au féminin* to reinforce Alice's speech:

I – who was more or less old fashioned – waited 50 years to become conscious. Before, I thought that politics was men's business; I didn't have the time either, I was a widow with four kids, I had other stuff to attend to. But now I understand women have to get moving if they want to get anywhere.[155]

The film opens in February 1977 with Renée and Christiane sitting on a park bench over-looking Besançon. The two women discuss their earliest work experiences as maids for bourgeois families and the absurd demands that were made on them as young girls. From this discussion of being children, the film cuts to children, first playing in the Lip factory and then in school, reading aloud about the situation of the workers in the region (Haut-Doubs). The images are shot in a direct style, with no apparent intervention other than the occasional glance at the camera by the children.

The first real formal intervention is an element of post-production. Subtitles explain that, as a result of a threat by the police, who told them to evacuate the factory (the image is of a night watchman's station with a large banner reading "Factory Occupied"), the night watchmen have organised. The sequence is accompanied by music, and as the camera tracks across images of banners inside the factory, Alice's voiceover explains that they had a lot to recount (referring to the development of the book *Lip au féminin*). The film then moves to the women's return to the factory after having won. The women first describe the incredible sense of victory upon returning to work. They also discuss how betrayed they felt by those at Lip who wanted to become bosses after the struggle of 1973 (Figure 3.24). Renée and Christiane, in some sense returning to the initial project of this film being a fiction film, begin to stage the interactions between these new bosses and the workers, each acting out a different role.

During the production of the film, Copans focused on and shot more politically oriented material. He was also responsible for shooting the sequences with Christiane, while Nahum shot the scenes with Renée:

When I filmed Renée, the question was how to get closer to the truth. I was more interested in fiction. I was more attracted by little scenes, stories. Some things are filmed very well quite simply because I was in the right place. Richard also filmed very well. We each had our own particularities. So we all participated as a collective, but with *À pas lentes*, we decided that each one of us would attach to a particular person, so each of us had a particular relationship with the respective character.[156]

At one point during the shoot, Renée invited the filmmakers into her home and introduced them to her sister and mother. This aleatory aspect of the film is what began to alter its construction and the way it was shot. Nahum described the experience of shooting this sequence as participating in a kind of "revelatory dialogue".[157] For the first time, during an otherwise contentious debate about women and political engagement, Renée's mother opens up about her own experiences of struggling as a woman. But more powerful is a sequence where Renée articulates her

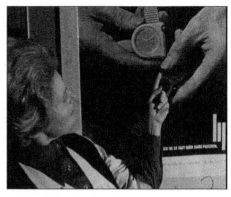

Figure 3.24 Pointing to some of the contradictions at Lip

own convictions in front of her mother and sister, who both oppose Renée's political choices. Renée insists that she yells not for the mere pleasure of yelling but rather because she absolutely must be heard. Her sister comments that there is a certain lack of dignity in demonstrating like that in the street, and their mother intervenes, saying that it would be very difficult to behave that way herself.

If Nahum described his revelatory moment as shooting in Renée's home with her mother and her sister, Copans described his as Christiane conducting a sort of "filmic psychoanalysis, really interrogating herself".[158] Christiane talks about her experience at school and the discomfort she felt in leaving at age 14. She discusses her relation to her daughter at school, particularly not wanting to become too authoritarian with regard to her daughter's success. Further, she recalls being conflicted owing to contradictory thinking, as she needs to push her daughter to do better if she wants to succeed. She doesn't want her daughter to be an OS like her, but that brings up issues for her about how she feels about her own work and the working class more generally. The sequence is quite moving, and as she says that the work she does is at least noble work, she suddenly has nothing left to say.

It is perhaps here, at the point of Christiane's silence, that we find the film's most significant departure from not only the previous Cinélutte projects but what has typified militant cinema more generally. *À pas lentes* is not a film based on the workers working, but rather a film that invents itself based on everything that happened there at the factory. It deals not only with the workers' self-management, their return to work and everything that made Lip so iconic, but also with all that happened in the social relations between the filmmakers and their subjects. It could contain surprise events, but this sudden inability to respond, this silence, is a productive aporia – a provocative moment in a film responding to a politics and an engaged cinema that had militated for answers. In fact, the real end to this sequence turns out to be Christiane and her daughter dancing together in their living room.

From these intimate sequences, the film starts moving to its close with slightly more general scenes. For instance, the women from Lip discuss their experience with a delegate from the CFDT. Charles Piaget (a key figure in LIP workers' struggle for self-management) and others recount the history of the female voices at Lip and how, for instance, early on the male workers would listen to the women speak politely, but then get back to business. Their discussion is particularly important historically, and in terms of what Lip represented in the cultural and political trajectory of French left-wing politics of the 1970s. One of the delegates says that the women at Lip focused their struggle on the liberation of the individual, in some sense turning away from the collective class struggle the CFDT was trying to continue. The sequence, while providing few answers, nevertheless follows on the heels of the previous sequence, which showed two generations of women wrestling with the questions of work and their place in the world.

The film ends, as a title-card states, "In the Office of the former boss Neuschwander", where the workers share a meal together, which eventually turns into a birthday party for Fatima, who starts crying. The sequence ends with Renée singing, while Christiane takes out and starts playing a harmonica. Nahum had this to say about this sequence:

> Then there is the birthday. We knew that was coming up, but we had no way of knowing that Christiane was going to get out her harmonica, which was magical, and that's the stuff that nourishes the film. With *À pas lentes*, we wanted to go deeper into the relationship with the people, to make a film alongside of them, and not insist that they say what we want to hear.[159]

The closing text of the film is written on a calendar:

> Renée, in disagreement with a new orientation of the struggle, quits the factory and goes back to house cleaning.
> Christiane stayed but refused to go back to being an OS. She now works in the childcare centre.
> Productions LES FILMS D'ICI

Reflecting on his experience with the film, Nahum said:

> If we made *À pas lentes*, it's thanks to all our prior experience that we were able to make it. If that was the first time that we had used a camera, we would have never made *À pas lentes*. And obviously the workers at Lip would not have made the same film as *À pas lentes* either. At the time, they probably would have filmed what interested them, unions, that kind of stuff. They weren't really interested in what we were making. Today, yes [people are interested], because it provides an incredible memory, something that hadn't been seen and that remains very rich. But when people make a film, they make what is most important for them. For us that was the most important.[160]

À pas lentes encountered an enormous synchronisation issue, which meant that Nahum eventually had to take responsibility for synching and editing the film alone. When Nahum took over the synching and editing of the film, his first step was to remove everything that was explicitly and didactically political. He narrowed the focus of the film to the characters, meaning that in the end, the film wasn't explicitly about the factory or Lip; rather, it always maintained a sense of subjectivity. He wanted to return to what he thought was important, that is, the subjectivity of the characters:

> The construction of the film is equally subjective; it's not that on one hand you have subjectivity and on the other a political position. The structure of the film is a little more fragile. In *Petites têtes*, for example, the structure is clear: the tracking shot, interview with the manage-

ment, and then the sequence with the cashiers. These are three clear moments, whereas *À pas lentes* is a little more like someone on a high wire, but who, in my opinion, makes it across.[161]

À pas lentes and the discussions surrounding this film point to and participate in a simultaneous cultural and political shift. The way this film was made (and how the positions vis-à-vis politics were incorporated), as discussed by Copans and Nahum, signals the beginning of the fracturing of the collective project undertaken in the '68/post-'68 period. Nahum has insisted that his desire at the time was to make a more personal, singular film, marking a distinct move away from the collective model.[162] Equally important, the collective was in its second phase and had already received a blow to its initial collective hopes with the departure of Bonan. As *À pas lentes* was finished, French progressive society as a whole had begun to undertake new political projects that, ironically, found their initial mutations in the movements at Larzac and Lip. In a further blow, in 1978, the right won the legislative elections. In an interview for another project, former *établi* at Renault-Flins Nicolas Dubost described the morning after the election at a meeting of Révolution!:

> We had 12 pages of text explaining what we would do should the left win, and half a page if it was the right. So there we were with what I called at the time something worth as much as a good editorial in *Le Monde*: nothing. That's the day I left.[163]

Society had become more closed, and thus the audience for *À pas lentes* was not as large as it might have been earlier in the decade. Consequently, the afterlife of the film does not really begin until the release of the DVD in 2010. Following the termination of the project, the review/collective *Cinéma politique* (the collective was the second incarnation of Cinéma Libre) published an interview with Copans in which he offered a balance sheet of the collective as it was coming to a close. The text is a seminal assessment of the decade from 1968 to 1978. It begins with the disintegration of the generalised political thinking of the '68 period and its fracturing or transformation into a thinking based more on multiplicities of politics. Copans poses the question as to whether or not, at this stage in the political moment, it is correct to reject the entirety of militant certainty and its concomitant illusions. He asks, "What is it that remains of collective work, of political work or of just plain work?"[164]

The period and the events that shaped Cinélutte provide the context for the response that Copans develops on the question of the collective. Collectivity itself had been the early inspiration for the creation of Cinélutte, defined in part by the belief that individuals were bourgeois "constructs". As the collective progressed, however, certain members were left behind or departed because they were not sufficiently Leninist; others, like Sainderichin, were excluded because they became anti-Marxist. As a result, the collective became homogeneous in an effort to be seen as unified, to

Figure 3.25 *Cinéma politique*, 11

Figure 2.26 *Pour un front culturel révolutionnaire*

be the bearers, if you will, of one signature. This organism functioned "collectively" for three years, before collapsing. Then several forces went to work to disintegrate it: the limits of collective work, the explosion of the unity of a certain political language, the desire on the part of some members to assume their roles as filmmakers within the group, and learning from the practice of shooting directly. All these trends gave rise to three consequences:

(1) Professionalisation,
(2) *Politique des auteurs*, and
(3) Cinema of inquiry.[165]

Until 1981, Cinélutte continued to distribute films. The production and distribution company Films d'ici started with *À pas lentes* and was initially created to distribute short films. In 1982, Copans and Paulo Branco created a production company (along with Robert Kramer, Raoul Ruiz and others) specifically for the distribution of feature films called Les films du passage. That project ended quickly, and Copans restarted Films d'ici. Nahum left and began working for Juliet Berto as an assistant, and it would take some thirty years for *À pas lentes* to reappear.

Chapter 4
Les groupes Medvedkine: Before and After Chris Marker

4.1 The adventure of Les groupes Medvedkine

This chapter examines the work of two closely associated collectives that have been grouped together under the name Les groupes Medvedkine. These groups ultimately formulated a cinematic response to the questions posed by figures we have looked at so far – particularly in their instantiation of the "cameras in the hands of the workers" debate. Further, in looking at Les groupes Medvedkine, another kind of engagement becomes apparent, one related to the mixing of culture and work, the likes of which were expressed in the phenomena of the *établis*. Les groupes Medvedkine's experiments exemplify what might be called an impure form of *établissement*, but one not centred on the creation of a Marxist–Leninist cell within an established union. Instead, it was a participatory *établissement* that functioned as a dialogue between cultures: cultural workers participating in factory life and factory workers participating in and transforming cultural life.

The story of Les groupes Medvedkine begins with an anecdote. When shown Chris Marker and Mario Marret's documentary film *À bientôt j'espère*, the workers who were the subject of the documentary overwhelmingly disapproved of the film's representation of the strike and the workers' experience. Marker's response to the critical reception was to insist that only the workers would be able to effectively represent themselves and their positions on film. Marker told the workers the story of the Soviet filmmaker Alexander Medvedkin's experience with his Cine-Train in the Ukraine, and the group adopted his name for their own filmmaking collective.

4.2 Medvedkin and the Cine-Train

Alexander Medvedkin's experience with the Cine-Train, an early historical (and explicit) precursor to the formation of the collectives, began in 1932, almost 40 years before the meeting between Marker and the workers of Besançon. Born in 1900, Soviet filmmaker and Red Army propagandist Alexander Medvedkin was the son of a railway man, and prior to his work as a filmmaker, he worked in political publishing, as an educator, and as a theatre director. He began his career in cinema as an assistant director and went on to direct short agitprop films. These short films had a tendency towards the comedic, and given laughter's often ambiguous derisive component, the trouble and time it took for officials to figure out what exactly was being laughed at left Medvedkin in the critical cold. When, as a result of this ambiguity in his work, he was nearly dismissed from his position as a filmmaker in 1932, Medvedkin and some thirty film technicians left Moscow aboard what would become known as the Cine-Train.

With the support of the Central Committee of the Communist Party, three out-of-service train cars were given to Medvedkin. He outfitted them with editing facilities, a processing lab and a screening room; the little space that was left over was dedicated to sleeping and eating quarters. For 280 days, the Cine-Train travelled into Ukraine and the Caucasus regions, where the technicians produced films on the life of factory workers, miners, farmers and peasants. The official aim of the project was to improve productivity in a given industry, with an ancillary goal of creating a kind of immediate socialism. The train would stop, for instance, at a factory that was not meeting the requisite production standards. The Cine-Train crew would film the workers at the factory, return to the train to process the film, and then screen the films for the workers in order to examine exactly what was slowing down production. In keeping with his more comedic (and perhaps dialectical) sensibilities, Medvedkin employed a technique in which, for example, two factories in the same industry (one meeting production standards, the other not) would be filmed separately. The workers of both factories would gather together and watch the films. Inevitably, the debate that followed would be heated and highly uncomfortable for those workers of the struggling factory. But like some sort of communist Johnny Appleseed, Medvedkin's Cine-Train would never leave a town until the factory in trouble had been straightened out and appropriate production levels had been met.[1]

Medvedkin left the project of the Cine-Train in 1933. In 1934, he made the comedy *Happiness*, the film that he is most known for and one that Eisenstein thought merited a comparison to Chaplin.[2] *Happiness* was also one of the films that Marker screened for the workers during the strike at La Rhodiacéta. Medvedkin continued to make films but remained relatively obscure until Marker began to take an interest in him. Marker made two films about Medvedkin, *Le train en marche* (1971) and *Un tombeau pour Alexandre* (1993), and, of course, following the story told by Marker to the factory workers of Besançon, Medvedkin and his Cine-Train found their appropriate heirs.

After the workers in Besançon heard this narrative, a series of film workshops were established which involved prominent filmmakers and technicians from Paris travelling to the Palente region of Besançon to teach these factory workers how to use the equipment.[3]

Two closely linked, though somewhat distinct, collectives were formed: the first in Besançon and the second further north in Sochaux. Between the two groups, 12 projects were created from 1968 to 1974. The fortuitous meeting with Marker and his already established SLON (Société pour le lancement des oeuvres nouvelles) was of decisive importance for the establishment of these film collectives (particularly the first of the two). However, other firmly entrenched features of *Bisontin* (emanating from Besançon) history and culture allowed for the emergence of the kind of collectivity required to create such a project. The embodiment of this tradition finds its apex in the CCPPO (Centre culturel populaire de Palente-les-Orchamps), a community centre that had ties to postwar popular education organisations like Peuple et culture and Travail et culture.[4]

Les groupes Medvedkine are conceivably one of the most diverse instances of French militant cinema from the period. The filmography for this collective crosses genres and relentlessly challenges and manipulates the traditional boundaries separating documentary, fiction and experimental film. Further, these groups address the myriad issues that informed the work of their contemporaneous film collectives: alternative modes of production; diverse forms of representation with respect to nationality, gender, race and community; the articulation of revisionist histories that seek to express marginalised voices; an engagement with Third World struggles; and alternative distribution channels and modes of reception. And, in escaping traditional genres and formal categories, the groups' body of work manifested the ways in which the cultural and cinematic practices of the era were being absorbed and produced – that is, montage, collective authorship and *détournement*. Like the films discussed in the preceding chapters, these works always posed the genealogical questions: In what way are these cultural processes an expression against, and a product of, their historical moments? and Why does this body of work emerge at this moment?

4.2.1 Beginnings

The story of Les groupes Medvedkine is recounted mainly as a narrative of how the group resulted from a fortuitous meeting between a group of professional, primarily Parisian, intellectuals and filmmakers and a handful of militant factory workers in eastern France. This mythic, almost hagiographical narrative tends, if not to undermine, then at least to divert attention from the manifold historical and cultural contexts of the era in which the experiment arose. Such an approach is highly sympathetic and concurrent with the increasingly hypercritical narration of the history of the events of May 1968 themselves.[5] Individual figures become isolated from their context and are invested with seemingly discrete and anomalous narrative power, all in an attempt to redeem or rescue some meaning from the events, and to escape culturally imposed disappointment; that is, their excision from history allows for a reflection that is precisely ahistorical and acontextual. But even if we were to forfeit fidelity to the events and consider them to be a failure, the question arises: Why was the proliferation of militant filmmaking in general, and the films of Les groupes Medvedkine in particular, so remarkable?

Again, the answer is that of all the collectives analysed thus far, Les groupes Medvedkine are the most synthetic: they combined the entire corpus of aesthetic strategies we have noted: collectivity, the reliance on various realisms, the use of *détournement*, the employment of hybrid film forms (at once experimental film, documentary film, pamphlet film and narrative fiction) and a turn towards and engagement with the Third World. They also represent the example *par excellence* of putting the camera in the hands of the workers. While Les groupes Medvedkine can easily be, and often are, analysed in terms of cultural production, we will see how they were equally at work on a form of historical representation – one that was specific to the epoch, namely collective authorship.

The period shortly before and through the decade following 1968 saw an increase in the establishment of collectives as a way of approaching and creating more participatory social and cultural forms of organisation. To these ends, the working class was approached to take part in the creation of a dialogue. Yet because of difficulties in shaking up class categories and intellectual hierarchies, the dialogue was often trapped in interrogation and objectification; that is, dialogue tended to devolve into monological explication. In opposition to this tendency to objectification, Les groupes Medvedkine managed to create (with the preliminary technical assistance of professional filmmakers) a filmic space in which an active and collective subject could emerge. Marker's response of relinquishing authorial control and of encouraging the self-representation of this group of factory workers – on their own terms and in their own syntax – was a purposeful move. It rejected the ethnographic position, with its attendant "sympathetic gaze" and its perennial activation of a monological representation.

In place of militant filmic fieldwork, Les groupes Medvedkine proposed a counter-model of popular cinematic historiography. In her book on May '68, Kristin Ross outlined the methodological aspirations of the history collective Revoltes logiques. She noted that the word "Logics" in their name served as a dialectical quilting point, which set up an interdependency between the logic of the historian and the logic of the object of study. Ross described the logic of the historian as depending on the transformation of historical data into historical knowledge. With the logic of the object (being an inverted homology of the logic of the historian), the study of the truth comes from the lived experience of the worker, who is unfit for the task of recounting this truth. So again, it becomes the task of the historian to pry the truth from the mouth of this allegedly mute body.[6] This argument translates well into those positions articulated by Cinélutte and their insistence that the filmmakers be the ones to film. Les groupes Medvedkine are able to stimulate the contradictory collusion of these two poles by taking the position of observer and observed and by working to create a collective, and immediate, filmic history.

This collective historical method, in keeping with contemporary methodologies, would draw on other aesthetic strategies in order to begin the process of representation. It called for strategies that would seek to understand reality as a nexus of interwoven social, historical and ideological processes, and would further reveal these processes in a practice. As David Faroult has remarked, an appropriate description of what these groups were attempting to do, each with their own respective methods, was to render the invisible visible.[7] That is, where a naturalist documentary approach might claim to have an unmediated window onto the real, it would perhaps be unable, through its primarily descriptive method, to account for the myriad economic, social, historical, ideological and aesthetic complications not immediately visible in the profilmic material. Thus, working out new cinematic articulations of various forms of realism was imperative.

Another notable strategy of Les groupes Medvedkine was *détournement*. This largely Situationist technique of recuperation is defined as "the reuse of preexisting artistic elements in a new ensemble". It adheres to two fundamental laws, the first being "the loss of importance of each *détourned* element", and the other "the organization of another meaningful ensemble that confers on each element its new scope and effect".[8] One of the collectives that made overt and consistent use of this technique was Cinéthique, particularly in their film *Quand on aime la vie, on va au cinéma* (1975, 90 min.).[9] Yet, when Cinéthique engaged in the process of *détournement*, it was largely in the context of a formal filmic strategy expressed through montage (see Chapter 5). In looking not just at the cultural production of Les groupes Medvedkine and the CCPPO but equally at their social formation, we can say that *détournement* and montage were also used as forms of social organisation. These techniques attempted ideological subversion by revealing contradictions in dominant cultural referents. This social *détournement* and montage was formed by, but not limited to, a multiplicity of voices speaking from the various margins of dominant and minor cultures. Further, and more important for cinema, Les groupes Medvedkine practised *détournement* as the reclamation of the forbidden dominant cultural practice (in this case, filmmaking) from the (mis)use of bourgeois culture. In demanding access to and participating in bourgeois cultural forms, the CCPPO and Les groupes Medvedkine were trying to effectively subvert the intended uses of those sociocultural practices.

4.2.2 SLON

One year before the May events, Marker established the production and distribution company SLON (also the Russian word for "elephant"). SLON was created in order to distribute the collective film project *Loin du Vietnam* (1967). This project brought together a number of the luminaries of 1960s filmmaking, including Jean-Luc Godard, Joris Ivens, Alain Resnais, Agnes Varda, William Klein, Claude Lelouch and Marker himself, in support of the North Vietnamese during the American military involvement in Vietnam. SLON was set up in Belgium because of their permissive censorship laws (and because of France's particularly strict ones). It went on to serve as the production and distribution company for Marker's 1967 documentary on striking workers in Besançon, *À bientôt j'espère*, which was the motivational spark for the founding of Les groupes Medvedkine.

What set SLON apart from some of its contemporary militant collectives was that although it would struggle against auteurist or star-centred directorial efforts, it was also very open to commercial distribution. It gladly exploited television in its effort to present the films to the widest possible audience. Further, to make things easier for film festivals, community centres or more commercial screenings, SLON did not enforce the tradition common to *cinéma militant* in which a spokesperson travelled with the film in an effort to direct the discussion after the screening.

Loin du Vietnam was ultimately considered something of a failure precisely because of the fidelity it maintained to auteurist cinema. However, the experience of the collective film was itself a success in that, at the very least, it provided the groundwork for the production and distribution of Les groupes Medvedkine's films.

4.3 CCPPO

In March 1967, Marker received a message that read, "If you are not in China or Cuba, come to Besançon, where some pretty interesting things are happening."[10] The message was from CCPPO founder René Berchoud, and referred to a workers' strike at La Rhodiacéta, a textile factory in the French town of Besançon. The response came in the form not of a letter but rather of a knock on the door at 7 rue des Pâquerettes: Marker stood at the door with soundman Antoine Bonfanti, and the two participated in strike actions and documented them on film.[11]

The CCPPO was established in Palente-les-Orchamps. It was inspired by Travail et culture, and the more catholic Peuple et culture, an organisation created after the liberation, dedicated to popular education, and which counted among its members both Marker and André Bazin. The CCPPO wanted to bring culture with a capital "C" to the workers. With that purpose in mind, they organised events that included performances by people like Colette Magny and Ariane Mnouchkine and film screenings with such fare as militant filmmaker René Vautier's *Afrique 50*. This early cultural animation helped establish the groundwork for the soon to be realised cultural production at the centre run by the group.

While the official founding of the CCPPO took place in September 1959, the organisation had a rich prehistory. The pre-CCPPO narrative benefits from a varied cast of characters as well as political geographical placement. Located in the Palente region of Besançon, a suburb of the already small city, the CCPPO sprung from a region steeped in political utopianism as well as with a solid grounding in collective practices. On the one hand, it was the birthplace of the Lumière brothers, Victor Hugo, Pierre Joseph Proudhon and the utopian socialist Charles Fourier. On the other, it was equally grounded in a more recent history of collectivity and cultural production created by and for the region's working class.[12] Micheline Berchoud remarked that

[I]t was this conjunction of a neighbourhood without a "soul" but rich with diverse and complementary inhabitants and personalities that made possible the emergence of the

CCPPO. What unified us all was the desire to share, and particularly to share the cultural *richesse* with those who had been excluded.[13]

When future CCPPO founders René Berchoud (a schoolteacher from a peasant family) and his wife Micheline arrived in Besançon, they encountered a spirit of militant collectivity that worked its way into the everyday life of the working class. Early on, the Berchouds made the acquaintance of Maxime and Lucienne Roland, a couple who were engaged in the collective activity of the region. Maxime, a former militant in the ACO (Action catholique ouvrière), was part of Les castors (the beavers), a group of workers who took over the construction of unfinished block housing and then lived in it. Lucienne was a housewife and a militant in the AFO (Association familiale ouvrière), an organisation that sprung from the MLP (Mouvement de libération du people), a progressive Christian organisation. Among its many activities, the AFO organised washing-machine collectives and collective coal purchases. The AFO also provided a forum to discuss and work through community problems.[14]

Another couple that would become major figures in both the CCPPO and Les groupes Medvedkine (both in Besançon and in Sochaux) were Pol and Jeannine (Zouzou) Cèbe. Pol, a worker at the Mischler factory who would go on to work in the library of La Rhodiacéta, was an autodidact who wanted to share his cultural discoveries with those who had not had exposure to such culture.[15]

These couples began meeting at the Berchouds' and sometimes at La Maison de Jeunesse, and new participants continued to join. These included future members not only of the CCPPO but equally of Le groupe Medvedkine Besançon, among them Roger Journot, current director of the CCPPO. Pol Cèbe brought militant workers from La Rhodia to participate. Among them were some who would go on to be significant figures for Les groupes Medvedkine, including Georges Lievremont, Georges "Yoyo" Maurivard, Claude Zedet and, later, Georges Binetruy.[16]

Most of the organised activities prior to the official foundation of the CCPPO took place in a local café, where the group would present poetry, slideshows, music and montage around a particular theme. Some of the films shown during this period were Vautier's *Afrique 50* and Marker's *Olympia 52*, a documentary about the 1952 Olympics in Helsinki. The latter film had characteristics that were important to the foundation of both the CCPPO and Les groupes Medvedkine. First, it was made by Marker, and second, it was produced using a crew composed of members of Peuple et culture. The group that made up the future CCPPO had already become familiar with Peuple et culture through the intermediary of a cultural workshop organised by the MLP.[17] Peuple et culture was one of several postwar popular education organisations that sought to bring together the working class and culture. This link between the CCPPO and Peuple et culture would be made explicit when, in 1959, with its official founding, the CCPPO would write the following in their statutes:

Figure 4.1 Page from Pol Cèbe's *Livre d'or de la grève de la Rhodiacéta*

The goal of the CCPPO is sociocultural promotion in the popular milieu. It is non-secular and addresses itself to all regardless of political or religious opinion. While forbidding all propaganda for any particular party, it puts emphasis on the extension of a civic culture to dominant economic and social [spheres], this approach alone being capable of rendering each citizen capable of taking an active part in the necessary and difficult edification of an economic, social, political and cultural democracy. To achieve that it borrows largely from the methods employed by Peuple et culture, and uses all the means of popular education, such as cinema conferences, exhibitions, listening sessions, study groups, etc.[18]

In January 1960, the first issue of *PLOCC* (the newsletter of the CCPPO, the title standing for Palente-Les-Orchamps Centre Culturel) announced the presentation of a series of texts by Jacques Prévert, entitled *Démons et merveilles*. The show/reading was directed by Pol Cèbe. A review in *Les Nouvelles de Franche-Comté*, on 25 February 1960, read:

Under the title *Démons et merveilles* the CCPPO presented a remarkable ensemble last Saturday dedicated to the work of Prévert and directed by the centre's president, Pol Cèbe […] With limited means the cultural centre adeptly put on a show like we have never seen in Palente, not even in Besançon. It is regrettable that without the space or the time (the principal performers being factory workers), they will be unable to perform this piece again. But the CCPPO has demonstrated that they know how to give life to anything they touch.[19]

This presentation was already the 20th cultural event since the foundation of the centre. In an effort to bring as much cultural activity to the CCPPO as possible, René Berchoud began reaching out to musicians, poets, filmmakers and artists. In the archives at the CCPPO are letters to Miro, as well as Picasso, Bertolt Brecht's widow, Hélène Weigel, and of course Marker.[20] With this cultural outreach, the centre began to offer a steady stream of events for the local community. Presenting films was a priority for the centre, and these were often accompanied by discussions with immigrant workers or students in the region. The CCPPO also held exhibitions of local artists' work, and in February 1961, in relation to events in Algeria, the CCPPO put on an immense "spectacle" dedicated to the work of Brecht: *Voix dans la nuit* (see below).

In 1964, at a farm in Urtière purchased by Les castors, the CCPPO evaluated where they were five years after the creation of their organisation. They made explicit the fact that they were engaged in a cultural revolution, one composed of spectacles, cinema, theatre and other media. They believed that the means at their disposal were those of popular culture. The question posed during this stay was about how to move from a cultural organisation to an explicitly political organisation. While in general they believed that they could be most useful in the realm of culture, they ultimately concluded that they had to liaise with leftist workers' organisations. The outreach began with many militant workers proving amenable to participating in the activities of the ccppo. After 1968, the majority of CCPPO members were also members of the PCF. Although this fact would be a source of contention, and ultimately contribute to the dissolution of Les groupes, in 1964 the Communist Party did not have much of a hold on the *Bisontin* population; therefore, a certain openness towards the question of culture remained in effect.[21]

An event of some importance took place on 5 February 1966. The CCPPO held an evening of poetry at the Salle des fêtes de Palente as part of a demonstration being held by the PCF. At one point during the evening, a group from the CCPPO spontaneously descended on the MJC

(La maison des jeunes de Palente), which was next door to the Salle des fêtes and was hosting a ball that night. The group from the CCPPO started reciting the poetry of Prévert to a less than receptive audience. This action once again raised the question of choosing between cultural and direct action – a question that remained central for the CCPPO. But these discussions were disrupted in the spring of 1967 by the strike at La Rhodiacéta.[22]

The 25th of February 1967 saw the commencement of the strike at La Rhodia, a textile factory with more than 3,000 employees in Besançon. What set this strike apart was that it was not primarily a strike over wages, but rather a strike that came with demands about improving the living and working conditions of the factory employees. In a sense, these demands were a precursor to the sort of demands made during May '68. Like the celebrated strike at Saint-Nazaire depicted in ARC's film, this strike caught the attention of journalists and filmmakers because of the importance the strikers accorded to culture. With the participation of Pol Cèbe and Georges Lievremont, the CCPPO was quick to put together improvised libraries (book shops), art exhibitions and film screenings followed by discussions. At this point, the now much-cited letter was sent to Marker from René Berchoud. Marker visited the site of the strike and returned many times with camera and sound operators. It is worth noting that Marker screened Medvedkin's *Happiness* for the strikers at La Rhodia.[23]

4.4 Two productions by the CCPPO

4.4.1 *Voix dans la nuit*

Before the meeting with Marker and the commencement of the Les groupes Medvedkine project, the members of the CCPPO had experimented with paracinematic forms of film-making. One of the earliest was *Voix dans la nuit* in 1961, which was a seminal multimedia piece performed six times at the Cité Universitaire and the MJC du centre ville.[24] *Voix dans la nuit* is composed of scenes from Brecht's *The Private Life of the Master Race*, the recital of poems by Brecht and others, multi-projector slide-shows, various audio recordings and film clips, and, finally, a screening of Alain Resnais' *Nuit et brouillard* (1956).

The following is a description of the production based on a mimeographed breakdown of the presentation.[25]

Voix dans la nuit opens with Jean Cayrol's closing lines from *Nuit et brouil-lard*:

> There are those of us who pretend to believe that this happened only once, and only in one place, and those who do not look around and who do not hear the interminable cry.

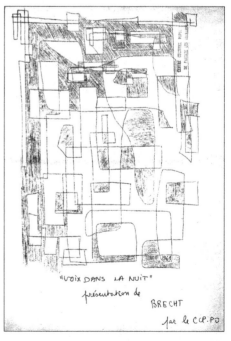

Figure 4.2 *Voix dans la nuit*

Over the next four minutes, scenes from the documentary *Fascism in Italy* are projected on a screen, but the soundtrack is replaced with Kurt Weill's "Cannon Song". The sequences chosen from the film show Hitler and Mussolini in conversation, military parades, civilian parades and Mussolini giving a speech with subtitles: "The Reds said they wouldn't make it, but we made it and I promise you we'll go on." Final images are those of battles, refugees and civilians. The film and sound are abruptly cut and replaced with a slide of a tortured Algerian prisoner. The music is "The Song of the Dead of Auschwitz". The audio begins:

This voice that you hear, coming from the night of the Nazi camps, is the song of the dead Jews of Auschwitz; it is also that of those tortured in all countries, that of the victims of fascism. To this tragic voice comes a response from another voice, from a German who lived with eyes wide open during the period that saw Hitler rise to power: it is the voice of Bertolt Brecht. To those who ask how we arrived at such a place, he responds by showing how we *can* arrive at such a place.

As a slide of Brecht is presented the soundtrack continues:

I, Bertolt Brecht, was born in the Black Forest. I came to the cities in times of disorder, and I revolted with them. What are these times, when to speak of trees is almost a crime, because it is to be silent on infamy. That's how the world is going, and it is going well.

A table and chair are then brought to the front of the stage, and a moustachioed "brave citizen" sits down to smoke his pipe. The first newspaper boy announces:

11 November 1918. The first and last world war is over ... economic and financial crisis in Germany ...

The lighting fades on him as it brightens in the theatre. Two people recite:

One day an old woman arrived who had no bread to eat ... then a man arrived all alone ... then came an inspector ... and then a lot of men in red ... but the military made their machineguns do the talking.

A second newspaper boy suddenly arrives on stage:

January 1919: the failure of the Spartacist revolution ... Communists Rosa Luxemburg and Karl Liebknecht are assassinated.

[First Voice:] February 1919. Birth of the anti-worker paramilitaries. Young people join small terrorist groups.

With each line delivered, an image of Brecht is projected onto one of the side screens accompanied by an audio recording:

Here comes the horde of the SA...

On the centre screen, a slide of the SA with arms raised in salute.

> Second Voice: September 1919. Adolph Hitler, laid-off officer instructor, becomes a member of the German Workers' Party.
>
> First Voice: August 1920. The German Workers' Party becomes the German National Socialist Workers' Party. NA_ZI
>
> Second Voice: July 1921. Adolph Hitler is elected president of the German National Socialist Workers' Party. NA_ZI.

Two newspaper boys announce the news and give the paper to a "brave citizen". While this dialogue is delivered, a slide of Brecht is projected onto one of the side screens, and on the other side screen the dates are projected. Images corresponding to the events are projected on the main screen. Two audio recordings play, one with poems by Brecht and excerpts from Hitler's speeches, the other with music by Kurt Weill. The montage then occurs in four steps:

> 1. Projected in white light are images of the aftermath of the war, nationalist movements, poverty and the fall of the Deutsche Mark in 1923. The audio accompanying these images is Weill's "Ballad of the Good Life".

> 2. Projected in orange light are images of the economic crisis of 1929; in parallel are the Nazi ranks and images of unemployment, projected onto the side screens. The audio is still "Ballad of the Good Life".

> 3. Projected in red light are images of Hitler attaining power and his first decisions. The two newspaper boys have left the stage, and two other young men with swastikas have replaced them.

The Brave Citizen yells, "Look, look! … 19 January 1933: Oreste Rosenfeld writes in *The Popular* that Hitler's disappearance from the political stage is foreseen!" This is followed by the First Seller, who announces, "28 January 1933: governmental crisis in Germany."

The First Seller exits the stage, leaving only the Brave Citizen in a red light with an audio recording of someone shouting, "The army to power!" (The recording was taken from Algerian radio in 1960.) The Third Seller, wearing a swastika, enters and announces, "30 January 1933: Hitler is named head of the government." The Fourth Seller shouts, "1 February 1933: Hitler dissolves the Reichstag and gives a speech broadcast on the radio!" This is accompanied by excerpts from the speech: "Oh German people, give us four years." Whenever a text by Hitler is presented, the central screen is backlit and serves as a theatrical screen behind which a performer gesticulates.

Now only the screen with Brecht is illuminated while the audio continues: "the house-painter speaks of great future epochs … the forests begin to grow anew, men breathe again." The score in this third part is military music, and spans from 23 March 1933, when the new Reichstag votes all power to Hitler, up to the "reorganisation" of the unions. This is followed by the tango of the sailors after the successive disappearance of all parties, except the Nazis.

> 4. The light becomes blue. The theme of war is introduced by the projection of a part of Alain Resnais' *Guernica* (1950). The audio is of goose-stepping boots.

In the theatre, the First Reciter asks, "And who gets the soldier's wife?" The Second Reciter announces, "A German mother complains." This is accompanied by a slide showing ruins.

The actor playing Hitler in shadow leaps onto the stage and recites: "You, learn to see instead of looking stupidly, act instead of just talking. Here's what almost dominated the world at one time. The people ended being right, but no one should cry victory out of season. The belly from which this foul thing sprung is still fecund."

Following this are four scenes from *The Private Life of the Master Race*:

- The Old Militant (hanging with the sign I VOTED FOR HITLER);
- The Jewish Woman (my sister Ayenne was obligated to flee, her husband let her leave);
- The Hour of the Worker (Everything is better in the Third Reich, don't you agree Mr. Mahn?); and
- The Snitch (Did that kid report his father's thoughts?)

The Coryphée is standing on an independently lit watchtower next to the stage. This is revealed by unravelling the sheet of the central screen; someone brings it down for a scene change, while a song from *Mother Courage* plays and a slide of the Nazis is projected. After the Snitch appears, the Coryphée says: "Mr Brecht affirms: a man is a man, nothing equals his docility, etc. We can, if we don't keep track of him, make of him from one day to the next, a torturer."

This is followed by a screening of Alain Resnais' *Nuit et brouillard*. After *Nuit et brouillard*, in the dark, a recording of the same quote plays: "Mr Brecht affirms", and so on.

And finally, the speaker from the beginning returns:

> Thus goes the world, and it's not going so well. But I ask of you with insistence to never say it's natural before the events of each day…. During an age when confusion reigns, when blood spills, when we organise disorder, when the arbitrary becomes the force of law, when humanity dehumanises, don't ever say it's natural so that nothing will pass for the immutable.

This production, while one of many staged at the CCPPO by its members, offers a prescient and concise portrait of the kind of work that would become the hallmark of the later film productions. While not wanting to make too serious or strong a link, a rather appropriate analogy emerges from this type of project. *Voix dans la nuit* resembles an expanded and mature form of the chained-sequence plays from early cinema. While the CCPPO performances were perhaps not theorised as montage at the time of their staging, the use of this practice in 1960s France was one of the dominant aesthetic strategies of the period. *Voix dans la nuit* effectively functioned as a complex expression of montage and *détournement* entirely in keeping with contemporary developments in cinema and the arts.[26]

Further, the piece registers many of the dominant influences of the later collectives to come, as well as those influences that were dominating the then contemporary film culture: specifically, the prominent use of Brecht was demonstrative of an aesthetic movement that would perhaps find its most evolved articulation in the films of Jean-Luc Godard. What makes the use of Brecht of particular interest in this piece is that not only was Brecht called upon as a dramaturge, but his strategies of defamiliarisation and distanciation were employed. In this way, the piece, while dependent on Brecht's plays, also became an object lesson in Brechtian theatre as a political and aesthetic strategy.

4.4.2 *Manuela* (CCPPO, 1967, 6 min., slideshow with audio accompaniment)

By 1962, the CCPPO had produced an 8 mm film entitled *Les cinglés du CCPPO* (The nuts from the CCPPO). And, throughout his participation with the CCPPO, Jean-Pierre Thiébaud created handmade "films" composed of a series of his illustrations on a partially transparent spool of paper. The spools were loaded onto a rudimentary projector intended for classroom use, which quite simply projected light through the spool of paper as someone turned a crank to pass the images in front of the gate. Recordings of audio montage and short narratives accompanied these "films". In April 1967, members of the CCPPO began production on another paracinematic endeavour entitled *Manuela*, a slideshow narrative accompanied by a recorded voiceover and musical score. The credits for *Manuela* contain many of the names that would figure in the future groupes Medvedkine projects. The names are presented without attribution: JP Thiébaud, Jacques Grandguillôm, Pol Cèbe, Yoyo Maurivard, Daniel, Micheline y René.

The voiceover – sounding entirely ambiguous with regard to age and gender, but suggesting that of a small child – recounts the narrative of the young and poor Manuela, her handicapped brothers Louis and Mariano and her criminal father Diego (Pol Cèbe). While the story follows the quixotic adventures of Manuela, it is also a film about the Palente region and a strike at La Rhodiacéta. Although the majority of the images for the project are staged, the images that accompany the strike are documentary photographs. The great turning point in the brief narrative is when, after Manuela runs off to Mexico, Diego and his two sons, while rummaging through a garbage can, find a strange document: *La Doctrine de Karl Marx* (Figure 4.4). It is the event of finding this document that reunites and restores all that has been turned upside down in the lives of this proletarian family, finally providing them with happiness. The voiceover explains that, with this happiness, "they understood that life had meaning".

The project made between the shooting of *À bientôt j'espère* and the formation of Le groupe Medvedkine Besançon is imbued with an aesthetic that would dominate later groupes Medvedkine films. It is a project created out of montage, albeit as still images. However, the reliance on montage in *Manuela* and *Voix dans la nuit* has re-orientated the idea of montage away from the merely formal filmic understanding and towards something that resembles a more generalised artistic, cultural and social form. While Cinélutte or Jean-Pierre Thorn clearly theorised montage to consist of techniques beyond just editing (for example, Thorn's use of placards and banners within a film to function as title cards, or multiple planes of simultaneous polyvocality), the CCPPO and the even-

tual groupes Medvedkine would take this strategy further by including extradiegetic formations, such as the social and cultural.

The other nascent aesthetic strategy that *Manuela* employs in particular is the use of generic hybridity. *Manuela* is on the one hand clearly a fictional narrative, but it fluctuates between being a quixotic fable and a documentary about striking workers in Besançon. In creating a slideshow the group not only experiments with genre but equally challenges any institutional concept of a "film" as a fixed medium or

Figure 4.3

Figure 4.4

Figure 4.5 Jean-Pierre Thiébaud in *Manuela*

Figure 4.6 Pol Cèbe in *Manuela*   Figure 4.7 Still from *Manuela*

form. Whereas *Voix dans la nuit* mobilises such a massive amount of media that it would never be considered simply a film, *Manuela* unfolds much more traditionally in the manner of a film. Although *Manuela* utilises a more or less causal narrative, projection, a soundtrack, and so on, it clearly lacks a key component of cinema: movement.

Finally, there is the collective aspect of the film. Those involved in making this project were also the subject of the film, and were also the distributors and no doubt the audience for the film. These two projects, along with the political history of the CCPPO, were the elements necessary for the encounter with Marker to be a fruitful one.

4.5 Le groupe Medvedkine Besançon

4.5.1 *À bientôt j'espère* (1967–1968, B/W, 44 min., 16 mm)

Produced by Marker's SLON and eventually screened in March 1968 on ORTF's (France's public radio and television agency) show *Caméra III* (cancelled after May '68), *À bientôt j'espère* was the cinematic salvo that would initiate the creation of Le groupe Medvedkine Besançon. One of the common assumptions about this project is that this was a meeting between militant filmmakers and militant workers. *À bientôt* certainly introduces its audience to the militant factory workers, or, as is revealed over the course of the film, factory workers *becoming* militant. However, when we return to the narrative of the CCPPO and its work with many of these same workers, we see that the tendency towards cultural production had a prehistory of at least a decade in the region. While the film merits analysis on its own terms, *A bientôt*'s dynamic historical character becomes much more apparent when it is put into a productive comparative analysis with the first groupes Medvedkine film, *Class de lutte*.

À bientôt j'espère opens in a snowy Besançon. As a number of men pick through piles of Christmas trees, a voiceover announces that it is a few days before Christmas (therefore, nine months after the March strike), just outside the factory doors of La Rhodiacéta. Off-screen Georges Maurivard (Yoyo) calls out to those who will listen to take a moment to hear about the difficulties of workers in Lyon. While his speech is one of solidarity, as he militates for striking workers in Lyon, the image of Yoyo and the group of hapless workers listening to him outside the factory suggests that solidarity has come apart. Those listening seem unreceptive to Yoyo's speech. They look down, almost appearing to be extras quickly brought together for the film so that Yoyo would have an audience. The voiceover goes on to recount the history of the strike in March, paralleled with footage from that strike and the current attempt in December. In this way the film proceeds – always combining location footage, stock images, interviews and voiceover. It thus participates in a predominantly *direct* style, with some authorial intervention.

Among the interviews in this film, one typifies the aporia the film confronted. In hindsight, the interview clarified the work that Les groupes Medvedkine would have to accomplish. While the representation of Yoyo and the other workers in the film may have seemed resigned and melancholic, they were given a modicum of autonomy as young militants represented in their various capacities participating in the strike. But given the emphasis on qualitative changes in life (and not mere quantitative changes in salary), the interviews in the homes of couples and families tend to be more revealing in terms of how present working conditions are affecting everyday life. One interview, which becomes the starting point for the first groupes Medvedkine project, is the one with Suzanne and Claude Zedet.

Figure 4.8 Suzanne and Claude Zedet

The interview takes place in the Zedet home, with Suzanne and Claude sitting together at the kitchen table, smoking. Claude describes his work schedule, and as he speaks, we see a close-up of his wife Suzanne, who timidly avoids the camera through a downcast look. Claude describes how they barely see each other, and remarks that when he comes home at eight, he wants to eat, but Suzanne's ready to go to sleep. The interview continues this way: Claude speaks while Suzanne listens and is looked at. At one point Suzanne

Figure 4.9 Suzanne Zedet

speaks out that working just to bring home money is useless, and that she hates working for others, but Claude more or less interrupts her.

The passage offers a précis of the film's general problem, which will be addressed and remodelled in subsequent groupes Medvedkine films. Claude's speech is not itself the critical stumbling block: in it, he clearly describes working-class life and insists upon the toll it takes on his wife. He is conscious of the immense responsibility that falls on a mother, particularly a working-class mother. His wife is present; she speaks once, which creates the impression that her voice is on the same plane as his own, suggesting an equivalence of speech. But there is an impasse that points to an imbalance: the image of Suzanne makes clear that she has desires, that she wants to speak, and so, like Yoyo's call to action in the opening, the image contradicts the logic of the speech. With the fragment of speech that we do get from Suzanne, her mournful stare momentarily aligns itself with the speech, as we hear her recount that she is working in a void and that she doesn't like working for someone else. The problem pointed to by Suzanne's sound and image is not *what* Claude says, but the fact that he speaks at all. His speech is an authorial, authoritative speech, which by no means seeks to invalidate or undermine what Suzanne says, but on the contrary seeks to legitimise it. Therefore, it forces us to ask the question: What power structures are in place at the level of speech and representation that mean some speech requires legitimisation?

This last question reveals one of the primary problems of *À bientôt j'espère*: Marker and his crew of sympathetic filmmakers create a filmed counter-history and seek out marginalised voices to recount it. They tell a story that must be told, but essentially, while in the presence of the workers, it is still the filmmakers who tell it. *À bientôt j'espère* maintains the legitimising voice of the author, even though the majority of the film is dedicated to discussion by and with the workers of the factory. Despite the fact that in those discussions, the author's voice takes second place through the *cinéma direct* technique of the non-amplified, off-camera interviewer's voice, the film ultimately creates only an illusion of the primacy of the workers' speech. It always lapses back into the voiceover of the authors. Further, within the diegesis, the film replicates the very structure of a marginalised history, within which the presentation of the history comes from the legitimised speech of those who normally speak – in this case, the men.

Much like *La reprise du travail aux usines Wonder*, *À bientôt j'espère* is a document about failure, and in particular about the failure of the strikes. While the empirical facts about strikes are undisputed, the film's presentation remains deeply locked into a discourse that appears to seek out this failure and to exacerbate it, by focusing on how this failure is reproduced in daily life. The only moment that seems to inspire hope is the final interview with Yoyo. There, a number of the workers are gathered around a table discussing why the December strike was unsuccessful. Yoyo turns to the camera as if turning towards the factory bosses and says, "À bientôt j'espère" (Hopefully we'll see you soon). The realisation of this hope is historical because, from the historical vantage point, we know that *Classe de lutte* will follow – that is to say, there will be a reverse shot.

4.5.2 *La charnière* (1968, 13 min., audio)

La charnière (The hinge, pivot or turning point) is an audio recording, recorded and edited by Antoine Bonfanti, of the workers' response to the screening of *À bientôt j'espère*. There is something decidedly telling about this document consisting only of a vocal recording. The importance of speech is brought to the fore, conveying the idea that the first thing that needs to be accomplished is the setting of all speech on the same plane. The audio recording consists only of diegetic sound; no one voice takes primacy over another, and no image can intervene to subtly persuade the audience to attribute more credibility to a particular speech. For a moment, away from images, a semblance of an entirely horizontal democracy takes shape.

The criticism from the workers is aggressive, as one of them yells out, "The director is inept!" Another worker explains, "Our solutions, and we do have solutions, weren't discussed at all." And another says, "Chris is a romantic. He looked at the workers and the unions with romanticism." The workers feel betrayed by the portrayal, and the volley of vociferous criticism is impressive. This criticism, however, doesn't fall on deaf ears. Marker responds by saying that he understands and believes that as long as he is the one filming, he can only be a sympathetic observer; the workers need to be the ones creating the films. And so he gathers a group of filmmakers and technicians to teach the workers at Besançon, over the course of six months, on weekends and evenings, how to use film equipment. The workers will film themselves and, indeed, represent themselves; after Marker's recounting of the story of Medvedkin and the Cine-Train, the first groupes Medvedkine and the film *Classe de lutte* will emerge.

4.5.3 *Classe de lutte* (1968, B/W, 40 min., 16 mm)

The first official project of Le groupe Medvedkine Besançon, *Classe de lutte*, immediately sets itself against the sullen opening of *À bientôt*. Silvio Rodríguez's song "La Era está Pariendo un Corazón" accompanies a soft-focus, black-and-white close-up of Suzanne Zedet taken from Marker's film. This is followed by a full shot of Suzanne crossing a room strewn with political banners, eventually arriving at a flatbed editing table, where another woman watches a demonstration on the monitor. There is then a Godardian intervention: a close-up of factory worker Georges Binetruy filming, matched with the sound of a bullet being fired and ricocheting. As the drama of Rodriguez's ode to Che Guevara builds, the camera moves away from the women at the editing machine and pans up to a wall covered in the kind of graffiti that only French militants are capable of. A spray-painted paragraph written in cursive reads, "Cinema isn't magic, it is a means and a science, a means born from a science and put in the service of a will: the will of the workers to free themselves" (Figure 4.10). Binetruy, the image of the working-class hero, crosses the frame, leaflets are printed, and one wonders whether the pleasures of revolutionary activity have ever been filmed with such spirited and ludic clarity.

After the opening sequence of Classe de lutte, we return to the Zedet home, where Claude works at a desk, Suzanne types and their child draws. An off-screen voice asks Suzanne, "What are you doing?" She responds, "I'm working for the cause." Already this is a remarkable change. The home life looks industrious and spirited – both work; the three of them work. But the first to speak is Suzanne. Her timidity is by and large gone; the weight of listening to another describe her is no longer a factor; she speaks for herself, and she speaks clearly.

The first image in *Classe de lutte* after the credits is a sequence not shown in *À bientôt j'espère* but from the same shoot of the interview with Claude and Suzanne. They now talk about the amount of time they are able to give to the cause. Suzanne

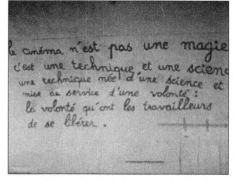

Figure 4.10 *Classe de lutte*

says she would like to be more politically active but doesn't have the time. Claude concurs that she doesn't have the time. While it remains true that Suzanne's demeanour suggests timidity, she does speak. These images and this speech were left out in *À bientôt j'espère*. Here we see the importance of her speech, in particular the importance of her speaking about the significance of her own political life. This sequence cuts to events of May 1968. Suzanne, in a black rubber trench coat, her hair tightly cropped, is at a demonstration of workers of the Yema watch factory. She yells, "We're not scared!" This cuts to Suzanne standing on a platform above the crowd addressing the people: "We can't accept this division. Until now we have decided to go on strike *together*, we have explained our demands *together*, we have spoken to management *together*, and we must continue our struggle *together!* If there's going to be a vote, it has to be done together!"

Figures 4.11–4.12 Suzanne in *Classe de lutte*

This is a very different Suzanne Zedet than the one portrayed in *À bientôt j'espère*, and it is precisely these images that indicate the major strengths of the groupe Medvedkine project: the acknowledgment of the indispensability of speaking for oneself and the imperative of self-representation. The film represents the workers as they wish to be shown because it is *they* who are doing the representing. Suzanne speaks for herself, by herself, but, as she insists, *together*. That is to say, she speaks as a worker for the workers. This is not the mere inversion of a power structure in which woman has replaced man as the authoritative or imperious voice. Instead, the film offers an image in the service of radical egalitarianism. When seeing these films in sequence, one notes a radical transformation of the individual directly corresponding to a radical transformation of social conditions; that is, owing to a political transformation of the political situation of these workers there appears to be a subsequent transformation of Suzanne. This transformation is seen primarily in *Classe de lutte*'s narrative of a working-class wife and mother becoming conscious of the impoverished conditions of her daily life. The Suzanne of *À bientôt j'espère* is passive, grey, timid and self-doubting; the Suzanne of *Classe de lutte* is radiant, self-assured and committed. She has become what appears to be a fully actualised militant.

Although Suzanne is the primary subject of the film, it is worth remarking on a few of the formal qualities of *Classe de lutte*. To begin with, Marker's imprint is more than apparent: the film employs voiceover, interview footage and many of the same elements that filled *À bientôt j'espère*. But the sombre tone of Marker's effort (even with his evident love for the people he films) is replaced by a political levity. The themes are still the perennial themes of the world proletariat, but it is they who speak and recount their events. Elements include music, playful intertitles, a lengthy handheld tracking shot along a brick wall (oddly reminiscent of the textured films of Jean-Daniel Pollet or *The House is Black* by the poet Forugh Farrokhzad), inserts that have the mark of Godard, and the continual appearance of slogans. The use of stills (primarily industrial-looking etchings) to accompany the recounting of Besançon's history, and the series of shots of water, townsfolk, the various textiles produced and the figures that correspond to production totals are all exciting demonstrations of a particular strain of materialist filmmaking. Here is

Figure 4.13

the director of *La jetée*, moved by the imperatives of *cinéma direct* to shoot with as much objectivity as possible in order not to obscure the subject with his own ideological residues, formally trumped by the working class of a town in eastern France.

Before *Classe de lutte* ends, the film returns to Suzanne for a final interview, in which she wears a dress, and appears more formal than in the previous representations of her (Figure 4.13). Suzanne explains that she no longer works in a void as a result of her militant work, even if she has taken a substantial pay cut. Images are shown of her with other women from the factory and of her in a library, and there is a brief interview with her as she drives. She speaks about Picasso, comparing him to Jacques Prévert, and says that she came to culture through the class struggle, and that the first book she read that she loved was *The Mother* by Gorky. This is the last we hear from Suzanne. Colette Magny's "La pieuvre" (a song about La Rhodiacéta) accompanies images of Suzanne during May of '68. The final lyrics of the song are from Suzanne's address to the workers at the beginning of the film: "Until now we have decided to go on strike *together*, we have explained our demands *together*, we have spoken to management *together*, and we must continue our struggle *together!*" The film ends with a black screen and then the words "à suivre" (to be continued).

4.5.4 *Rhodia 4/8* (1969, B/W, 4 min., 16 mm)

Following the collective jubilation of *Classe de lutte*, the group created their next project, *Rhodia 4/8*. The film is a four-minute piece that employs most of the aesthetic strategies that would be the mainstay of Les groupes Medvedkine. This short film emphasises a realism that is based on recounting and representing the workday, and which thus functions as a kind of *mise-en-mimesis*. *Rhodia 4/8* also foregrounds generic hybridity and *détournement*, particularly in relation to the recycling of images from *À bientôt j'espère*. The film sets the narrative of the workers' struggle with factory life to a song by the French popular singer Colette Magny and employs a sequence of shots, both moving and still, of factory work at La Rhodiacéta.

Magny's song describes the working conditions and the system of "4 × 8" in place at La Rhodia. The 4 × 8 system, which functions on a 32-hour, 4-day week schedule, rotates two 8-hour days in the morning, then two 8-hour days at night, followed by two days of rest. It was considered an abusive system that, because of the continual rotation, never allowed for a liveable life outside of work. The system is still used, but there is a substantial movement against it in favour of a straight 5-day, 39-hour week without rotation.

The film opens with familiar illustrations by Jean-Pierre Thiébaud. Thiébaud's drawings had been a staple of the CCPPO experience, always adorning the flyers for their events, the *PLOCC* newsletter and paracinematic films. Magny's "La pieuvre" (The octopus) was recorded for her album *Mai '68* and was specifically about La Rhodiacéta. The narrative, told in images, opens with the entry into the factory, punching the time clock, and such familiar faces as Yoyo and Lievremont. Footage of work on the industrial looms and gigantic spools of nylon follows. The images move to exterior shots of the town of Besançon near the factory, and there is a brief insert of a clip from a magazine ad of a tennis player, matched to Magny's lyrics, announcing the "*patron*" (boss). The final sequence comprises a series of stills of Lievremont, the waving of banners and finally a sea of factory workers demonstrating.

The narrative arc of the film, both in its explicit visual trajectory and in the more implicit emotional path of the song, moves from tedium to a ludic or euphoric conclusion. Thus, even though this is only the first production after *Classe de lutte* and May of '68 attributed to Le groupe Medvedkine Besançon, a first attempt at performing a comparative synthesis has already been accomplished.

Considering first the visual trajectory, we could say, tracing the various aesthetic procedures from *À bientôt j'espère* to *Classe de lutte* (as discussed earlier), that the works were distinctly moving away from the melancholy representation of the workers' endeavours to a far more polyvocal and formally dynamic view. In miniature, a similar progression takes place over the course of this four-minute film.

Second, this work gives primacy to a commonly marginalised voice and positions it in the place traditionally reserved for the dominant discourse. Where Suzanne Zedet was the subject of *Classe de lutte*, Collette Magny plays a primary role in *Rhodia 4/8*. And, like Suzanne's, Magny's personal story is one of moving from relative silence to a vocally militant position. Once referred to as France's Ella Fitzgerald,[27] *La Magny*, as she was often referred to, was no stranger to Les groupes Medvedkine or the region (she had performed at an event on 30 April 1968, celebrating the first of May, that was organised by the CCPPO). She ultimately participated in the struggle and act of self-creation Les groupes Medvedkine were engaging in.

In 1962, when Magny was 36 years old, she quit her job as a bilingual secretary at the Organisation de coopération et de développement éconimiques in order to pursue a better life. Although she had never played music in her life, not even knowing how to hold a guitar,[28] her first single, "Melocoton", would have some success. However, it was after witnessing a violent confrontation between supporters of French Algeria and the FLN (Front de libération nationale) that Magny introduced politics into her repertoire. She picked up a guitar and began a singing career.

Magny's position in *Rhodia 4/8* points to another of the most pronounced elements that this film shares with the work made, thus far, by Les groupes Medvedkine in response to *À bientôt*. This element is the at least doubled number of marginalised voices, engaged in a process of self-realisation whose source is the sometimes-suppressed conception of individual freedoms that seem to be opposed entirely to the social. Yet the singular voice of Magny and her own transformation narrate the collective desire for transformation. At the same time, the images attest to the practical realisation of such a transformation, namely, the banners, demonstrations and other militant symbols.

Finally, an autosyncretic recycling of imagery is equally part of a process of *détournement*. Much of the footage of the factory interior came from an industrial film, as factory workers were forbidden to bring cameras into the workplace. The footage had already been used in *À bientôt j'espère*. Again, the choice to appropriate images (that were in effect already appropriated) expands even further two central themes of the early groupes Medvedkine efforts. One is the use of *détournement* as cultural strategy, and the second is the proliferation of the multiplicity of marginalised voices. These themes are expanded by building on the formative *À bientôt* in order to continue to create new films. In this final synthetic filmic strategy, Les groupes Medvedkine maintain a direct link to the collaboration between the Parisian intellectuals and the *Bisontin* working class.

4.5.5 *Nouvelle société* series

Following *Rhodia 4/8* the group produced *Images de la nouvelle société* (Images of the new society), often referred to simply as *Nouvelle société*, which was a series of numbered films (numbers five through seven appear, for the time being, to be the only ones available). Of all the groupes Medvedkine films, this series most resembles the traditional militant pamphlet film. Each film in the series addresses a particular issue related to working-class life. Thiébaud described the process of making these films as being the quickest of all the groupes Medvedkine projects.[29] Each film relies on voiceover and interview, and Thiébaud remarked that these films are *for* themselves and *about* themselves, effectively creating a collective link among the *Bisontin* working class.[30] The films were shot on reversal stock (eliminating the need for negative cutting) donated by SLON, and while the group had become more or less autonomous in terms of montage (the CCPPO had managed to acquire an old Atlas editing table), the image and sound editing for the *Images de la nouvelle société* films was nevertheless done in Paris after hours, with Antoine Bonfanti in charge of sound.

Aesthetically, the films in the *Images de la nouvelle société* series all resemble *À bientôt j'espère*, but it is worth noting the differences between the two projects. *Images de la nouvelle société* focuses on the various miseries of working-class life, and in this sense, the presentation is steeped in a downtrodden and melancholic tone. *À bientôt j'espère* had been critiqued for just this type of presentation. However, the critique was directed not so much at the stylistic choices as modes of cinematic representation as at the fact that these choices had been made for the representation of a strike that sought qualitative changes in the everyday life of the workers. Further, in *À bientôt*, the style had been imposed from outside, so it was not the representation the workers involved in that strike thought appropriate to the event. *Images de la nouvelle société* does not try to present solutions, such as a strike, but rather directly represents those miseries that a strike might seek to change. In this sense, the aesthetic choice of direct representation functions as an appropriate mode of communicating the collective's critique.

The critical thrust of the films, while on the one hand related to the general poverty of everyday working-class life, also specifically and ironically evoked Jacques Chaban-Delmas' political slogan "La nouvelle société". As prime minister under Pompidou, Chaban-Delmas' idea for the creation of a *Nouvelle société* was inspired in part by a centrist need for French unification after *Les trente glorieuses* ("The Glorious Thirty" years from 1945 to 1975), a need intensified by the events of May '68.[31] Chaban-Delmas' proposal was

Figure 4.14

considered to represent at best a centre-right position, and Pompidou's conservative policies ultimately forced Chaban-Delmas to resign and forfeit aspirations for his *Nouvelle société*. However, Les groupes Medvedkine took up what the radical extensions of Chaban-Delmas' proposal might have looked like, while explicitly demonstrating the ways in which the actualisation of the so-called *Nouvelle société* was being held back in the everyday struggles of working-class life.

Figure 4.15

Each film in the series has the same opening and closing credits. The opening shot zooms in to a close-up of a young girl standing her ground in the middle of a large crowd (Figure 4.15). This image will be seen later in the groupes Medvedkine Sochaux film *Sochaux, 11 juin 1968*. This shot is an image from the funeral of one of two workers killed at a demonstration on 11 June 1968. After a brief freeze-frame on the girl, military drumming commences. The drumming is accompanied by a rapid montage of newspaper headlines describing international class struggle – from the Philippines to Guinée-Bissao to Sweden.

The closing credits for each film use the drumming to punctuate the final statement. A series of titles are intercut throughout the closing montage:

> The class struggle / exists / on a global level / Everywhere the administrative class / invents itself with new masks…

Up to this point, the text is revealed uninterrupted by accompanying images, until "new masks", which is immediately followed by an insert of Pompidou accompanied by the following text:

> To survive / in France the most recent name is / *Nouvelle société*… / We don't / believe in it / We don't / want it / We will build the New Society / without them [here there is an insert of Chaban-Delmas] against them /

Here there is an insert of a sketch of what resembles some sort of wooden administrator with a large "CNPF" (Conseil national du patronat française) written above his head. The CNPF was essentially a kind of protective union for bosses and employers. Today it is known as the MEDEF (Mouvement des enterprises de France).

The last line of the closing credits is "With you". The last image is the same zoom-in on the girl at the funeral.

4.5.5.1 *Images de la nouvelle société No. 5: Kelton* (1969, B/W, 8 min.)

The first film of the *Images de la nouvelle société* series is *No. 5: Kelton*, which recounts the narrative of a young worker at the Timex Kelton watch factory. The film opens with a series of interviews recounting commuting time, waking and returning from work, and schedules in general. Although the questioning is brief, the repetition of the question and response gestures towards the same mimetic function we saw in *Rhodia 4/8*. The film expresses the exhausting nature of the work schedule in the exhausting nature of the series of questions and their responses. *Kelton* starts out as a tract against inhuman working conditions but presents a somewhat generalised portrait of them. Thus, a kind of confusion reigns about the specificity of the narrative. But within the short eight minutes of this film, an equally humorous and appalling turn is taken.

As the worker describes his schedule and his work life, he begins to discuss a specific project that the factory undertook: the creation of a Sylvie Vartan watch (Vartan was a *yé-yé* singing sensation, dancer and performance artist). The film ends abruptly with the closing punchline that all the workers at Kelton were given a Sylvie Vartan record. It is ultimately this comic turn that allows the film to escape the melancholic mould of *À bientôt j'espère*.

4.5.5.2 *Images de la nouvelle société No. 6: Biscuiterie Bühler* (1969, B/W, 9 min.)

Biscuiterie Bühler addresses the effect of working-class life on the family. The film is narrated by a young girl (an intertitle offers the subtitle "The Story of a Little Girl"), who describes her parents' work schedule, which, as she announces at the outset of the film, is "not so great". The young girl describes the cookie factory where her mother works and focuses specifically on the heat in the factory her mother has to endure. Again, the film emphasises the work hours, and the young girl adds that with these hours, she is unable to see her mother very often. This last statement is followed by an insert of an advertisement featuring a young girl eating one of the cookies from the Bühler factory.

The young girl is then followed around the exterior of a public housing complex in Besançon. She insists that her mother spoils her. The voiceover is often difficult to hear. She begins to describe her father's job as a trucker; she sees her father even less than her mother. There are inserts of trucks on the road. She climbs onto her parents and describes how she sees them only during vacation. Her father watches TV and sleeps on Sunday. The film closes with a nursery rhyme about bells, followed by a night-raid siren, which winds down as the image of the young girl eating the cookie is inserted again.

4.5.5.3 *Images de la nouvelle société No. 7: Augé découpage* (1970, B/W, 11 min.)

While the films in this series each present a particularly forceful critique of the actual life of the French working class, *Augé découpage* is by far the most dramatic. Whereas the previous films in the series ultimately described the fatigue and alienation of proletarian time, *Augé* describes the physical violence that results from the necessity of perfecting and increasing production in the workplace. The film is similar to the rest in its presentation, and it also works by using the mimetic re-creation of the narrative in a kind of *mise-en-abyme*.

This time, the opening shows commuters running to work. A shot is heard from within an automobile; simultaneously, a 31-year-old worker describes his working hours, as well as the time allotted throughout the workday for breaks, and the time it takes to accomplish his tasks. The film cuts from scenes within the factory to the commuters running, which is matched with the accelerating description of the time of the day and then punctuated with a still image. These sequences move inexorably to a point where tedium becomes tragedy. There is a discussion about the resistance of the factory administration to adding a second towel in the bathroom, when there is only one towel for 25 workers. The speed of this film accelerates in both image and voiceover, culminating in the description of a worker who loses his hand in the machine he runs. It is at this moment that the film is composed almost entirely of still images. In other films in this series, stills had often served as instantiations of the reifying effects of *Bisontin* proletarian life. But their use in this film, while still alluding to these effects, manages to emphasise the cutting of film and therefore denotes violence, referring to the cutting off of the worker's hand.[32]

4.5.6 *Lettre à mon ami Pol Cèbe* (1970, B/w, 17 min., 16 mm)

The last two films attributed to Le groupe Medvedkine Besançon are *Lettre à mon ami Pol Cèbe* and *Le traîneau-échelle*. These two films form distinct departures from the collective's previous films, in that they make a decidedly formal turn away from the pamphlet film or anything resembling advocacy. I have attempted to make clear that the body of Les groupes Medvedkine film work is always replete with formal concerns that enable the films to transcend some contemporary militant film productions. However, the following two films move the formal aspect, which has up to this point been largely an aspect of advocacy, to the fore. When montage is used as a formal strategy in the *Nouvelle société* series, it makes visible the tedium of the workday recounted in the voiceover. Here, however, montage and voiceover remain present as formal strategies, but they prevent us from directly engaging with militancy. These two films, while still political in nature, are attempts at employing the *essay film*.

If *Lettre à mon ami Pol Cèbe* can be considered a documentary, the term has to be understood in its most rudimentary definition – meaning something that is a document. It is precisely here that the hybridity of Les groupes Medvedkine films is most evident. The film chronicles members of the group driving to Lille to screen *Classe de lutte*. The opening credits consist of the title handwritten on a reel-to-reel tape recorder as the reels revolve, immediately making visible the motif of rolling. This visual metaphor links to the car in which the film is being made, the turning of the film spools, Medvedkin's Cine-Train and, of course, revolution more generally. Equally, opening with the image of the audiotape gives some sense of the importance of sound for this project, as both sound and image are manipulated and experimented with equally.

In a car driven by Antoine Bonfanti, with Michel Desarois, credited as the film's director, in the passenger seat, and José in the back seat, a camera is passed back and forth between the two passengers. There is a running concern throughout the film to maintain sync by clapping. This technique is strangely out of place in a film that progressively becomes obscured by the arrival of night, and in which the audio is often totally incomprehensible. As night falls, the trio approaches a tollbooth, and there is a brief discussion about the fact that the toll taker won't understand cinema, and they ruminate on how much the man gets paid. The film begins to move from direct sound to a voiceover that is modulated through an effects filter. A recording from a train station addressing passengers to Besançon in English is repeated and eventually processed through an echo filter.

Slowly the image becomes increasingly degraded as a letter is read to Pol Cèbe, matched with close-ups of street lights and tail lights. There is a discussion about hands at the end of the film, recalling the hands of the worker in *Augé découpage*. A free-form jazz score is woven throughout the film. The film ends with a tympani

Figure 4.16 *Lettre à mon ami Pol Cèbe*

version of "La Marseillaise", and the credits are announced as they pull up to a tollbooth. The film ends with a shot of the toll taker continuing his work.

4.5.7 *Le Traîneau-échelle* (1971, colour, 8 min., 16 mm)

Continuing in the experimental tradition of *Lettre à mon ami Pol Cèbe*, *Le Traîneau-échelle* is the final film attributed to Le groupe Medvedkine Besançon. Although *Lettre* had recourse, from the opening and throughout, to formal concerns and experimentation, the political discourse, hidden as it may have been, was still present in the conversations of the passengers about the conditions of the working class. *Lettre* also employed a direct style that was encroached upon primarily by the experimental audio track and the visual abstraction that took place as lighting conditions changed over the course of the film. *Le Traîneau-échelle* almost entirely abandons this style in favour of formal experimentation.

Le Traîneau-échelle is composed largely of still images, opening with a voiceover meditating on pastoral themes, reinforced by equally pastoral visuals. Something resembling a political discourse begins to develop in the form of a global reflection on war, instantiated by images from WWII and Vietnam, as well as the poem recited in the film. After moving through its images of war, the film returns to nature: we see quasi-religious imagery of the sky cracking open and the sun pouring through, while the audio begins to assert the necessity of humankind awaking to – and recognising – what makes us human.

One of the issues that arises in describing these last two works is that one might be able to make the claim that the descriptions try to separate a kind of formally enlightened cinema militant from the other "*cinéma militant, cinéma chiant*". To counter this assumption, the descriptions should be considered as an elucidation of what some of the possibilities are when the camera is put in the hands of the workers. Equally, they should serve to point out the range of possibilities within the overarching rubric of *cinéma militant*. That is, to generalise *cinéma militant, cinéma chiant* is to make an assumption about what that cinema is. These last two works do not have to be considered as the highest achievements of the genre simply because they manipulate form in relatively sophisticated ways; rather they could be considered a contribution towards the expansion of an engaged filmmaking canon.

That these are the last two films of the Besançon group is not remarkable. The melancholy tone of both films is apparent, and one cannot help but see in this the portended end of the group being put into filmic practice. One of the causes of the separation and disintegration of Le groupe Medvedkine Besançon came from the pressure from the unions and the PCF on members of the collective. Two workers who took part in the film collective, Henri Traforetti and Georges Binetruy, have each described their experiences with the difficult relationship between the PCF and Le groupe Medvedkine Besançon.

Traforetti began work at La Rhodia in 1964 at the age of 23. In 1965, he witnessed his first strike but did not participate. After being harangued by his friends and co-workers for not striking, he began to participate in the workers' movement.[33] His work with Les groupes Medvedkine was an extension of the workers' movement – one that adopted a new mode of thinking that favoured the plural over the singular. Eventually, the PCF leadership in Doubs approached Traforetti about choosing between the party and the film collective. Traforetti suggested that the PCF was uncomfortable with the leftist heterogeneity of the film collective and that they wanted the political engagement to focus more on the monological ideas of the party. Traforetti slowly stopped participating in the events at the CCPPO.[34]

Georges Binetruy had been a member of the CGT Peugeot since 1961. He started working at La Rhodia in 1964 and in 1967 was elected as the person responsible for the CGT Christmas tree and summer camp. One morning at 4 a.m., in the company's library, Binetruy met Pol Cèbe for the first time. He recounts the dialogue he had with Cèbe: "'Good morning sir', I said, and Cèbe responded, "Here we don't say sir, we say comrade.'" This meeting convinced Binetruy to join, and become a militant for, the PCF.[35]

Binetruy also described his initial mistrust of Marker and the other filmmakers who came to film the strike in 1967. Despite his reservations, he eventually joined the group, and Jacques Loiseleux taught him how to use a camera. He said that the experience of Les groupes Medvedkine created links with other workers that he had never felt before, which in turn created a sense of being less isolated culturally. By the time the filmmakers left, he said that he wished they had taken him with them.[36] The PCF asked Binetruy (as they had Traforetti) to quit Les groupes Medvedkine, and he did. In 1971, he left La Rhodia to become treasurer of a CGT section for which he became a committed militant.

4.6 Le groupe Medvedkine Sochaux

Just as Le groupe Medvedkine Besançon had been inspired by and formed around the experience of *À bientôt j'espère* and cultivated by the cultural work of the CCPPO, the Sochaux group sprung from an encounter with a film and was equally cultivated by a cultural centre. The film was *Sochaux, 11 juin 1968*, a documentary made to commemorate the killing of two workers during what is considered to have been the bloodiest day of the May events (apart from the deaths, there were a number of amputees and hundreds of injured demonstrators). The cultural centre of Sochaux was the Centre de loisir et culture Clermoulin, which was owned and operated by Peugeot Sochaux, and of which, after having been fired from La Rhodia, Cèbe became the director.[37]

Christian Corouge, a militant worker at Peugeot Sochaux between 1969 and 2011, participated in Le groupe Medvedkine Sochaux.[38] He recounted the experience as follows:

> Pol Cèbe functioned as the intermediary with the filmmakers. Peugeot's Works Council, at the time managed by the CGT and the CFDT, bought a recreation centre in a town on the Doubs called Clermoulin and they hired Cèbe to manage it. Standing before this man, it was reassuring for young guys like us, to have this sort of father figure, who was a bit like a militant but with something more: this something more was the spreading of culture, a completely new way to approach literature and cinema [...], which we were completely lacking in a region where we were totally isolated, where we had no outside contact, in terms of culture, with anything or anybody. Pol was able to be the link between all these young workers and a powerful idea: how to begin a debate about reality. Could we really let these young, and old, workers live in the factories without ever seeing light, the space of intellectual enjoyment, without ever getting the slightest glimpse of a different life?[39]

Cèbe again began the process of introducing culture to the local worker community. He had famously erected a banner at the cultural centre that read, "Culture is like fishing, you learn it."[40] A group of workers from Peugeot began to congregate around Cèbe and his cultural efforts, and it was precisely this group that became Le groupe Medvedkine Sochaux. Just as in Besançon, weekend workshops and reading groups were established, and the first project to emerge from this work was *Sochaux, 11 juin 68*. The film was not necessarily credited as a groupes Medvedkine film at the time of its release. However, the 1971 issue of *Image et son* profiling two militant collectives (Dynadia/Unicité and SLON) cited *Sochaux, 11 juin 68* as a SLON-produced film, directed by Bruno Muel, Marie-Noelle Rio, Pol Cèbe and a group of workers in Sochaux.[41] But it was the work performed as a whole that established the intimacy in the region between Cèbe, Muel and the workers, giving way to the following explicitly groupe Medvedkine Sochaux projects.

4.6.1 *Sochaux, 11 juin 1968* (1970, B/W and colour, 20 min.)

In preparing *Sochaux, 11 juin 1968*, Cèbe called on Muel to help him with the project. Muel had been designated by the "*Groupe action*" of Les états généraux to cover the workers' work in Besançon. He was accompanied by the sound recordist Elvire Lerner. Together they filmed the scene used in *Classe de lutte* of Suzanne Zedet militating before the gates of the Yema watch factory. They shot a total of about 20 minutes of footage, which was edited for *Classe de lutte*. Muel has remarked that this image of the militant young woman was a kind of inverted image of that other famous face of '68: the anonymous woman from *La reprise du travail aux usines Wonder*.[42] Such a face was full not of hope and conviction, but rather of rage and disappointment.

While Cèbe and Muel were trying to come up with ways to represent the events of 11 June on film, rumours began to circulate that a "non-militant" taxi driver had managed to shoot the events with his Super 8 camera. Cèbe took on the task of locating the driver and convinced him that he should turn over the footage.[43] Muel then projected the Super 8 footage and simply reshot it on 16 mm. This accounts for the odd colour of the film during the colour sequences, as the technique produced a bluish hue. Marker was contacted and took on the role of editor for the film, which was cut in Besançon on an editing table in the basement of the CGT headquarters. *Sochaux, 11 juin 1968* was finished in time for the two-year anniversary of the events. While a number of demonstrations commemorated the events, the film was projected continuously throughout the day to a consistently packed theatre.

Sochaux, 11 juin engages most of the formal strategies in the *cinéma militant* arsenal: title cards, a focus on montage, contrapuntal audio and still images. However, most of the film is devoted to interview footage with workers who participated in the strike. The first interviewee recounts the typical workweek of an OS at Sochaux: difficult hours, no sleep, days without eating, and so on. This account is followed by interviews in which workers describe the violence of the strike. The interviews are intercut with the colour footage from the Super 8 film described earlier. Finally, the film ends with a voiceover taken from a speech given at Pierre Beylot's funeral (one of the workers killed during the strike), accompanied by shots of the funeral. The last shot is the one in the opening credits of the *Nouvelle société* series of the young girl (described previously).

While *Sochaux, 11 juin* is certainly a militant film, it is also one that steers clear of the particularities or ideological affiliations of the far-left critique of the CGT and the PCF. In this sense, the film presents more generalised politics and terms for its representation of the strike. Again, Muel, while often critical of the party, was a long-standing member of the PCF, and Cèbe was equally faithful in his own way to the party. Cèbe had spoken out against the extreme left in a tract entitled *L'acne*,[44] but he also summarised his critical, if faithful, stance towards the CGT, writing, "If my presence disconcerts the CGT then it's because it knows very well that I'm engaged in a *class combat* that is in complete conformity with everything the CGT has taught me."[45]

The film, like *À bientôt j'espère*, is the product of a collaboration between filmmakers and workers. The difference with *Sochaux*, however, is the position of Cèbe, who, while always championing the dissemination of culture among the working class, was nevertheless from a working-class background himself. By the time he reached Clermoulin, he was on quite familiar terrain with filmmaking – aware of the possibilities of formal experimentation as well as shooting in the direct cinema tradition. The culmination of this history is evident in the film. It has its political function, in that it recounts the narrative of the strike and the death of the two workers. At the same time, it also mixes black-and-white with colour footage, employs title cards in a productive way (namely, showing the increasing tension created in the opening sequence), mobilises sound in a manner that demonstrates an understanding of how audio can serve as a counterpoint to the image, and, ultimately, is constructed out of montage. Yet for Le groupe Medvedkine Sochaux to form as a workers' film collective would require the participation of workers confronting filmmaking for the first time.

In late 1970, Cèbe and Muel, with the assistance of younger CGT members, organised a week-long workshop on filmmaking.[46] Cèbe included in this workshop more than just technical training; he continued his militant cultural agenda by also screening films and introducing the workers to the literature he treasured.[47] Following this workshop, the group accomplished two films: *Les trois-quarts de la vie* (1971) and *Week-end à Sochaux* (1971–1972).

4.6.2 *Les trois-quarts de la vie* (1971, 18 min.) and *Week-end à Sochaux* (1971–1972, 54 min.)

Two films were produced by Le groupe Medvedkine Sochaux. The first was *Les trois-quarts de la vie*, which became a kind of sketch or test run for the more elaborate *Week-end à Sochaux*. Both films demonstrate an aesthetic development that goes beyond the work accomplished in Besançon, in terms of formal experimentation and equally in terms of expanding the filmic palette of *cinéma militant*. Rather than giving an evaluative or qualitative judgement, this assessment suggests that the work done in Besançon articulated its historical moment. That is, the Besançon films reflected the kind of work the group had been exposed to and the filmmakers they had worked with and learned from; the Besançon group produced films entirely in dialogue with contemporary *cinéma militant*. The group at Sochaux, by contrast, had benefited from the experience of the workers in Besançon, particularly given the role that Cèbe played in training this new collective. This latter group pushed its political film project into seemingly uncharted territory.

Trois-quarts and *Week-end* (clearly a reference to Godard's *Weekend*) both utilise strategies that Cinélutte would exploit in their 1977 film *À pas lentes*, in particular the restaging of certain workers' experiences. But the works go further than just restaging. Unlike the Cinélutte film (which constantly straddled the two film forms of documentary and fiction), the Sochaux films each combine traditional elements of fiction and documentary forms, mixing highly scripted and highly acted sequences with talking-head interviews and strike footage. These elements make the films made at Sochaux some of the most cinematically elaborate in the tradition of French *cinéma militant*.

Les trois-quarts de la vie is shot entirely in black and white, is just under 20 minutes long and mixes documentary with staged sequences. The first very brief image shows demonstrators marching, accompanied by a piece of music from the Spanish Civil War. The shot lasts barely five seconds before it cuts to a man on an apartment floor looking through the wanted ads, where he finds that Peugeot Sochaux is hiring. He calculates his salary minus an unaccounted for sum to arrive at what he will make monthly. This cuts to the exterior of the Montbéliard SNCF station. Again, this first sketch by the Sochaux collective was more inclined than its more developed iteration, *Week-end à Sochaux*, to mix fiction and documentary. As one of the protagonists of the film exits the station (ignoring the camera that films him), a sharp contrast is seen with those bystanders who look directly into the camera or watch the protagonist as he crosses the parking lot. When this principal character (scripted) asks for directions to get to Peugeot, the response given by the onlookers is earnest and quite obviously unscripted. He then meets up with another principal actor in the film and asks directions, only to find that this new character is also heading to Peugeot for work. The two walk off together.

The following sequence is a collective interview/discussion with a young immigrant worker who has come to Sochaux after having lived in Avignon. This worker describes the method by which he was hired: a representative from Peugeot went into high schools looking for workers, and those interested were subjected to an aptitude test. The sequence shows the young worker surrounded by other Peugeot workers, including the two who were previously filmed at the SNCF station (in this shot, these two principals are not acting but rather participating in the filmed interview in their respective roles as workers from the Peugeot factory). The sequence does nothing to suggest it is anything other than a documentary interview, making the following sequence all the more striking.

The interview of the young immigrant worker segues into a very staged and theatrical re-enactment of the recruiting process. The recruiter stands in a darkened room giving all the information the young worker has just given, almost verbatim. The young worker from the previous scene and other workers ask the recruiter questions about the hiring and working conditions. This sequence, entirely staged, is followed by another staged sequence, showing the aptitude test, followed by job placement. The staged sequences do not attempt to conceal the fact that they are acted and lean more towards being overtly theatrical with no trace of a naturalist documentary style.

The last section of the film, totalling roughly five minutes, is given over to interviews both on- and off-screen. These are accompanied by quotidian scenes of life at Peugeot: getting food at the canteen, eating, brushing one's teeth, and so on (the majority of the workers represented in the film live in Peugeot-owned dormitories on the factory grounds). While *Les trois-quarts de la vie* is the first official groupe Medvedkine Sochaux film, it ultimately remains a précis or sketch for the fully fleshed-out *Week-end à Sochaux*, in which entire sequences from *Les trois-quarts de la vie* are restaged and assembled into a more accomplished and determined work.

Week-end à Sochaux opens in a dormitory where a number of young workers live, but the film quickly moves to a restaged sequence from *Les trois-quarts de la vie*. What had already been a re-enactment in the first film is now reproduced and restaged in an overtly theatrical manner. The sequence is of the recruiter, and whereas in *Les trois-quarts de la vie* the lines for the sequence were taken from the interview with the worker from Avignon and dramatised, in *Week-end* the sequence is staged outdoors on a raised platform.

Figure 4.17

The same actor plays the recruiter, but this time he wears a Napoleonic soldier's uniform and gesticulates wildly, reinforcing the overacted quality of the performance. This early sequence establishes a different approach to making *cinéma militant*. While documentary is far from abandoned, the engagement with staging and acting set the film apart from the work accomplished in Besançon. The film will maintain this distance for the duration, eschewing the staples of the *cinéma militant* repertoire that we have become accustomed to. There are no title cards, no stills except for the final image, and no images of Marx, Mao or Lenin (or Stalin for that matter).

Further, in *Week-end à Sochaux*, the strike footage only occurs at the end of the film, at which point there is first an integration of the demonstration footage from *Sochaux, 11 juin*. This is followed by what appears to be Portapak-shot footage of a demonstration showing certain participants of the film, and then finally a sequence of the film's participants passing out tracts at the Peugeot gates[48]. This choice to leave the political action sequences to the end is compelling, and it is a key aspect of the way that the collective structured the narrative. The film, while never disavowing its political affiliations, is not an incessant tract. It does not mobilise the whole arsenal of its predecessors, opting instead for something that creates a narrative in which the *dénouement* is the political intervention.

One of the significant moments in the film is a discussion with the workers, who describe what it means to them to work on a film, and further what film can be in terms of a tool for changing the working class:

> The cinema could become a viable weapon for the proletariat, given that it has already proven that it is an effective tool for the bourgeoisie. On Monday morning when you [...] show up at the factory he talks about the films he saw on Sunday or on TV [...] Why wouldn't he talk about films made by the workers and which are made to destroy precisely this class that uses cinema to put false ideas into our heads?

For the majority of the films thus far discussed, such an intervention on the part of the actors has not really occurred. Suzanne Zedet in *Classe de lutte* talked about her experience with culture, and the film showed us the transformation in her that resulted from this experience. Yet in *Week-end à Sochaux*, this direct address to the camera about film, as reflected upon by the workers responsible for creating it, is a singularity. Such an intervention mirrors a similar process in a film like Egar Morin and Jean Rouch's *Chronique d'un été* (1961), a film to which, conceivably, these workers were no strangers. *Chronique d'un été*, however, never entirely breaks with its documentary form, even if the filmmakers go to great lengths to make the viewer aware of the constructed nature of the film (the scenes of Marcelline walking through Paris recounting her experience in the Nazi camps were arguably also staged, and thus break to some degree with documentary *sensu stricto*). *Week-end à Sochaux* goes a step further in this process in that it stages fiction, documentary and the meta-commentary from the workers who form the collective, both within and exterior to the diegesis.

The moment of direct address comes in the middle of *Week-end à Sochaux*, unlike in *Chronique d'un été*, which saves for its *dénouement* the screening of the film for those involved.[49] This placement at the end of *Chronique* in turn serves to slightly privilege the formal mediations over the narratives of happiness the actors of the film portray. Forgoing this strategy, *Week-end* stages its intervention much earlier, in turn giving the spectator formal knowledge about the film that can be included in the understanding of all that follows. Another worker remarks:

I made this film because it really shows all that has happened to me in the last year and a half since I've been at Peugeot. All the trickery they use on you in the beginning. They get you all excited to come work here. Then you're exploited. When you put all that kind of stuff in a tract, people just read it and then forget it. But with a film you're pretty much sticking them in front of a mirror: they see themselves through us.

Again, counter to those films that militate in no uncertain terms from the outset, *Week-end à Sochaux* constructs a rudimentary narrative arc that is interspersed with various formal manipulations that affect the spectator's understanding of the film as it progresses. The film engages the spectator as a participant, as another member of the collective. Given this tactic, the arrival of the demonstration and strike footage at the end offers teleological hopefulness that is presented in less didactic terms than in many of the other films discussed thus far.

The final sequence follows a 14-year-old, Annette Paleo, the daughter of Antonio Paleo, a Spanish immigrant worker at Sochaux who figures in the film.[50] The decision to use Annette for the ending of the film came about as a result of a discussion held at the cultural centre at Clermoulin. Muel describes how the group had got together to try to figure out the ending, and they started with the question, "How do you see the future?"

There was a long silence, and we were about to move on to something else when a little voice spoke up: "Me, I know what I see for the future." It was Paleo's daughter Annette, who was barely 14 and who often attended our meetings. We all breathed a sigh of relief. She quite simply dared to recount her utopia, without worrying about being judged, and she was ready to do it for the camera, right away on the quiet little street behind Clermoulin. Today she's a doctor.[51]

Figure 4.18 Annette Paleo

One of the formal elements the group emphasised was the use of sound. Much of the score consists of distorted electronic sounds with echo effects for the voiceover. This sound accompanies the last strike sequence prior to Annette's monologue. In this way, the cut distinguishes between the climax of the tentative narrative arc and this beatific afterword (it takes us from the cacophonous and massive march from screen left to screen right to Annette on the quiet road, alone and smiling, walking right to left). The camera follows Annette up the road as she describes the way in

Figure 4.19

which she imagines the future: open elections, total democracy in the workplace, well-lit factories, the destruction of housing projects and their replacement by houses with gardens and unlocked doors. The last image is a still close-up of Annette. The credits run to her left, once again making the collaboration between the seasoned filmmakers, the workers and this child all a part of the same militant project.

This is formally the last image of the groupes Medvedkine films. Muel went on to make a film with some of the workers at Sochaux entitled *Avec le sang des autres*, but he quickly found himself finishing this film alone. According to Muel, the dissolution of the second iteration of the groupes Medvedkine collective came about owing to internal issues rather than external ones.[52] Whereas the group in Besançon faced pressures from the party and the unions, the Sochaux group, according to Muel, quite simply could not maintain the energy needed to work on an automobile assembly line and make films during their time off.

Avec le sang des autres had a run in Paris, and it received positive reviews. However, in Sochaux the film wasn't received quite as well. It was as if the film had consumed the whole of our collective work. As if, after everything we shared, the documentary was a kind of violence without sharing. It took a number of years before those from Sochaux accepted the film and claimed it as their own.[53]

Chapter 5
Of Theory and Peasants: Groupe Cinéthique

5.1 Groupe Cinéthique

Après l'ultra-chic Aragon-Cardin, passons à l'ultra-flic "Cinéthique"…
– *Peinture: cahiers théoriques1*

Of the many film collectives that emerged from the May '68 movement, Groupe Cinéthique (Cinéthique) was among the most theoretically rigorous. The inclination towards theory was unsurprising given that prior to being a filmmaking collective Cinéthique was first a film journal, and a film journal that marked film theory indelibly with its publication of Jean-Louis Baudry's canonical "Cinéma: effets idéologiques produits par l'appareil de base".[2] The publication of this essay and *Cinéthique*'s temporary alliance with the writers at *Tel Quel* render the group's film-making practice all the more interesting and begs the question: if one of the upshots of the variations on the early apparatus essays was that the cinematic project was so wholly tainted with bourgeois ideology that an effective radically political cinema was impossible from the outset, how could this Marxist–Leninist collective create a work that escaped this aporia, one that the group's own associates had constructed? Perhaps the group's work could be understood – in what could stand almost as a motto for the politicised cinephiles of this period – as a quasi-Althusserian case of cinema in the last instance.

In late 1968, during the still vibrant aftermath of the May events, Jean-Paul Fargier, a young left-wing film critic, attended a screening of Jean-Daniel Pollet's *Méditerranée* at the Cinémathèque

Figure 5.1 *Cinéthique*, issue 4

Française. Fargier had been writing for the PSU's (Parti Socialiste Unifié) weekly paper *Tribune Socialiste*, as well as for the Fédération Loisirs et Culture Cinématographiques' journal *Télé-ciné*.[3] A former seminarian, Fargier considered himself to be a member of the Christian left, who, after seeing Godard's *La Chinoise*, sided with the pro-Chinese movement that was attracting many disillusioned leftists at the time.[4] Fargier remained after the screening of *Méditerranée* to discuss Pollet with some other fervent cinephiles, and here he was approached by Gérard Leblanc. Leblanc explained that if Fargier was interested in seeing the film again he would be showing it the following week at a ciné-club he organised in Boulogne-Billancourt. Leblanc also informed Fargier that he was starting a new film journal and they were looking for editors, if that was of interest to him. The journal was *Cinéthique*.

Filmmaker Marcel Hanoun initiated the creation of *Cinéthique*, and according to both Leblanc and Fargier, Hanoun's principal impetus for starting the journal was that he felt he was being ignored as a filmmaker, particularly by the critics at *Cahiers du cinéma*.[5] To remedy this Hanoun gathered a group of people around him who were enthusiastic about his films and with whom could undertake this project of a film journal. Fargier had already had some contact with Hanoun when in October 1968 Fargier organised a week of political cinema at the arthouse movie theatre Studio 43 for the PSU. The theatre's owners had transformed Studio 43 into what they were calling a "national popular cinema" in reference to the TNP (Théâtre National Populaire), and the host of this CNP (Cinéma national populaire) was the film critic and scholar Jean Collet.

The first editorial meetings were at Marcel Hanoun's apartment near Rue De Moufetard. Nearby there was a private film school, established in 1967, where Noël Burch, André Fieschi, Jean Rouch and Marcel Hanoun all taught. Students from this school, the IFC (Institut de Formation Cinématographique), joined the meetings, and eventually the first issue of *Cinéthique* was published in early 1969. But, while there was an editorial board in place, the majority of the writing was done by Leblanc and Fargier. This continued to be the case over the course of the subsequent issues, and as a result writers were dismissed from the journal, so that by the time of the fifth issue, according to Fargier, even Hanoun himself was discharged.

However, it was not just the burden of being responsible for the content that pushed the editors to change the direction of the journal; rather, both Fargier and Leblanc were becoming progressively more Marxist–Leninist in their political orientation, and they wanted, contrary to Hanoun's desires, to align the journal with this perspective as well. This political and theoretical turn was illustrated in a way similar to the way the *Cahiers* indicated its development some years later, namely through the removal of images from the cover of the journal.

While the direction of the journal was increasingly Marxist–Leninist, the editorial board of *Cinéthique* was not formally associated with any party. Fargier had been with the PSU but eventually left the party, in part due to an attack levelled at him by Jean-Louis Comolli. Comolli unearthed articles that Fargier had written for the *Tribune Socialiste*, articles that had been written quickly and without any real elaboration, and he criticised them for their lack of rigour, and for the alliance with a party that was not entirely within the political line *Cinéthique* touted. This critique, coming from the *Cahiers*, which was *Cinéthique*'s rival film journal, was enough to inspire Fargier to quit the party. Leblanc on the other hand had no formal party affiliation. However, the group found and met with militants who belonged to certain parties, for instance those from the PCR or Ligne rouge. *Cinéthique* wished to think of itself as the cultural branch of a future Marxist–Leninist communist party, a party that did not yet exist, but once it existed, Fargier noted, "we would be its ministers of culture; that was our fantasy".[6]

Jean-Paul Fargier had entered the experimental university Paris 8 (at the time it was called the Centre Universitaire Expérimental de Vincennes)[7] as a student. Because the university was equipped with modern film facilities, Fargier was able to carry out a detailed frame-by-frame study of *Méditerranée* using a 35 mm copy of the film.[8] Once finished, Fargier held a conference on *Méditerranée*, still in the role of a student, for Marie-Claire Ropars' seminar, and he invited Philippe Sollers (see below) to attend the conference and discuss the voiceover.[9]

Following the presentation, Marie-Claire Ropars asked Fargier if he would be willing to teach at the university. At that point Fargier had no real academic credentials, but was known as a film theorist and critic, and the students had also told Ropars that he was the editor "of the most important Marxist film journal".[10] Fargier accepted and brought Leblanc in with him, and from February to June 1970 the pair co-taught their first course on political economy and cinema. The following year they would co-teach again, this time a course on Dziga Vertov. Following that they each taught their own courses, two per semester.

Early in its publishing history *Cinéthique* had two particular alliances that influenced the political and cinematic tenor of the journal: Jean-Luc Godard and the literary journal *Tel Quel*. According to Fargier, when Godard finished a film, *Cinéthique* were the first to be invited to the editing room for a screening. Fargier had already established a working relationship with Godard prior to his affiliation with *Cinéthique*. When he organised a week of post-'68 cinema with his friend Jean Puyod, Godard saw the ad for the programme in *Tribune Socialiste* and contacted the programmers to see if they would like to screen a film he had made during May '68. That film was *Un film comme les autres*. Fargier and Puyod went to Godard's place on Rue St Jacques, and left with the film, which was screened for the first time within the framework of their programme. Jean Narboni from *Cahiers du cinéma* was there, along with the others from the journal, and they were astounded that this group had been able to acquire Godard's film.

This relationship with Godard carried over to the work at *Cinéthique*, and this was a particularly privileged relationship for such a young journal. Further, by turning his attention to *Cinéthique*, Godard was in a sense turning his back on *Cahiers du cinéma*. This critical position was compounded by Godard's contribution to the first issue of *Cinéthique*, wherein he criticised *Cahiers*. Thus it was this relationship with Godard that in part accounted for the initial distance between the two journals. But of equal importance in further creating and defining *Cinéthique*'s materialist political and aesthetic orientation was its relationship with Philippe Sollers' literary journal *Tel Quel*.

Tel Quel was founded in 1960 by the writer/critic Philippe Sollers. Sollers maintained a close relationship to film and even wrote the dialogue for Pollet's *Méditerranée*. The editorial board consisted of members such as Marcelin Pleynet, Jean-Louis Baudry and Julia Kristeva (Sollers' wife), while Roland Barthes, Michel Foucault and Jacques Derrida were some of those who were close to the journal and helped define *Tel Quel*'s language and approach to literary scholarship.

In 1971, in issue 226–227 of *Cahiers du cinéma*, the temporary rapprochement between *Cinéthique*, *Tel Quel* and *Cahiers* was instantiated in a collective editorial entitled "Cinéma, littérature, politique" written by Jean-Louis Comolli, Jean-Paul Fargier, Gérard Leblanc, Jean Narboni, Marcelin Pleynet and Philippe Sollers. To acknowledge the established critical differences between them, the writers noted that the "joint signature of this text by the three journals involved does not in any way aim to deny the contradictions, past and future, that exist between them".[11] What appears to have linked them, if temporarily, however, was the common enemy of yet another journal. In what appears to be an attempt to define the points of political and aesthetic commonality amongst the three journals, the entire short text constitutes a critique levelled at what they saw as symptomatic of the political position of rival film journal *Positif*, where the editorial board sought

> To mask or distort the development of theoretical work that draws more and more consciously on Marxism–Leninism;
>
> To exploit the delays and difficulties of Marxist–Leninist theory in the area of signifying practices, and more generally in the area of ideology, by recourse to political opportunism (whatever the context) in order to justify all smokescreen activity in this field;
>
> To censor that part of Marxism–Leninism which forms its irreducible scientific base: historical materialism and dialectical materialism, in their radical opposition to idealism in all areas of social practice.[12]

In describing the alliance with *Tel Quel*, Fargier has suggested that the connection was solidified by the mutual admiration for *Méditerranée*. During that period *Cinéthique* said that there were only roughly five revolutionary films, amongst them *Méditerranée* (along with the films of Philippe Garrel and Jean-Pierre Lajournade); the rest could be thrown away. For *Cinéthique* the film was materialist, but not yet *dialectically* materialist; rather it remained idealist materialism. In this sense *Méditerranée* was for *Cinéthique* something prior to a revolutionary cinema, even if the montage was based on formal attractions, and there was a quasi-ideology of transversality of culture that was equally structuralist in its capacity to draw on Marx, Freud and Greek classicism. But Fargier has also acknowledged that, for all the theoretical justification, much of the admiration came from the fact that it was Sollers who wrote the text.

Both Fargier and Leblanc have acknowledged that *Tel Quel* had another interest in bringing *Cinéthique* into the fold, a reason that they suggest had an ostensibly imperialist side to it. According to them *Tel Quel* wanted to have some control over every domain in the arts, and therefore wanted a journal to function as their mouthpiece in each domain. They already had *Peinture: cahiers théoriques* for the plastic arts, and given that *Cinéthique* was politically militant but remained autonomous, *Tel Quel* saw in it the possibility of participating in a federation. Thus, *Cinéthique* represented the domain of cinema for the *Tel Quel* network.[13]

When *Tel Quel*'s Marcelin Pleynet began writing for *Cinéthique*, he encouraged Jean-Louis Baudry to do so as well. It was in this context that Baudry published his famous essay on the cinematic apparatus in the journal. While Baudry's essay

Figure 5.2

was to be a highly influential essay in the history of film theory, there was an interpretation of that text which led to the idea that one could no longer make films, because the photographic lens was stained with bourgeois ideology. While this was a very restricted and limited understanding of the apparatus as a whole, it was in any case one of the practical upshots of the critique. But in the following years *Cinéthique* would become more than just a film journal, as the group would first distribute films that they believed had political merit, and then make films. For the *Cinéthique* critics, as a group that would go on to make films, what was important with regard to Baudry's insights and much of the apparatus theory was that one could still make films, but could no longer do so in bad faith with regard to the issue of representation, and so the *Cinéthique* group ultimately sought to make films that integrated these questions and tried to work with them in a politically progressive manner.

One of the chief adversaries of the apparatus theory was Jean-Patrick Lebel, and he challenged the position by making a comparison to the airplane: at its base the technical cinematic apparatus was neutral, just as the apparatus was in an airplane. *Cinéthique* argued that such a position denied the importance of representation and an investigation into the techniques of representing. However, the question of the apparatus couldn't entirely cover the investigation of the dominant modes and methods of representation in society and the necessary struggle against them. It is here that *Cinéthique* worked on the idea of an objective idealism: there was a form of objective idealism that was not yet entirely materialist, and to counter this it was not enough to critique just the technique or technology; one had also to undertake the struggle against the dominant representations. This struggle against the representations was manifest in two of Cinéthique's most widely seen films: *Quand on aime la vie, on va au cinéma* (1975) and *Bon pied, bon œil et toute sa tête* (1978).

5.1.1 *Quand on aime la vie, on va au cinéma* (1975, 90 min.)

Film production by Cinéthique began prior to 1975's *Quand on aime la vie, on va au cinema*; Fargier suggests that the idea of making films had been there from the beginning at the journal. Leblanc wanted to make films, and by the third issue of *Cinéthique* they came up with the idea to create a video journal that could accompany the print edition. The group began by interviewing Jean Rouch and Glauber Rocha using a Portapak. During that period the group had become quite militant about the use of video. Jack Haie, who was a technician at Beaux Arts and who inspired Godard, Jean Genet and Carole Roussopoulos to exploit the possi-

bilities of video, initiated Cinéthique into the new technology. But this preference for video was expressed in texts outside the domain of *Cinéthique* and written under pseudonyms. Leblanc and Fargier wrote polemical parodies of cinema and odes to the superiority of video over film in Jean-Edern Hallier's journal *L'idiot international*. However, in the pages of *Cinéthique* the writers' positions remained faithful to cinema/film.

In 1970, independent of Leblanc, Fargier and two other writers from Ciné-

Figure 5.3

thique, Simon Luciani and Eliane Le Grivés, were joined by Antoinette Fouque from the MLF (Mouvement de libération des femmes) to make a film ultimately entitled *Le Politique*. The collective creation of the film was articulated in the division of labour, resulting in a process whereby each of the participants shot and directed one scene. The film was shot on 16 mm and took as its subject a film shoot about the Kronstadt uprising on which the crew revolted against the filmmaker, subsequently taking control of the film shoot to create a different film, one that

Figure 5.4

was replete with political disquisitions. When the group showed *Le Politique* to Leblanc he dismissed it, telling them that he thought it was a "pre-revolutionary film".[14] Leblanc wanted to make a more theoretical project, a desire realised in the film *Quand on aime la vie, on va au cinéma*.

The history and theory of *Quand on aime la vie, on va au cinéma* unfolded over a period of six years in a series of texts published in *Cinéthique*. The origin of the film was a two-part text titled "Politiques de la censure" published over two issues of the journal, 11/12 (1971) and 13/14 (1972).[15] The text expressed the group's alignment with apparatus theory and the conception of ideology as formulated by Louis Althusser. But *Cinéthique*'s work was clearly seeking to break with any kind of aporia that might stem from the apparatus theory vis-à-vis film production. In "Politics of the contemporary moment", the closing section of the two-part essay, the *Cinéthique* critics outlined what they saw as the then current "contradictions that determined the current politics of the bourgeoisie with regard to film censorship".[16] The group noted:

> The objective aimed for by the bourgeoisie in terms of film censorship is to elicit, by all means, the creation of cinematographic representations that allow it to transform society according to its conception of the world. Of representations *guaranteed to conform* to the ideological apparatus inside the Commission de controle des films[17] (again, where representatives of the educational apparatus, the familial apparatus, the psychiatric apparatus, the cultural apparatus, etc. are all accounted for).[18]

Key in this discussion was this issue of representation (or what they would refer to as the "representational apparatus"), an issue that would remain at the heart of their two most developed film projects. At this stage of the collective's development towards a filmmaking practice, the hope of creating a counter-intervention with regard to cinematographic representation on film was evidenced in this seminal two-part text.

The next significant indication of Cinéthique's move towards filmmaking was the 1974 publication of the shooting script for *Quand on aime la vie* in issue 17/18 (a shooting script that demonstrates a few sequential discrepancies when put side by side with the final film).[19] Then in 1975, the year the film was finished and ready for distribution, issue 19/20 saw the publication of a presentation of, or introduction to, the film. Finally, in 1977, in issue 23/24, the last text by the group on the film was published, and by this time the editorial board was largely different from the board at the time of the publication of the first text, the most significant change being the departure of Jean-Paul Fargier.

The title, *Quand on aime la vie, on va au cinéma*, comes from a promotional campaign in 1972 by the movie theatre chains of UGC Gaumont Pathé Parafrance. Cinéthique noted that one of the film's first goals was to

> lead the struggle against the capitalists who are at the front of this monopolist concentration in the film industry; to undertake the struggle against the ideological themes developed in their promotional campaign – themes that aim to organise, based on their own economic interests, the expanded reproduction of cinema of which they control the financing and distribution along with the ever-increasing number of spectators.[20]

Whereas *Le Politique* had revolutionary content and was also organised politically in terms of the film production, *Quand on aime la vie, on va au cinéma* was created in a different manner, as it was a film primarily created through the process of montage. Cinéthique saw as part of its task the creation of a new kind of montage, one that struggled against a montage based on the organisation of representations favoured by the ruling class. The group sought "to substitute for the old bourgeois montage a new montage, subordinated to the process of the revolutionary organisation of the exploited classes on the economic and political fronts".[21] Such a montage would establish contradictions in which "the most typical representations" of bourgeois life could be juxtaposed with the "most simple acts of the everyday life of the masses".[22]

Quand on aime la vie on va au cinéma is divided into chapters, in this way gesturing towards its function as a text or thesis to be read. The film opens with a prelude that serves as a kind of critical ode to cinema as it is constructed by its own myths: the score is reminiscent of any typical Hollywood epic film and images flash from the eponymous promotional campaign evoking the importance and passion of cinema. The tone of the prelude caters to the cinephilic fantasy par excellence, until the sequence's disruption by a blank image of a movie screen on which different aspect ratios unfold in silence.

A central question that continues to resurface throughout the film is the comfort of the spectator. Two types of comfort, distinct but interconnected, are evoked in the film. First is the physical comfort of the spectator in the theatre, passing his or her leisure time. This finds its most concise and explicit

Figures 5.5–5.7

definition in Chapter 18 of the film, in the form of an ironic appeal from the voiceover: "Please, please sirs, film professionals, make comfortable films for us, build us comfortable movie theatres, you'll have all the money you'll need from the spectators' money." And in Chapter 17 there is a long take of the construction of movie theatre seats, again evoking the idea of being comfortable – this comfort being a result not just of cinema seats but of the organisation of representations offered by the audiovisual products of the ruling class (Figures 5.5, 5.6 and 5.7).

This latter comfort is the second kind of comfort: the ontological and ideological comfort that the spectator experiences through the identification with various (and frequently, according to Cinéthique, bourgeois) subjects in cinema. In one sequence, after presenting a long list of the various types of images one might be confronted with at the cinema, the narrator concludes that these are "images in which you are invited by your exploiters to see yourself and to live". The corresponding graphics are a series of film stills in which characters have been cut out and pasted onto different backdrops. The images are then reduced to a black silhouette; the space

Figures 5.8–5.13 (l. to r.; t. to b.)

where the characters were has been vacated, suggesting that they are there to be filled by the spectator's identification. The characters, when not mere silhouettes, are shown on a black background, pointing to their roles as cut-outs that can be placed in any situation (Figures 5.8, 5.9, 5.10, 5.11, 5.12, 5.13 and 5.14).

Exploring this issue of comfort as a critical analysis of the ideology of the ruling class, *Quand on aime la vie* turns to the question of cinematic forms, for instance in a brief engagement with the question of

Figure 5.14

popular political cinema, such as the *série-Z* films. Cinéthique uses images from the credit sequence for Costa-Gavras' *État de siège* (1972), and these recur throughout the film. Clearly the politics of representation that Cinéthique worked tirelessly to develop were on the opposite side of the spectrum to those of political thrillers such as *État de siège*. But Cinéthique's use of these images also evoked the issue of censorship, because even if the political approaches to film forms adopted by Costa-Gavras and Cinéthique were, if not antithetical, at least theoretically incompatible, Costa-Gavras' films were no stranger to censorship.

Regarding these conceptions of leisure time, work time and film form, Leblanc noted:

> The idea for us was this strategy: a rupture with politics signified a rupture with aesthetics. That means we were in direct opposition to Hennebelle, Costa-Gavras, etc. We couldn't use the old cinematic forms; politics had to find its extension in a specific aesthetic. And this aesthetic was itself coherent with the political objectives that we were pursuing. For example, we wanted to break with the opposition work/leisure: when we leave work, we're exhausted and we want to empty our heads. Our point was above all, don't empty your head! We tried to make films that were as rhythmical and intense as the gestures of work could be. Because everything is unified in society, there's not a time for work and a time for play, a time for prison and a time for freedom.[23]

In Chapter 10 there is a focus on the issue of censorship, and its role in maintaining the ideological comfort of the spectator in both working life and leisure life. Cinéthique calls out the functions of the repressive state apparatus and its agents of repression: "when capital refuses to satisfy the demands of the workers, the ministers and the police of that same capitalism intervene to censor films and to suppress strikes, occupations and sequestrations". This chapter features images from *Histoires d'A*, a reproductive rights documentary that was censored, as well as the iconic image of Gauche prolétarienne militant Pierre Overney being shot in front of the

Figure 5.15 Still from *Quand on aime la vie, on va au cinéma*

Renault-Billancourt factory by Renault security guard Jean-Antoine Tramoni.[24] Again, the pairing of such images points to what Cinéthique saw as the collusion of repression/censorship in cinema and in political struggles in maintaining the ruling ideology. In this way, while the film has certain aesthetic similarities to Guy Debord's *The Society of the Spectacle* (1973, B/W, 90 min.), is it theoretically much more Althusserian than Situationist.[25]

The end of the film again refuses the separation of productive and leisure spheres. The contradictions the worker faces in proletarian life are subsumed into and confronted on the terrain of representation and reworked into psychological, individual and dramatic conflicts in cinema:

Figure 5.16 and Figure 5.17 Citing other political films in *Quand on aime la vie, on va au cinema*

> It is necessary that the relations of production reproduce themselves [...] outside of the company as well, in other practices than that of production, in all the practices of social life. Outside of material production the worker must transform him/herself into a bourgeois, so that he has the impression that he is bourgeois. Television and cinema have as their principal role to inculcate the bourgeois way of life, the bourgeois conception of the world.

As the film closes there is a call to arms: "a new cinema = new society".

When the film was completed and ready for distribution in 1975, Cinéthique published an auto-assessment of the work they had accomplished. They initiated their evaluation by asking, what ideas and practices was the film capable of promoting? And equally, which classes and subsections of classes were implicated?[26] In their relation to much of the *cinéma militant* community, Cinéthique were often accused of elitism, and in their evaluation Cinéthique evoked this issue precisely with regard to the question of the intended audience of the film. If it seemed on the surface that the film was for a very small segment of a given class, namely, the petit-bourgeois intellectual, Cinéthique tried to turn the question around by rephrasing it as, who had the right to enjoy? Or, what conditions were necessary for the love of life and the capacity to locate the leisure time for going to cinema?

Cinéthique's assessment was that there were very few members of the working class going to the cinema (apart from a certain kind of working-class youth deemed "violent").[27] Television was, to their mind, the more accessible domain of the working class: no need to spend extra money to go out, the whole family could be together, and so (Figure 5.17). However, again, the critical lynchpin of *Quand on aime la vie* was neither the specific cinematic nor the specific televisual apparatus, but rather what Cinéthique referred to as the *order of representations* enacted by the ruling class under the minister of culture's slogan "the unification of audiovisual activities".[28] The task at hand was "the destruction of *all* the apparatuses (television, cinema and others) which create and broadcast the representations of the ruling class. These apparatuses make up an *integral part* of the state apparatus, which will be destroyed by the proletarian revolution."[29]

Figure 5.18 Representing the televisual apparatus in *Quand on aime la vie, on va au cinéma*

5.1.2 Anti-imperialist films in sub-Saharan Africa

While *Quand on aime la vie, on va au cinéma* was perhaps the most audacious and widely seen Cinéthique project during that period (the film was in competition at the 1975 Cannes film festival), 1975 also saw the production of three other Groupe Cinéthique films: *Même combat, Vive la lutte des peuples de Guinée-Cap Vert! Impérialistes dehors!* and *Etudier, produire, combattre.*

Même combat (B/W/, 50 min., 16 mm) was presented in issue 19/20 along with part of the shooting script (the remainder of the shooting script was published in issue 21/22) and was Cinéthique's contribution to the cinematic account of the *circulaire Fontanet* that both Jean-Pierre Thorn and Cinélutte had also documented (Figures 5.18 and 5.19). The group's goal was to make a film that dealt with the question of "working-class unity and situating the immigrant worker within the revolutionary process in France".[30] While focusing on documented and undocumented workers in France, the film fell under the rubric of "les luttes de classes en

Figures 5.19–5.20 *Cinéthique*, 19/20, front cover (left); back cover

France" (class struggles in France), one of the three rubrics the distribution wing of Cinéthique organised films under. *Quand on aime la vie* equally figured with this this rubric. The other two categories were "les luttes des peuples pour leur indépendance et pour la liberation nationale" and "les luttes pour l'edification socialiste".[31]

Under the first rubric Cinéthique distributed films such as Charles Belmont and Marielle Issartel's *Histoires d'A* and Front Paysan's *Des Dettes Pour Salaire* (see below). Under the third rubric the group distributed Dziga Vertov films as well as the Chinese documentary *Le dieu de la peste* (Farewell to the god of plague, 1971, colour, 35 mm),[32] concerning the meeting of scientific research and a revolutionary party line to combat Bilharziasis. But it was category two, that of "les luttes des peuples pour leur indépendance et pour la liberation nationale", where Cinéthique distinguished itself from many of the militant collectives of the period. While Jean-Pierre Thorn, Cinélutte and Les groupes Medvedkine were interested in the experience of the immigrant workers or undocumented immigrants in France, Cinéthique was equally concerned with integrating the fight against French imperialism into its cinematic practice, namely, writing, producing and distributing.

Under this rubric Cinéthique distributed the other films: *Etudier, produire, combattre* and *Vive la lutte des peuples de Guinée-Cap Vert! Impérialistes dehors!*. *Etudier, produire, combattre* took as its subject a FRELIMO (Frente de Libertação de Moçambique) secondary school in Bagamoyo, Tanzania. FRELIMO, which is still the principal political party in Mozambique today, began as a liberation movement in 1962, strongly influenced by Marxist–Leninist thought, ultimately becoming an officially Marxist–Leninist party in 1977. Cinéthique shot at the secondary school, which was collaborating heavily with the Marxist–Leninist contingent within the party at that time.[33] The collective's hope for the film was that it would open up a discussion about revolutionary education, and they set among its intentions the struggle for women's liberation, the struggle against elitism and the uniting of the people "to conquer the enemy [...] and produce an original national culture".[34]

Vive la lutte des peuples de Guinée-Cap Vert! Impérialistes dehors! (colour, 75 min., 16 mm) was credited principally to Tobias Engel, who was on the editorial board of *Cinéthique*. The film recounts the struggle of the people of Guinée-Cap Vert against Portuguese imperialism "and shows how this precipitated the crumbling of fascism in Portugal".[35] Where *Etudier, Produire, Combattre* made common cause with FRELIMO, *Vive la lutte des peuples* aligned itself with PAIGC (Partido Africano da Independência da Guiné e Cabo Verde), the liberation party co-founded by Amílcar Cabral. Another project under this rubric was the 15-minute audio-slide montage *Revolution jusqu'à la victoire*, about political organisation in Palestinian refugee camps.[36]

5.2 Le Front Paysan

While Cinéthique was making political alliances with the liberation movements in Lusophone Africa, they were also practising the same militant networking in France. While never officially members or representatives of a party, the group shared political affinities with the PCR(ml), although they ultimately undertook a lengthy critique of the PCR(ml) in a pamphlet published by Cinéthique entitled *Obstacles et difficultés dans la création d'un parti communiste en France et quelques éléments pour les surmonter: pour caractériser la ligne du PCR(ml)*.[37] Cinéthique also affiliated itself with the collective Front Paysan, and this affiliation was articulated in issue 21/22, when they published a text entitled "Les Paysans dans la lutte de classes – France, 72–75: bilan de la pratique cinématographique du groupe de militants-cinéastes du 'Front Paysan'" (Peasants in the class struggle – France, 72–75: balance sheet of the film practice of the militant-film collective 'Front Paysan'). In that same issue Guy Chapouillé of Front Paysan joined *Cinéthique*'s editorial board.

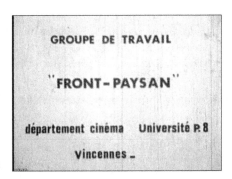

Figure 5.21

Front Paysan emerged in July 1972 when Guy Chapouillé and a group of five cinema students from Vincennes, including Claude Bailblé, began discussing the creation of a political cinema alongside the working class, particularly factory and agricultural workers. The group wanted to travel around France investigating the various struggles and strikes within these domains. The group went to Bretagne to research a strike undertaken by dairy workers that started in May of that year. Discovering that the dairy workers were suspicious of the students, the contingent quickly aligned itself with La gauche révolutionnaire.[38] Unfortunately the difficulties in maintaining the political trust between the students, the militants and the workers resulted in the majority of the students leaving the project. Thus for their first film project, *La Guerre du lait* (The milk war, 1972, B/W, 51 min.), which was the popular name given to this strike, Front Paysan was composed of just two members: Guy Chapouillé and Claude Bailblé.[39]

The strike did not begin in May of 1972 without precedent. Since at least 1969 there had been political agitation in the domain of dairy production, particularly in three departments of Bretagne, namely Finistère, Morbihan and Loire atlantique, as well as in the Midi.[40] The demands were largely typical, an increase in salary for instance, but what set this movement apart, particularly for the militant tradition as it was represented on film, was that while factory workers and students had held a primary place within the tradition of *cinéma militant*, here the agricultural sector was being represented. Further, one of the defining movements of the decade for France was the movement of the Larzac plateau, and the subjects of the films of Front Paysan were instrumental in engendering this movement.

For Front Paysan there were issues with *La guerre du lait*, what they referred to as traces of false ideas and unclear principals.[41] In trying to address all the issues that emerged during the strike, from the workers' salary to the status of women in agricultural work, the group felt that the film they had created, as it was edited together sequentially, was simply a "series of previews of films to come".[42] Yet certain ideas, ideas that would be shared principals with those at Cinéthique, came to the fore in the assessment of this project – in particular the question of representation and how to film the struggles they would investigate:

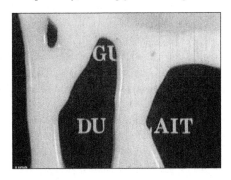

> Through the film we wanted to *re-establish truth* that had been completely deformed by *bourgeois objectivity*. We chose to use the formula *Vérité-Cinéma*. This in opposition to the very bourgeois and cinephilic

Figure 5.22 Title card for *La Guerre du lait*

Cinéma-Vérité. It is about setting the truth-taking-over-the cinema against the cinema-looking-to seize-the truth. The truth-taking-over-the cinema is the restitution of authentic facts by the peasants themselves…[43]

Figure 5.23

An equally important tactical outcome of the project was the alliance with Bernard Lambert's (a militant for Gauche Ouvrière Paysanne) radical agricultural union Paysans-travailleurs, a group for whom Front Paysan would go on to be the filmmaking wing.[44]

The critical self-analysis of *La guerre du lait* and the alliance with Paysans-travailleurs motivated Front Paysan to undertake a second project, this time about pig and cattle farmers in the Lot-et-Garonne department of southwest France, entitled *Des dettes pour salaire* (1973, colour, 26 min.). The group had now grown to include Pierre Coste, Monique Taris and Jacques Taris. The film recounted the struggle of roughly forty farmers against Sanders, a livestock feed company attached to the multinational corporation Cavanham Limited. The film was shot in colour and used dramatic recreations as part of its method. Given this, the film also functions as a fiction film within the *oeuvre* of Front Paysan.

Once completed, *Des dettes* was screened at a market in Agen-Boé, and the local and regional press were in attendance. One writer from the daily paper *Sud-Ouest* wrote:

Des dettes pour salaire makes no claims to aestheticism. It is a combat film, chopped up to a staccato rhythm, percussive, intercut with still images, shot on the very locations where the story unfolded, the local farmers as the actors. The multiple accounts constitute an assault without concession. The representative of the firm is here caricatured to the extreme. Successively cunning, threatening, arrogant, sarcastic or timid and manipulative, he plays the role of the brute and the bully.[45]

One and a half months after the screening and the *Sud-Ouest* article appeared, Sanders sought a court order to have the film banned. Following the hearing, the judge ruled that the film be censored in part; ultimately all of the reconstructed scenes, that is the fiction scenes, needed to be removed from the film. Sanders, unhappy with the judgement, appealed the

Figures 5.24–5.25 Stills from *Des dettes pour salaire*

decision. However, over the course of a second hearing the first ruling was overturned, and no censorship was required.[46]

Front Paysan continued with a third film, *La reprise abusive* (1974, B/W, 46 min., 16 mm). Claude Bailblé was not credited on this project, and Front Paysan now consisted of Dominique Bricard, Juliette-Janine Caniou, Nadine Charesson, Hubert Guipouy, Yves Lachaud, Joëlle Le Moigne and Bernard Pellefigue. This was a project that solidified the relationship between Front Paysan and Paysans-travailleurs and took as its subject the more global question of private property and land ownership in relationship to the peasants who work that land.

In 1976 the group undertook a project with the wine growers in the Languedoc-Roussillon department. Initially entitled *La guerre du vin*, the film was distributed under the title *N'i a pro* (1976, B/W, 68 min.) and followed the wine growers associated with the wine growers union MIVOC (Mouvement d'Intervention des Viticulteurs Occitans) as they attacked and emptied wine trucks that were importing cheaper wines, primarily from Italy.

The year 1976 also saw the announcement of another project, this time specifically addressing the condition and status of women within agricultural work; however, it wasn't until 1978 that production got underway, and ultimately the project was realised in 1979. Two particularities of this project distinguished it from the previous Front Paysan projects. First, it was not a film *sensu stricto*, but rather a paracinematic project, referred to as a *montage diapositives* similar to the CCPPO's project *Manuela* (see above), under the title *Femmes agricultrices*. Second, *Femmes agricultrices* not only took women agricultural workers as its subject, but was also specifically the work of the five women members of Front Paysan: Dominique Bricard, Nadine Charesson, Joëlle Le Moigne and Juliette and Janine Caniou.

For Cinéthique the group, Front Paysan made films that militated for the political objectives of Paysans-travailleurs. There was nothing ambiguous about Front Paysan films; they had very real objectives, which were dependent on collectivity:

> The militant filmmaker can't count on the "magic" value of his/her medium of expression – the technique of cinema – to be useful for certain struggles and/or to make films intending to lead an ideological struggle about such themes as racism, justice, etc. If she/he wants to participate in the transformation of the social reality in France, she/he has to understand that alone she/he represents no serious threat to the power established by the bourgeoisie.[47]

So even if the concrete goals and practice of Front Paysan were not precisely the same as those of Cinéthique, they were closer in tactic than other then contemporary groups. Leblanc, considering the difference of Front Paysan from the other groups, noted:

> For a group like Cinélutte there wasn't really any concrete political finality; it was struggle, struggle, struggle and then... With Paysans-travailleurs and Front Paysan it is important to pay attention to the articulation between the film and the politics. The films of Front Paysan could resemble the films of Cinélutte, in certain aspects, and certain members of the group [could also resemble each other], but in terms of their finality they were completely different.[48]

5.3 Les Handicapés méchants and Bon pied bon oeil et toute sa tête (1978, 80 min.)

While Cinéthique had made its alliance with Front Paysan by including Chapouillé on its journal's editorial board, another alliance was created that resulted in the production of a film under the direction of Cinéthique. Again, the group demonstrated its interest in different sectors of revolutionary activity, something that had been evident since its earliest film productions, if not clearly in the subjects of the texts published in the journal: Third World liberation movements both inside and outside France, the experience of the factory worker (as articulated in their film on the *circulaire Fontanet*), militant agricultural workers. And before turning to a film on nuclear energy, *Tout un programme*, Cinéthique undertook a long and in-depth investigation into the experience of the

Figure 5.26 *Handicapés méchants*, issue 1

politically radical special needs community in France. In particular they began collaborating with Les Handicapés méchants (The mean handicapped), ultimately creating alongside this activist group the film *Bon pied bon oeil et toute sa tête*.

Alongside the factory workers, the agricultural workers, the women's liberation movements, the documented and undocumented immigrants and a number of other specific revolutionary groups and causes, there were also the demands made by the special needs community in France. In 1964 a group of students, then considered physically handicapped, organised the GIHP (Groupement des Intellectuels Handicapés Physiques) and maintained a platform that demanded integration, autonomy and the refusal of charity. The group was founded in Nancy but spread quickly, and with the framework of May 1968 the movement gathered steam.

In 1974 Les Handicapés méchants developed out of an earlier militant organisation within the special needs community, Le comité de lutte des handicapés, which was founded in 1972. Le comité de lutte des handicapés were associated with the anarchist organisation Organisation révolutionnaire anarchiste, and it was in their journal *Front Libertaire* that the first issues of *Les Handicapés méchants* were published as a supplement. In January 1975 the group published the first autonomous issue of *Les Handicapés méchants*, with a print run of 5,000.[49] The creation of the group along with its journal had as its principal objective the autonomy of the special needs community: the group wanted to speak for itself, instead of (as we saw with the working class in Besançon of Les groupes Medvedkine) being talked for, or talked about by charities and specialists. The group was against institutionalisation, and expressed itself in autonomist terms: desire, autonomy, freedom and the refusal of marginalisation.[50]

In 1977 Jean-Luc Heridel of Les Handicapés méchants collaborated with Sabine Mamou, a film editor who had worked with Agnes Varda and Claude Lanzmann, to make a feature-length Super 8 film entitled *Âmes charitables s'abstenir* (100 min.). Mamou described the project in terms of all marginalised people being able to locate their own experience in that of the special needs community:

For this film we wanted everyone to be able to see himself or herself as I see myself: the immigrant is also marginalised, or a woman is also someone who can be considered to need assistance, and in this sense also lives handicapped.[51]

Heridel distributed the film independently, and following a screening by the B.D.H. (Bureau de Diffusion sur les Handicaps),[52] the Centre Beaubourg purchased the film.[53]

Following this experience, Cinéthique began working on a project with Les Handicapés méchants. At this point in 1977 the journal took what would be a near three-year hiatus in publication in order to devote itself entirely to their forthcoming project. While *Quand on aime la vie* had been an early example *par excellence* of Cinéthique's deployment of cinematic theory and practice, their collaboration with Les Handicapés méchants and their resultant film, *Bon pied bon oeil et toute sa tête*, in 1978, along with the publication of issue 25/26 in 1980, was the most elaborate articulation of their political approach to cinema.

As we've seen in the domain of *cinéma militant* during the 1970s, there were tendencies towards certain approaches to filmmaking, and groups like Cinélutte and Front Paysan and figures like Jean-Pierre Thorn aligned themselves in their filmmaking with a kind of unionism, even if it was within the framework of radicalising or replacing the existing unions, especially the CGT. When questioned about Cinéthique, many of these groups suggested that they were detached from the working class, and that their films were intentionally obscure and too theoretical. While most of the groups discussed maintained a theoretical base to inform their film practice, this pairing of theory and practice was a distinguishing component of Cinéthique.

For Cinéthique the critical investigation of a given subject was as important as the final film. It was this approach, Leblanc suggested, that separated their work from something like the work of Jean-Pierre Thorn:

> With Thorn, he was someone who, at the time, we felt didn't really undertake a concrete analysis. And that was it for us. If you look at the issue dedicated to the role of the special

Figures 5.27–5.28 *Cinéthique*, 25/26, front cover (left); back cover

needs community, there is over 90 pages of analysis, based on a long and thorough investigation. In terms of those working within the domain of *cinéma militant*, we were really the only ones doing that kind of work. It was a kind of academic work.[54]

This also meant that some of the key issues from so many of the collectives were not really of interest to Cinéthique, for example the perennial question of putting the camera into the hands of the workers. Of course the first question for Cinéthique was, which workers? And further, it was imperative to understand the intention of the workers with regard to a self-representational film practice – otherwise it didn't ultimately signify anything simply to turn the camera over to the workers. What did these workers want to make? Were they leading the struggle and searching for a cinematic means to represent and disseminate ideas and information about that struggle? Or did they want to make amateur films, or home movies? Leblanc said of the concept that "it's a slogan that demonstrates the political blindness of those who would support this term. The important thing is the goal."[55]

Cinéthique's ideal process for the creation of a film was to conduct a political-economical analysis (an *analysis de la conjuncture*), which was then realised in choosing a strategic subject/theme. Once the theme was chosen, the group would set about analysing the various representations of that subject. For *Bon pied*, this process began with the special needs community, where they saw representational themes such as the destruction of the body and the mind under capitalist production.

Bon pied opens with the five senses:

In the beginning it seemed so simple to open one's eyes to look, to look at what one enjoys looking at. And not only looking, contemplating these landscapes that we enjoy looking at, but also moving, walking, running, jumping and climbing and swimming.

The images that accompany this voiceover are effectively landscapes: a rugged coastline, a tropical beach, a waterfall. But once the other actions besides looking are mentioned, the image shifts to a group of people with prosthetic legs learning to walk with their crutches under a doctor's supervision. The film is again, like *Quand on aime la vie, on va au cinéma*, a film constructed through

Figures 5.29–5.31

montage, and we quickly arrive at an insert of an ad for Kodachrome film stock (Figures 5.29, 30 and 31). There are several different Kodachrome ads, but each carries with it the title "Les cinq sens" (The five senses), and these ads in turn became the focus of a short text about *Bon pied* published in *Cinéthique* issue 25/26 entitled "Les cinq sens selon Kodak".[56]

In "Les cinq sens selon Kodak" the group notes that with *Bon pied* they wanted to

> *re-establish* the unity of the senses and representations within the contradictions of the society. But for the film we also looked for a construction that would *support* the aspirations recuperated by advertisements and para-advertisements. For the film we sought a *poetic* construction.[57]

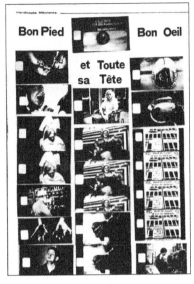

Figures 5.32

With this most developed articulation of Cinéthique's methodological approach to a critical cinematic practice, we still find that the initial theoretico-political concerns and the formal aesthetic approach (and sensibilities) remain intact: analyse a given topic, align it with the critique of the representational strategies of the dominant ideology and put together a film that remains very close in spirit to the founding aesthetic glue of Cinéthique, Jean-Daniel Pollet.

Figures 5.33–36 Stills from *Bon pied bon oeil et toute sa tête*

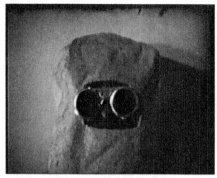

Figures 5.37–38 Stills from *Bon pied bon oeil et toute sa tête*

Bon pied's opening aerial shot of the ocean is indeed similar to the opening tracking shot of the sea in *Méditerranée*, but as the film progresses other elements resemble Pollet's work (Figure 5.32). One of the primary foci of *Bon pied* is the body: what constitutes a body, or what constitutes a complete and functioning body, under capitalism? The approach to filming the body – often disfigured, often "handicapped" – echoes Pollet's 1973 film *L'ordre*, about a Greek leper colony. By foregrounding the sometimes difficult images of those who have sustained disfiguring injuries, or those born with a congenital handicap, the Cinéthique project, in line with a traditional Brechtian programme of distanciation, insists that the spectator "must not relax, but rather become even more awake".[58]

The film traces a trajectory from the question of the "handicapped" body to the worth of the "handicapped" body and ultimately to the revolt of the "handicapped" body, while always rhythmically oscillating between a multitude of voiceovers. By the end of the film, the formal strategy breaks from an almost pure montage or even collage film to emphasise the militant organisation of the special needs community and their demonstrations. The concluding voiceover strikes out with militant fervour:

> Our concrete situation obliges us to unite the struggle against the most disastrous inhuman effects of capitalism and the struggle for its definitive and total liquidation in every domain of life, to destroy the society that destroys us utterly and entirely, and in the same movement we will build another, radically new society, a society where those who create all the wealth will have no difficulty adapting, because it will be theirs. But accomplishing that won't happen in the blink of an eye, we can't close our eyes, we can't just dream, even if dreaming stimulates us to struggle.

Cinéthique continued to make films, and the last official project of the group was 1978's *Tout un programme*, about the nuclear programme in France. In reflecting on Cinéthique's practice, Leblanc said of *Bon pied*:

> It was really the type of cinema we wanted to do. Which meant for us there was no contradiction between the fact that we worked with real social actors and the fact that we worked fundamentally with a political analysis, and with a strategic objective, and that was the

destruction of the state. And this is something that you just didn't see in Cinélutte, or any other group of militant cinema. It's what isolated us, but also what made us necessary.[59]

Cinéthique not only continued to make films, but continued to publish the journal until 1985. That year they published the last issue, number 37. Leblanc concluded, with regard to that time:

In 1980 *Bon pied* was screened in theatres, and at this point almost all *cinema militant* had disappeared, and in a way it was linked to Mitterand. We were the only ones who didn't vote Mitterand. Cinélutte all voted Mitterand. But we never really said we were *cinéma militant*, because all cinema militates for something. But that period was the end of politics as much as it was the end of *cinéma militant*.[60]

Conclusion

When Jean-Louis Baudry intervened with his apparatus essays, he suggested an impasse vis-à-vis any real cinematic production that could break with the ideology inherent in a bourgeois spectatorial position. Clearly, since the arguments of that period, the apparatus theory (as it was then expressed) has been challenged and even rearticulated in new and productive ways.[1] But at the time of its publication and reception, it served as a corrosive shibboleth that suggested that a filmmaker engaged in politically militant work would ultimately fall prey to the failings of a monological perspective and all its concomitant ideological trappings. The most often-cited response to this mode of theorising was Jean-Patrick Lebel's essay "Cinéma et idéologie". However, his response was not sufficient to undo the more elaborate theoretical arguments coming from *Cinéthique*, *Tel Quel* and, for a period of time, *Cahiers du cinéma*.[2] Yet as this study has attempted to demonstrate, there was another rebuttal, one that could function as an object lesson, as it emerged from the realm of cinematic practice: *cinéma militant*.

The theoretical elaborations of the cinematic apparatus based the core of their arguments on technicity, calling for a consideration of the position of the spectator, an engagement with Lacanian psychoanalysis and Althusserian interpretations of Marx. A response to this mode of theorising, as the collectives have demonstrated, started with not approaching bourgeois ideology as a singular, discrete, monolithic, logical or stable discourse. These groups took the approach (in a sense, more orthodox) that if the base was determinant in the last instance, then an attack on the social formation and control of production would perhaps be a more appropriate intervention than the more classically superstructural approach of the increasingly formalist *telquelians*.

Against this seemingly insurmountable politico-theoretical elaboration, the collectives and filmmakers chose a different path. Instead of responding directly to the critical aporia, they instead elaborated their own counter-theoretical models. The result was not simply a pat response that could deflect all argumentation; rather, it was the elaboration of a body of theoretical problems these groups found to be more pertinent to the critical issues of how to undertake a politically progressive, even communist, cinema. The problems the filmmakers posed addressed issues of distribution, modes of production, control of the means of production, aesthetic parameters (particularly regarding the issue of naturalism) and, finally, putting the camera in the hands of the workers.[3]

The work of Jean-Pierre Thorn provided a nascent idea of what this new political cinema could look like. His engagement with Russian formalism and more contemporary strands of a direct documentary cinematic style laid a foundation that many militant filmmakers who followed would build upon. His integration into the working class as an *établi* and his early focus on the factory reframed the the question of how, or whether, to hand over cameras to the workers to make films themselves.

Cinélutte advanced, both in practice and in theory, the idea that a film collective that was engaging the subjects of its films as collaborators was effectively using film in a way that struggled against the ideological constraints of the Renaissance perspective. Their *dispositif* included the mode of production and not just the means, and their intervention was on the terrain of modes, particularly that of collectivity. Like Thorn, Cinélutte was wary of putting the "camera in the hands of the workers". They shared his concern that the result would be diffuse citizen journalism that was both politically unfocused and technically weak. Yet for all the clamouring against this idea, the best examples of the camera being placed in the hands of the workers were the experiences in Sochaux and Besançon with Les groupes Medvedkine.

Both iterations of Les groupes Medvedkine presented a rather striking argument against Thorn, Cinélutte and those who rejected the political valence of workers making films for themselves. Given the period in which these workers' collectives produced films, they provided some of the most shining achievements of *cinéma militant*. Where in terms of politics they may not have militated as forcefully from a far-left (Marxist–Leninist) perspective, their films' inventiveness with regard to staging, re-enactment and even narrative construction put them technically on a par with those films made by filmmakers' collectives. Cinélutte may have been correct in their hesitation about the unfocused political message of films produced by workers, but the technical aspect of such collective efforts was shown to be equal to that of many of the militant films that preceded and followed the work of Les groupes Medvedkine.

Cinéthique found their own models for overcoming the stumbling blocks described by the publications of their own journal. They located a hard kernel of Marxist–Leninist film theory that enabled them to eschew the failings of direct cinema and wildcat shooting and employ something closer to the films of Guy Debord and the Situationists. Yet, they grounded this perhaps theoretical and experimental process in practical struggles faced by the working class in France and in developing nations.

However, even if the issue of worker-created films remained unsettled (ultimately, it may have ended up being a question of respective sensibilities), it nevertheless led to a substantive intervention on the part of technicians in an otherwise theoretical debate. Further, the intervention was not simply about responding to the *telquelian* critique; it was equally, if not more forcefully, about creating a new set of theoretical problems. Again, instead of debating spectator positioning and the a priori ideological components of Quattrocento optics, the groups put forward the notion that the social organisation was equally important – something that could be modified, reworked and tested. Who was filming, who was watching and who was being filmed were all equally significant considerations when facing down bourgeois ideological cinematic conventions.

This latter idea points to one of the many issues unable to be addressed in this book, which is the turn to video. While the collectives examined here were predominantly film-based (with a few minor forays into video as a tool to assist in the development of a particular project), there were collectives premised entirely on the use of video. This tradition merits its own study, not merely because of the practical technological changes that resulted from video, but equally because it was a technology frequently employed by feminist collectives. Recently in France, Hélène Fleckinger has undertaken the process of historicising the many strands of this broad domain. Some of the most prominent collectives which emerged from this tradition were Vidéa, Vidéo Out (within which Carole Roussopoulos produced much of her substantial body of film work), Vidéo 00 and Les Cents fleurs.[4]

Finally, outside the more hermetic territory of *cinéma militant* and the theoretical debates among partisans of the explosive combination of Maoism and structuralism, the practice of *cinéma militant* provides us with an historical chronicle. These works always attempted to move past the idea of a mere *document* (that filmic product that seeks to represent with total objectivity) and to push the limits of what constituted a film, a tract or a documentary. While doing so, they nevertheless opened up the possibility of seeing the events of May '68 and their reverberations across the following decades. This aspect flies in the face of the deprecatory turn that the narrative of May began to take. For those who would try to insist that the May movement was composed only of students, *cinéma militant* offers an historical body of work that insists on the participation of the French working class.

In the early 1980s, with the ascension of François Mitterrand to the presidency and the hopes that came with his socialist project, the militant avant-garde cinema in France began to settle down as other forms of avant-garde filmmaking took hold. At the same time, historical reflection on political avant-garde cinema remained, if not derogatory, then at best sparse. In assessing the political avant-garde's work, particularly that which surrounded the events of '68, the idea is to be able to expand the canon by adding these films to the history of French cinema. And yet there is also a hesitation. One of the lessons of the sometimes too reductive Third Cinema model (given to us by Octavio Getino and Fernando Solanas[5]) was that, according to its own designations, there was an almost inevitable degeneration of Third Cinema to the status of Second Cinema. That is to say, what made Third Cinema "third" was in part its temporal status: that of the (critical) present. This downgrade in status suggests that one of the most adept machines of reification is historical reflection – that practice wherein an object once in process is now, from the current vantage point, looked upon as a static and terminated materialisation. In this way, for example, *Hora de los Hornos* (1968) is no longer the same revolutionary exemplar of Third Cinema that required interruptions during a screening in order to discuss the political insights and possibilities of the film. Instead, it is now an auteurist (albeit political) masterpiece, which in turn reduces it (or promotes it, according to who is assessing) to Second Cinema status.

If the Third Cinema model is too limited, we still have recourse to the idea that history can take a film that once had a contemporary vitality and strip it of that *élan*, perhaps in favour of making it into an art historical document. Two possibilities for assessing work that engaged in the political processes of its time are as follows: to appreciate the work's artistic merits apart from its political aspirations (often considered a by-product or remainder of the aesthetic vision) or, more simply, to reject the work as useless to the contemporary cultural landscape. (In the case of *cinéma militant*, previously held political positions actually became a source of shame for some of the filmmakers, as we have seen.) The object of this presentation has been to take a somewhat practical approach: it is hoped that the consideration given to these works may help them to find some space in the Anglophone conception of French film history.

As this book opened with a quote from the most ardent supporter of precisely this *cinéma militant*, it seems only just to give him the last word. It would take almost 30 years for *La reprise du travail aux usines Wonder* to be given its deserved reverse shot in the film *Reprise*. Perhaps one of the greatest ironies of the original film is also one of its greatest successes: the fact that Le Roux is unable to find the woman from *Wonder* allows collectivity (of the many interviewees and the expressions of their respective experiences) to trump the perhaps fetishised individual. In the closing paragraph of Guy Hennebelle's posthumously published article on this tradition of filmmaking, he writes:

> Suddenly Hervé Le Roux's *Reprise* announced that the work of mourning was finally over – Mitterandism being in its last throes – and that we could go back and think about that damned *cinéma militant* and find some merit in it after all.[6]

Notes

Introduction

1 Sections of this chapter were published in an earlier version as "Just some of the ways to shoot a strike: militant filmmaking in France from ARC to Groupe Medvedkine", *Situations: Project of the Radical Imagination*, 4(1), Fall/Winter 2011, pp. 117–131; and in "The rumble of the anoetic", in T. Palmer and C. Michael (eds), *Directory of world cinema: France*. Bristol, UK: Intellect, 2012, pp. 100-139.

2 Guy Hennebelle, "La vie est à nous", *Écran*, 78(74), 1978, p. 75. This translation and all subsequent translations are my own, unless otherwise stated.

3 *Les trente glorieuses* refers to the thirty years from 1945 to 1975 in which France emerged as a fully modern country with an expanding economy and a growing consumer population.

4 See S. Harvey, *May '68 and film culture*. London, UK: BFI, 1978, pp. 14–15. Also see R. Roud, *A passion for films: Henri Langlois and the Cinémathèque Française*. New York: Viking Press, 1983.

5 In Christophe Bourseiller's study of French Maoism, he relates an anecdote about Godard being expelled by Tony Levy early on from meetings of the UJCML (Union des jeunesses communistes marxistes–léninistes) he was trying to film. Godard's unshakable commitment to form was undoubtedly anathema to the decidedly austere organisation. While those specifically interested in film and criticism, e.g. *Cinéthique* and *Cahiers du cinéma*, maintained their enthusiasm for Godard's work during the militant period, this work was also poorly received in other far-left militant cinema *milieux*. Coincidentally, Bourseiller was the actor who played the young boy in Godard's *Weekend* and *Deux ou trois choses je sais d'elle*. See C. Bourseiller, *Les Maoïstes: la folle histoire des gardes rouges français*. Paris: Éditions Seuil, collection "Points", 2008, p. 109.

6 Because this work has become increasingly available and documented, I have chosen to leave the Groupe Dziga Vertov out of this study, focusing instead on those collectives who have not yet received treatment in Anglophone film studies. For more on this group see C. MacCabe and S. Shafto, *Godard: a portrait of the artist at seventy*. New York: Faber and Faber, 2005; R. Brody, *Everything is cinema: the working life of Jean-Luc Godard*. New York: Metropolitan/Henry Holt & Co., 2008; A. de Baecque, *Godard*. Paris: Grasset, 2010.

7 Manchette is an interesting figure in this history of militant cultural practice, albeit critical of much of the French Maoism of the 1960s and 1970s (see, e.g., his dismissal of Kessel's two-volume

collection of tracts and circulars from the dominant Maoist currents leading up to the dissolution of La Gauche prolétarienne in his diaries). He specifically identified himself as pro-Situationist. See Manchette, J.-P. (2008). *Journal: (1966-1974)*. Gallimard., pp. 36-37.

8 See, e.g., Hennebelle's disparaging remarks about both Chabrol and Truffaut in a letter to the editors of *Cahiers du cinéma*, 248, p. 57.

9 See G. Hennebelle, *Quinze ans de cinéma mondial, 1960–1975*. Paris: Cerf, 1975.

10 Good examples of such work are, again, J.-P. Manchette's Eugene Tarpon novels and the early works of Frédéric Fajardie and his Inspector Padovani novels. Both writers, in the series cited, took the motifs of the private detective novels as their starting point and wove highly contradictory political parables that expressed at once the authors' respective political affiliations and the doubt inspired by the political transformation that occurred in the wake of the May '68 events. Perhaps one of the most fascinating developments that emerged from this predominantly leftist genre was the writing of A.D.G. (Alain Dreux Gallou, the pseudonym of Alain Fournier), a far-right author exploiting the *polar* much in the same way as his nemesis-compatriots of the *neo-polar*.

11 Where Guy Hennebelle had been suspicious of the *série-Z* in general, he was nonetheless concerned with the ability of cinema to be both pleasurable and political at once. Thus, it is worth noting that in his 1975 *Guide des films anti-impérialistes*, Hennebelle not only included *Dupont lajoie* but even gave it a rare two pages of treatment (rare, given that the majority of the films are treated in one-page entries). His book was dedicated in large part to concretely political world cinema generated in the southern hemisphere. Hennebelle said of the film that, even if it remained mired in the ideo-logical assumptions that plagued the *série-Z*, it was "unequivocally one of the best and most opera-tional films that has been made in France on the subject [anti-Arab racism]. The merit of the author is to have known how to effectively mobilize the cinema in the service of a cause that urgently needs attention and more than ever films that are capable of exercising an impact on the largest amount of spectators." *Guide des films anti-impérialistes*, Paris: Éditions du Centenaire, 1975, p. 22.

12 Boisset, while often lambasted by the critics of the far left, received praise from the Gauche prolé-tarienne-affiliated (and much-debated; see below) Cinéastes révolutionnaires prolétariens, who thought the popular reception of *Un condé* was a sign of a progressive shift in the French public. See the 1970 *Cinéma* interview for more on this filmmaking collective. Hennebelle, Guy and Martin, Marcel. "Les Cinéastes révolutionnaires prolétariennes". *Cinéma*, N° 151, 1970, pp. 100-104. J.-P. Manchette also noted his appreciation of this film in his diaries, which is unsurprising, given that Boisset would go on to adapt Manchette's *Ô Dingos, Ô Chateaux!* under the title *Folle à tuer*. See Manchette (2008), p. 299.

13 See Jean-Luc Godard's assessment of Groupe Dziga Vertov's film *Pravda*: "On a tourné un film politique au lieu de tourner politiquement un film" (We made a political film instead of making a film politically). Godard, J.-L. (2007). *Des années Mao aux années 80*. Flammarion, pp. 71–72.

14 J. Rancière, *Les Scènes du peuple*. Lyon: Horlieu, 2003, p. 7.

Chapter 1

1 See P.J. Maarek, *De mai 68 aux films x: cinema, politique et société*. Paris: Dujarric, 1979; and C. Zimmer, *Cinéma et politique*. Paris: Seghers, 1974.

2 Hennebelle, G. and Serceau,D. "L'Irresistible ascension du cinéma militant". *Écran*, N° 31, December1974, p. 46.

3 Ibid., p. 74.

4 Vidéo-doux was Jean-Paul Fargier's video collective that he formed shortly after leaving Ciné-thique. The group eventually changed its name to Les cent fleurs.

5   The first few issues of *CinémAction* were published either as special issues or as dossiers within existing journals.

6   Hennebelle, G. *Vous avez dit : "Cinéma d'intervention" ?*, Ecran, N°80, 1979, pp. 17–32.

7   Ibid., p. 17.

8   G. Hennebelle, "La vie est à nous", *Écran*, 79(86), 1979, p. 71.

9   G. Hennebelle, *Cinéma d'aujourd'hui: Cinéma militant*, 5–6, March–April 1976. Rumont: Film Editions, pp. 12–13.

10 Interview with Michel Andrieu, 11 January 2010, Paris.

11 See, e.g., a Slate.fr article titled "Nicolas Sarkozy, le plus soixante-huitard des présidents" by Jean-Marc Proust (26 October 2011), which suggests, among other things, that while his campaign insisted on turning the page of May '68, it was also an exploiter of the events' most notorious slogans. Retrieved from http://www.slate.fr/story/45451/sarkozy-mai-68 (accessed 12 June 2012 [e.g.]).

12 V. Linhart, *Le jour où mon père s'est tu*. Paris: Points, 2010.

13 What is interesting to note is that her previous book was a passionately sympathetic account of *l'établissement*. See V. Linhart, *Volontaires pour l'usine: vies d'établis (1967–1977)*. Paris: Seuil, 2010.

14 B.-H. Lévy and S. Žižek, "Violence and the Left in dark times: a debate instigated by Paul Holdengräber". Celeste Bartos Forum LIVE from the New York Public Library, 16 September 2008. While one would be curious to know Žižek's take on this, he unfortunately responded by turning to the Prague Spring.

15 H. Hamon and P. Rotman, *Génération*, 2 vols. Paris: Seuil, 1990.

16 K. Ross, *May '68 and its afterlives*. Chicago: University of Chicago Press, 2002.

17 It should also be remarked that the filmmakers mentioned here all created works that could equally be charged with hermeticism regarding their subjects. In fact, Solanas and Gettino have suggested that a film like *Hora de los Hornos* and its corresponding text *Towards a Third Cinema* need be read against the specific historical and national backdrop of contemporary Argentina. F. Solanas and O. Getino, "Towards a Third Cinema". In B. Nichols (ed.), *Movies and methods: an anthology*. Berkeley: University of California Press, 1976, pp. 44–64.

18 See, e.g., S. Shafto, *Zanzibar. Les films Zanzibar et les dandys de mai 1968*. Paris: Paris Experimental Editions, 2006. The Zanzibar group was a loose collective of experimental filmmakers, including Philippe Garrel, who remained relatively unknown outside of France but who increasingly achieved notoriety in the late 1990s in the United States. This example is striking because, given the films were highly experimental in nature, they were not easily assimilable to a general film-going public. Further, this collective had a very small body of work and existed for a brief period of time. The difference with *cinéma militant* was that it became part of a tradition that lasted for at least a decade and had a far larger body of film work attributed to it.

19 See Ciné-Archives at http://www.cinearchives.org.

20 What is interesting about this group is that it is one of the very few which receive mention in Anglophone film studies, particularly Sylvia Harvey's work (see section 1.4, below).

21 J.-P. Oudart, "Cinema and suture", *Screen*, 18(4), 1977–1978, pp. 24-34. Originally published in *Cahiers du cinéma*, 211–212.

22 Comolli, J.-L., "Technique and ideology: camera, perspective, depth of field". In P. Rosen (ed.), *Narrative, apparatus, ideology: a film theory reader*. New York: Columbia University Press, 1986, pp. 421–43. The two seminal essays on apparatus theory by Jean-Louis Baudry, "The ideological effects of the cinematographic apparatus" (pp. 286-98) and "The apparatus: metapsychological approaches to the impression of reality in cinema" (pp. 299-318) , appear in the same volume.

23 S. Žižek, *The fright of real tears*. London, UK: British Film Institute, 2001.

24 Again, my concern here is not to re-examine this theoretical strand, which has been more than amply dissected, but rather to return to the reality of film production.

25 Issue 241 (September–October 1972) saw the disappearance of a cover image. It was not until issue 262–263 (January 1976) that the magazine began running cover images again, and the first image was a cartoon drawing of a police officer with a pair of scissors about to castrate Charlie Chaplin.

26 Not a surprising choice, given *Tel Quel* editor in chief Philippe Sollers' role as writer on the film.

27 This grouping of films might also be categorised, along with the post-New Wave and the *série-Z*, as yet another response to '68. My decision to exclude these films in the introduction was made principally owing to the fact that the films lumped together in this malleable category were made across the decade of the 1960s and did not in themselves consistently respond to the events of May. Further, as will be discussed, this small genre or canon is largely rooted in theory and features very few concrete examples of production based on the *Tel Quel* line.

28 G. Hennebelle, *Quinze ans de cinéma mondial, 1960–1975*, Paris: Cerf, 1975, p. 363. Alongside this argument, it is relevant to point out that *Cahiers du cinéma*, having been the bastion of auteur appreciation, managed even in their "ultra-leftist" period to maintain a focus on auteurs.

29 R. Barthes, *Le degré zéro de l'écriture*. Paris: Seuil, 1972, p. 15.

30 Ibid.

31 Ibid., p. 17.

32 Ibid., p. 19.

33 G. Hennebelle, Letter to the editors, *Cahiers du cinéma*, 248, 1973, pp. 53–64.

34 It is also imperative to recall that the theoretical positions of *Cinéthique*, *Cahiers du cinéma* and *Tel Quel* were not synonymous, and there were fierce debates among these journals as well as debates with those like Jean-Patrick Lebel and the writers at *Positif*.

35 G. Hennebelle, Letter to the editors, *Cahiers du cinéma*, 248, 1973, p. 53.

36 Ibid.

37 See J.-P. Lebel, *Cinéma et idéologie*. Paris: Éditions Sociales, 1971.

38 G. Hennebelle, Letter to the editors, *Cahiers du cinéma*, 248, 1973, p. 54.

39 Ibid.

40 Ibid.

41 G. Hennebelle, *Quinze ans de cinéma mondial, 1960–1975*. Paris: Cerf, 1975, p. 369.

42 Ryan, M. "Militant documentary: *Mai '68 par lui-même*", *Ciné-tracts*, 8(3–4), Summer–Fall 1979, pp. 1-20.

43 S. Harvey, *May '68 and film culture*. London, UK: BFI, 1978, p. 1.

44 Ibid., pp. 27–43.

45 Ibid., p. 33.

46 "Politique et cinéma". *Cinéma*, N° 151, 1970, pp 81-104.

47 Sébastien Layerle makes reference to three other titles for this film: *Flins, Continuons le combat (juin 1968–juin 1969)*, *Flins 69* and simply *Flins*, this being the title of a copy of the film (attributed to the "Collectif Renault") at the International Institute of Social History in Amsterdam. See Layerle, *Caméras en lutte en mai '68: par ailleurs le cinéma est une arme*. Paris: Nouveau Monde, 2008, p. 442.

48 See G. Hennebelle, *Guide des films anti-impérialistes*. Paris: Éditions du Centenaire, 1975, p. 43.

49 Interview with Jean-Pierre Olivier de Sardan, 2 February 2012, Paris.

50 Having conducted extensive research, including verifying the names cited in the interview of those who allegedly made up this group (none of whom knew anything about the group), I would suggest that it is most likely that the group did not exist in the form suggested by the text.

51 See S. Harvey, *May '68 and film culture*. London, UK: BFI, 1978, pp. 131–137.

52 A. de Baecque, *Les Cahiers du cinéma: histoire d'une revue*. Paris: Cahiers du cinéma, 1991, p. 253.

53 Ibid.

54 Ibid.

55 Hennebelle, G and Leblanc, G. (1972) *"Coup pour coup*. Polémique entre Gérard Leblanc et Guy Hennebelle"*Écran*, 72(4), pp. 41–44.

56 Ibid, p. 42.

57 Ibid, p. 44.

58 E. Lunn, *Marxism and modernism: an historical study of Lukács, Brecht, Benjamin, and Adorno*. Berkeley, CA: University of California Press, 1982, p. 34.

59 C. Zimmer, *Cinéma et politique*. Paris: Seghers, 1974, p 180.

60 Ibid., pp. 178–179.

61 P.J. Maarek, *De mai 68 aux films x: cinema, politique et société*. Paris: Dujarric, 1979.

62 A. de Baecque, *Les Cahiers du cinéma: histoire d'une revue*. Paris: Cahiers du cinéma, 1991.

63 Ibid., p. 223.

64 G. Gauthier and T. Heller, *Le cinéma militant reprend le travail*. Condé-sur-Noireau, Paris: Corlet Télérama, 2004.

65 C. Foltz, "L'expérience des groupes Medvedkine (S.L.O.N. 1964–1974), histoire d'une aventure cinématographique révolutionnaire". Université Paris I, Panthéon-Sorbonne, UFR 03 (thesis advisor: Nicole Brenez), 2001.

66 These DVDs were distributed by Éditions Montparnasse.

67 *Cinéma et politique: actes des Journées du cinéma militant de la Maison de la Culture de Rennes, 1977–78–79*. Paris: Éditions Papyrus, 1980.

68 Comité d'action cinématographique, "Rencontres internationales pour un nouveau cinéma" (conference). Agence de Presse Libre de Québec, Montréal, 1975.

69 G. Gauthier and T. Heller, *Le cinéma militant reprend le travail*. Condé-sur-Noireau, Paris: Corlet Télérama, 2004.

70 See S. Daney, *Postcards from the cinema*. Trans. P. Grant. Oxford: Berg Publishers, 2007, p. 129.

71 An expression of this ambivalence can be found in Hennebelle's assertion about the influence of Godard on world cinema: "what is important today is to stop the ravages of an insidiously reactionary 'Weltanschauung' while at the same time welcoming the wonderful linguistic arsenal that constitutes the international god-art". G. Hennebelle, *Quinze ans de cinéma mondial, 1960–1975*. Paris: Cerf, 1975, p. 407.

72 Hennebelle, *Cinéma d'aujourd'hui*.

73 See G. Sadoul, *Dictionnaire des cinéastes*. Paris: Microcosme/Éditions du Seuil, 1965.

74 See T. Perron, "À la recherche du cinéma ouvrier: périodisation, typologie, définition", *Les cahiers de la cinémathèque* (Cinémathèque de Perpignan), 71, 2000. Retrieved from http://www.peripherie.asso.fr/patrimoine_activites.asp?id=15&idDossier=2. (accessed 10 February 2011.)

75 See Hennebelle, *Cinéma d'aujourd'hui*, p. 20.

76 See Bert Hogenkamp's contribution "Film, propagande et Front Populaire: à la défense des intérêts des cinéastes et des spectateurs", in: Jean-Pierre Bertin-Maghit (ed.), *Une histoire mondiale des cinémas de propagande*, Paris: Nouveau monde éditions, 2008, p.215-232.

77 See J. Buchsbaum, *Cinema engagé: film in the Popular Front*. Urbana, IL: University of Illinois Press, 1988.

78 See D. Tartakowsky, "Le cinéma militant des années trente, source pour l'histoire du Front Populaire", *Les Cahiers de la cinémathèque* (Cinémathèque de Perpignan), 71, December 2000, pp. 15–24.

79   Hennebelle, *Cinéma d'aujourd'hui*, pp. 19-31.

80   Ibid., p. 23.

81   Ibid.

82   Ironically, *Afrique 50* began to receive recognition from the French state as a necessary and important document of France's colonialist past.

83   See Vautier's autobiography: R. Vautier, *Caméra citoyenne: mémoires*. Rennes: Apogée, 1998, pp. 29-54.

84   G. Gauthier and T. Heller, *Le cinéma militant reprend le travail*. Condé-sur-Noireau, Paris: Corlet Télérama, 2004, pp. 152–158.

85   Hennebelle, *Cinéma d'aujourd'hui*, p. 75.

86   CoBrA was a postwar art collective made up of artists from Copenhagen, Brussels and Amsterdam, the first letters of the names of the cities being used to make up the quasi-acronym CoBrA. Some of its most prominent members were the painters Karel Appel and Asger Jorn and the Dutch architect Constant.

87   *Détournement* is defined as "The reuse of preexisting artistic elements in a new ensemble", and it has two fundamental laws, the first being "the loss of importance of each *détourned* element" and the other being "the organization of another meaningful ensemble that confers on each element its new scope and effect". In "Methods of détournement", the practice is described as a "powerful cultural weapon in the service of a real class struggle [...] It is a real means of proletarian artistic education, the first step toward a *literary communism*." In the early essays, the method was thought to be largely applicable to literary forms, but the practice was found to be applicable to a number of spheres of artistic and cultural production, the cinema being one of the most important. See K. Knabb, *Situationist international anthology*. Berkeley, CA: Bureau of Public Secrets, 2007, p. 55.

88   See P. Carpita and P. Tessaud, *Paul Carpita: cinéaste franc-tireur*. Montreuil: Échappée, 2009.

89   See S. Layerle, *Caméras en lutte en mai '68: par ailleurs le cinéma est une arme*. Paris: Nouveau Monde, 2008, pp. 113-15.

90   Hennebelle, *Cinéma d'aujourd'hui*, p. 26.

91   OCI was a Trotskyite group that split with the PCI (Parti communiste internationaliste) under the influence of Pierre Lambert (Pierre Boussel).

92   G. Dauvé, *Eclipse and re-emergence of the communist movement*. London: Antagonism Press, 1997, p. 1.

93   See L. Estrade, "Pour un cinéma éthique: Hervé Le Roux", *Critikat*, 20 May 2008. Retrieved from http://www.critikat.com/Herve-Le-Roux.html (accessed 15 June 2009).

94   See D. Fairfax, "'Yes, we were utopians; in a way, I still am...': An interview with Jean-Louis Comolli (part 1)", *Senses of Cinema*, 62, April 2012. Retrieved from http://sensesofcinema.com/2012/feature-articles/yes-we-were-utopians-in-a-way-i-still-am-an-interview-with-jean-louis-comolli-part-1/ (accessed 1 May 2012).

95   Comolli gave a series of lectures at the Centre Pompidou in January 2008 entitled *Regards critiques Histoire du cinéma sous influence documentaire*. Among the films addressed were works by both Cinélutte and Les groupes Medvedkine.

96   Ironically, this is almost the precise expression of one of Comolli's favourite theoretical formulations, Octave Mannoni's "Je sais bien, mais quand même", developed in Mannoni's *Clefs pour l'imaginaire ou l'autre scène*. Paris: Éditions Seuil, 1985.

97   "*Les Cahiers* aujourd'hui", *Cahiers du cinéma*, 250, May 1974, pp. 5–10.

98   P. Anderson, *Considerations on Western Marxism*. London: Verso, 1976.

99   Bourseiller, C. (2008). *Les Maoïstes*, p. 154.

100 Interview with Jacques Kébadian, 7 April 2010, Paris.

101 The series was created by Laydu in the early 1960s and consisted of three- to five-minute episodes which aired at bedtime.

102 See Ciné-Archives. *Grande grève des mineurs*, 1 March–4 April 1963. Retrieved from http://www. cinearchives.org/recherche_avancee_GRANDE_GREVE_DES_MINEURS__LA_-424-237-0-2.html?ref=ad63ae36b0e7ede42d8841907ab25222 (accessesed 15 June 2010).

103 In an interview with Tanguy Perron, he suggested that this attribution had no foundation in an actual connection between Daquin and ARC at that particular moment, and that the film was most likely confused with the 1948 *Grande Lutte des mineurs*, directed by Daquin with a scenario by Roger Vailland. Interview with Tanguy Perron, February 2012, Montreuil.

104 Together, these two, along with Richard Copans and other students from IDHEC, would go on to found the militant film collective Cinélutte in 1973.

105 "I wanted to direct films, thanks to Jean Rollin, who was also working at Actualités Françaises as a sound editor. He was great, an anarchist militant, a member of the Anarchist Federation. He produced my first film in '66, *Tristesse d'anthropophages* (short film, 23 min., shot on 35 mm since we had everything free) – which in January 1967 was censored by the CNC. The film was a metaphorical critique, a man who has to work in a restaurant where they eat shit. Phillippe Joyeux was a programmer who had L'Arc en Ciel, a cinema where he showed what he wanted to, censored or not. He showed *Anthropophages*, and it was also projected during the May events at the occupied Les 3 Luxembourg." Interview with Jean-Denis Bonan, May 2010, Paris.

106 Ibid.

107 CERFI was established in 1965 by Felix Guattari as a subgroup of the existing FGERI (*Fédération des groupes d'études et de recherches institutionelles*) at the experimental La Borde clinic. The group's project was largely described in their publication *Recherches*, which took as its guiding principle that the problems communist organisations were experiencing during that period were related to changes in global capitalism. The group was transdisciplinary, publishing texts on, among other topics, psychoanalysis, ethnology, mathematics and political economy. CERFI continued to exist until 1987.

108 Not to be confused with Lionel Soukaz's film of the same name.

109 Born in 1913, Deligny was a French educator who specialised in working with adolescents with special needs. The definition of "special needs" for Deligny was an extended one. It included not only those with, for example, autism or schizophrenia, but also teens characterised as delinquent or socially marginalised. He wanted to provide a place for these kids that was neither a prison nor a hospital (in many ways, Deligny was a forerunner of the antipsychiatry movement with his near total disdain for institutionalisation – although this attitude was complicated by a fascination for/ love of the asylum life). In 1948, under the guidance of Henri Wallon, Deligny undertook such a project and founded La Grande Cordée, a therapeutic educational network that made use of the youth hostels across France. This experiment was an attempt to introduce the children he had been working with to a new method of addressing their various diagnoses. After a few years, the first incarnation of La Grande Cordée dissolved, and Deligny left Paris for eastern France and then travelled to Vercours, Allier and the Cevennes with other educators and some of the young students from the project. It is during this period, in 1956, that Deligny met the principal actor/character of his eventual film project, *Le moindre geste* (1962–1971): a former student from La Grande Cordée named Yves who had been diagnosed as psychotic. *Le moindre geste* was first undertaken in 1962 and was eventually screened at Cannes in 1971. The loose narrative follows Yves, who escapes with another boy (Richard) from an asylum; the two then wander the Cevennes. The film was shot in black and white, and much of the often asynchronous audio was recorded each night after shooting, when Yves would recount into an audio recorder his adventures, which would then serve as voiceover for the film. The film was distributed by the militant collective ISKRA.

110 A long-time collaborator of Guattari's, he co-founded the journal *Chimères* along with Deleuze and Guattari.

111 Interview with Bonan, May 2010, Paris.

112 S. Layerle, "Les murmures du monde. L'Atelier de recherche cinématographique en Mai '68", 2008, p. 2. Text accompanying the DVD *Le cinéma de Mai '68, une histoire. Volume 1: 1968–1969.* Paris: Éditions Montparnasse.

113 The JCR mutated into the better-known LCR (Ligue communiste révolutionnaire) in 1969. Many of those involved in this project would go on to participate in the Situationist-inspired Mouvement du 22 Mars.

114 Following the attempted assassination of Dutschke, a television channel bought footage of *Berlin 68* from the group. See Layerle, "Les murmures du monde", p. 5.

115 "But it's important to know that a film isn't made collectively – there is a collective of people who are associated with the film but really one or two people take up the majority of the responsibility for the film, which is something we kept under wraps at the time." Interview with Bonan, May 2010, Paris.

116 "I was lucky enough in high school to have a philosophy professor who had been active in the Resistance; his name was Pierre Fougeyrollas. He quit the PC [Communist Party] in 1956 and was very anti-Stalinist. He brought us to the editorial board of a journal called *Arguments* where Edgar Morin was, so here's this guy bringing his students to a post-Marxist journal, which in turn rooted me in a particularly convinced anti-Stalinism. For me, everything that was Mao, was Stalin, was state capitalism. This is what I thought – I was close to Socialisme ou barbarie. So I couldn't be with the Maos. But everybody was doing different things, and we wanted to do things together; it was a movement that was bigger than whatever church of ideas each member belonged to." Interview with Andrieu, 11 January 2010, Paris.

117 Interview with Kébadian, 7 April 2010, Paris.

118 Hennebelle, *Cinéma d'aujourd'hui*, p. 47.

119 Interview with Andrieu, 11 January 2010, Paris.

120 André Glucksmann wrote the voiceover for ARC's *Le droit à la parole*.

121 Interview with Andrieu, 11 January 2010, Paris.

122 Ibid.

123 Ibid.

124 Towards the end of the May events, ARC began to make connections with the North American political film collective Newsreel. The result of this relationship was that ARC's *Le droit à la parole* became one of the very few militant films from '68 to be subtitled in English. The resulting film was entitled *The Right to Speak*. See Layerle, "Les murmures du monde", p. 7.

125 "Near the end of May, we were in the old IDHEC, in an old studio. Godard said, 'Look, go to the lab, and grab me one minute every ten minutes. Don't choose, don't look, just do it totally randomly.' I was the one who was in charge of getting the footage, and I did try to stop at the end of the shots/ sequences, but in general I did what he asked. And it was a shock, both aesthetically and ethically. It was for *Un film comme les autres*, and everything that isn't shot by him is ours; everything that isn't in the interview. I understood something then that I hadn't understood before: it was the eruption of modern art in cinema, the aleatory, something that I had never imagined. I didn't realise we could not choose the images. I thought it was extraordinary to think that way." Interview with Andrieu, 11 January 2010, Paris.

126 See Hennebelle, *Cinéma d'aujourd'hui*, p. 47.

127 "The minute that editing started, the conflicts started, so there was a forced position by Françoise Renberg and André Glucksmann. Glucksmann was very present in ARC, and I never got along with him and Renberg; I had no idea what he was thinking. We wanted to make a big film about May '68. But to do that quickly, we just shot whatever was in front of us, assuming that afterwards we could figure it out in the editing. I shot and edited this film about fighting in the streets; ultimately, it was a film that wasn't really linked to anything." Interview with Bonan, May 2010, Paris.

128 Interview with Kébadian, 7 April 2010, Paris.

129 Ibid.

130 Valentine paint factory in Gennevilliers.

131 *Albertine, le souvenir parfumé de Marie Rose* (1972, 25 min.).

132 See N. Dubost, *Flins sans fin*. Paris: Maspero, 1979.

Chapter 2

1 J.-P. Thorn and T. Perron, *Le dos au mur*. Montreuil: Scope éditions, Périphérie, 2007, p. 36.

2 *Emmanuelle* (or *Mi/Vie*) won first prize *ex aequo* at the Évian film festival in 1966. Thorn recounted his experience with this film: "I had made a couple of shorts and I was in conflict about it. My producer was Pierre Braunberger; he produced a film of mine that was edited by someone else. I made a short called *Emmanuelle*, and this allowed me to meet Joris Ivens. It was about a generation, lost and unsure how to act politically in the face of Vietnam, very influenced by Godard. I wanted to use sounds from the war, not sound effects, but actual recordings of sounds from the war in Vietnam. At that time *Le ciel, la terre* (1966, B/W, 30 min.) was being projected in universities, and after a projection I introduced myself and he was very nice, and he said come see me and tell me about your film, so I did and he gave me some sounds for the project on the condition that I show him the film when it was done. I did, and since then we were friends. He was shooting in China at the time, the series made while I was an *établi*, and we remained in contact. For me, he was kind of a spiritual father." Interview with Jean-Pierre Thorn, April 2010, Paris.

3 Ibid.

4 This history of this group is discussed in more detail later in this chapter in the section on Thorn and his experience with *établissement*. See "2.5 *Les établis*".

5 Tangui Perron relates a biographical story that he suggests, in some sense, to be the reason for Thorn's total abandon to militancy and Maoism. According to Perron, Thorn and his then girlfriend had made a trip to Madagascar, where both caught malaria. While Thorn eventually recovered, his girlfriend unfortunately succumbed to the illness. His turn towards the extreme positions that he would go on to hold was in some respects for Perron "a way of escaping an entirely unbearable reality". See Thorn and Perron, *Le dos au mur*, p. 38.

6 Workerism emerges from within the far-left milieu and places a central focus on the working class. Interview with Thorn, April 2010, Paris.

7 See Bourseiller, *Les Maoïstes*.

8 Interview with Thorn, April 2010, Paris.

9 "Jean-Michel Normand was part of the first wave of *établis*, and he wasn't at Flins very long. Afterwards he couldn't take the conflict at the heart of the UJC(STET UJC original in interview), meaning between the *Toulousains* and those who founded La cause du people. He participated in the Long March in Bretagne, but then he left for Latin America with his wife (with whom he later split), and the guy had a lot of problems. He was a junkie, he ended up in prison, and then eventually San Francisco. He tried to get well, he lived with a new woman, and he invited me to screen my work with a group of Trotskyites in San Francisco that animated a television channel." Ibid.

10 See Thorn and Perron, *Le dos au mur*, p. 38.

11 Interview with Thorn, April 2010, Paris.

12 See P. Dauty. "Du documentaire à la fiction, l'itinéraire de Jean-Pierre Thorn". *Cinémaction, 76. Le Cinéma "direct"*. Paris: Cinémaction–Corlet, 1995, p.121. The quote here is taken from my interview with Thorn, April 2010, Paris.

13 Ibid.

14 A tentative agreement between the Pompidou government and the unions to increase the minimum wage and wages in general, in an attempt to quell the rioting and the strikes. The agreements took place on 25–26 May 1968.

15 For accounts of the death of Gilles Tautin, see H. Hamon and P. Rotman, *Génération*, 2 vols. Paris: Seuil, 1990, pp. 570-72 (vol. 1); and Bourseiller, *Les Maoïstes*, p. 141.

16 See Thorn and Perron, *Le dos au mur*, p. 23.

17 Ibid., p. 21.

18 Interview with Thorn, April 2010, Paris.

19 Thorn and Perron, *Le dos au mur*, p. 21.

20 Interview with Thorn, April 2010, Paris.

21 "Godard made copies of the films for me; he had helped us a lot, he was often the one who paid the lab fees for ARC. I had finished the editing of my film, and Godard, who was at Les états généraux du cinema, asked me how many copies I needed of the film. I told him four, and he said, leave the negatives and I'll attach them to the end of my film and my producer won't see a thing. We met three weeks later, he gave me my four copies of the film, said go to work, and I've never seen the guy since." Interview with Thorn, April 2010, Paris.

22 On the *film de synthèse*, see *Le cinéma s'insurge. Les états généraux du cinéma, 2*. Paris: Eric Losfeld, 1968, pp. 15–17.

23 Interview with Thorn, April 2010, Paris.

24 V.I. Lenin, *What is to be done? Burning questions of our movement*, rev. ed. New York: International Publishers, 1969.

25 A. de Baecque et al., *Cinéma 68. Cahiers du cinéma*, 2008, p. 109.

26 S. Layerle, "… Que rien ne passe pour immuable entretien avec Jean-Pierre Thorn", *Cinémaction*, 110, January 2004, p. 138.

27 See Thorn and Perron, *Le dos au mur*, p. 39.

28 See Hennebelle, *Cinémaction, 76. Le Cinéma "direct"*, p. 119.

29 Ibid., p. 52.

30 Ibid., p. 122.

31 Ibid.

32 See *Coffret le cinéma de mai 68* (DVD). Paris: Éditions Montparnasse, 2008.

33 See Bourseiller, *Les Maoïstes*, pp. 94–109.

34 Ibid., pp. 245–246.

35 Ibid., pp. 94–109.

36 Jacques Jurquet, founder of the PCMLF, during a trip to China in 1970 asked the Chinese Communist Party to break all ties with Ligne rouge, citing them as a divisive group. Bourseiller, *Les Maoïstes*, p. 214.

37 "Vive le cinéma, arme de propagande communiste !" *Cahiers du cinéma*, 245–246, 1973, pp. 31–42.

38 "The debt was a problem for almost ten years; it wasn't until much later that we were able to pay it back, when we were forced to sell the archives to Gudie Lawaetz. Which hurt, because here's this film, one of the few about '68, and it's made with our footage, and our films hadn't been seen. During '68 and Les états généraux du cinema, we wanted to establish a cooperative called La cooperative nouveaux printemps. We went to Brussels and made a deal with the Belgian Cinematheque; we thought we were being really slick, and now we know: we made a deal that for every image they developed (they're the ones who would pay for the development) they could keep a copy, but without the sound, which means that all the images should in theory be at the cinematheque but without sound. Afterwards we had networks that smuggled the reels around; my film was entirely developed in Belgium. One Christmas I smuggled the negatives back under a Christmas tree on the roof of my car." Interview with Thorn, April 2010, Paris.

39 *Vive le cinéma, arme de propagande communiste !*, p. 31.

40 Ibid.

41 *Vive le cinéma, arme de propagande communiste !*, p. 31.

42 Ibid.

43 Ibid., pp. 32–33.

44 Ibid., p. 33.

45 Ibid. On Cinéma Libre, see below.

46 Ibid.

47 See Chapter 1 on this group.

48 All of the information on the CRP comes from Hennebelle, Guy and Martin, Marcel. "Les Cinéastes révolutionnaires prolétariennes". *Cinéma*, N° 151, 1970, pp. 100-104, discussed in the introduction. It is unknown who participated in that interview, but Sardan says that the film was under his direction and claims to have never heard of the CRP. Iterview with Sardan.

49 Hennebelle, Guy and Martin, Marcel. "Les Cinéastes révolutionnaires prolétariennes". *Cinéma*, N° 151, 1970, p. 102.

50 Ibid.

51 Ibid.

52 Ibid., p. 104.

53 Again, that this is "their" film and not Sardan's is questionable.

54 Hennebelle, Guy and Martin, Marcel. "Les Cinéastes révolutionnaires prolétariennes". *Cinéma*, N° 151, 1970, p. 103.

55 See V. I. Lenin, "The spontaneity of the masses and the consciousness of the Social-Democrats". In *What is to be done?*

56 "Vive le cinéma, arme de propagande communiste !" *Cahiers du cinéma*, 245–246, 1973, p. 34.

57 Ibid., p. 35.

58 Ibid.

59 Ibid. On Overney, see Hamon and Rotman, *Génération*; M. Sportès, *Ils ont tué Pierre Overney*. Paris: Grasset & Fasquelle, 2008; and J.-P. Le Dantec, *Les dangers du soleil*. Paris: Presses d'aujourd'hui, 1978.

60 "Vive le cinéma, arme de propagande communiste !" *Cahiers du cinéma*, 245–246, 1973, p. 36.

61 Ibid.

62 Ibid.

63 Ibid.

64 Ibid.

65 Ibid.

66   Ibid., p. 37.

67   Ibid.

68   Ibid.

69   Ibid, p. 39.

70   One of the questions that arises is, when confronted with this practical concept, who exactly was in favour of this idea, and what films resulted from it? The problem that emerges from this question is that the most common and best-known example of this practice was the experiment between filmmakers and factory workers who participated with Les groupes Medvedkine, and each of those who suggest that they are opposed to the idea of such a practice cite Les groupes Medvedkine as an exception and acknowledge the remarkable quality and results of this project.

71   "Vive le cinéma, arme de propagande communiste !" *Cahiers du cinéma*, 245–246, 1973, p. 39.

72   See Chapter 3 on Cinélutte.

73   See P. Roussopoulos. In *Cinéma et politique: actes des journées du cinéma militant de la Maison de la Culture de Rennes, 1977–78–79*. Paris: Éditions Papyrus, 1980, pp. 25-7.

74   "Vive le cinéma, arme de propagande communiste !" *Cahiers du cinéma*, 245–246, 1973, p. 40.

75   Ibid., p. 41.

76   Ibid.

77   See "Débat sur 'En renvoyant le dieu de la peste'", *Cahiers du cinéma*, 242–243, 1973, pp. 87–94.

78   "Vive le cinéma, arme de propagande communiste !" *Cahiers du cinéma*, 245–246, 1973, p. 41.

79   "Cinéma Libre: une experience de diffusion (1971–1975)". *Cahiers du cinéma*, 257, 1975, p. 44.

80   Secours rouge was an organisation created by Jean-Paul Sartre in 1970 to protect the people (militants) from increasingly strict laws concerning the right to demonstrate and the so-called *anti-casseurs* laws, penalising demonstrators for any damage they caused.

81   "Cinéma Libre: une experience de diffusion (1971–1975)". *Cahiers du cinéma*, 257, 1975, p. 44.

82   Ibid., p. 45.

83   Ibid., p. 44.

84   Ibid.

85   Ibid.

86   Ibid., p. 48.

87   Ibid., p. 44.

88   Ibid., p. 49.

89   Hennebelle, G. and Serceau, D. "L'Irresistible ascension du cinéma militant". *Écran*, N° 31, December 1974, p. 49.

90   "Cinéma Libre: une experience de diffusion (1971–1975)". *Cahiers du cinéma*, 257, 1975, p. 46.

91   Ibid.

92   Ibid.

93   Ibid., p. 47.

94   Ibid., p. 49.

95   Ibid., pp. 49–50.

96   Ibid., p. 45.

97   Ibid.

98   Ibid.

99   Ibid., p. 51.

100 See P. Roussopoulos. In *Cinéma et politique: actes des journées du cinéma militant de la Maison de la Culture de Rennes, 1977–78–79*. Paris: Éditions Papyrus, 1980, pp. 25–27.

101 "Cinéma Libre: une experience de diffusion (1971–1975)". *Cahiers du cinéma*, 257, 1975, p. 51.

102 Ibid.

103 Interview with Thorn, April 2010, Paris.

104 P. Schneider, *Lenz*. Köln, Germany: Verlag Kiepenheuer & Witsch, 2008.

105 See J.-P. Warren, *Ils voulaient changer le monde: le militantisme marxiste-léniniste au Québec*. Montréal: VLB, 2007.

106 A reference made by Marnix Dressen in an interview with the author, January 8, 2009, Paris.

107 Speech at the Chinese Communist Party's National Conference on Propaganda Work, 12 March 1957. *Selected Works of Mao Tse-Tung*, vol. 5. Peking, China: Foreign Languages Press, 1975, pp. 422-435. There is a certain oddity about the word *établi*, which sounds almost conservative even in its English translation as "settling down". And yet as we will see, the practice was quite radical and far from the process of "settling" in nature.

108 See M. Dressen, *De l'amphi à l'établi: les étudiants Maoïstes à l'usine 1967–1989*. Paris: Belin, 2000.

109 See M. Ragon, *Histoire de la littérature prolétarienne de langue française*, revised and expanded edition. Paris: Le Livre de Poche, 2005.

110 S. Weil, *La condition ouvrière*. Paris: Éditions Gallimard, 2002.

111 "There is a tradition in France, even today, in engineering school where the students have to go work on the assembly line, or at least manual labour. But the next big experiment in the nineteenth century was in Russia, this movement towards the people en masse by the children of the aristocracy, many of whom were Russian students studying in Switzerland. It was called the Mouvement vers le peuple." Interview with Dressen by the author, January 8, 2009, Paris..

112 This adherence to the school year indicated the student orientation of the group. It would be in breaking with this scholastic tendency that the dissolution of the UJC(ml) and the subsequent development of the Gauche prolétarienne, Vive le communisme, Ligne rouge, etc., would take place.

113 Cited in P. Kessel, *Le mouvement "maoïste" en France – 1*. Paris: Union Générale d'Édition, 1972, p. 272.

114 Le Dantec would go on to write an account of his experience during this period. See J.-P. Le Dantec, *Les dangers du soleil*. Paris: Presses d'aujourd'hui, 1978.

115 See Bourseiller, *Les Maoïstes*, pp. 115–116. Bourseiller recounts how the male members of the delegation, upon arrival at the Albanian border, were forced to shave and the female members obliged to exchange their jeans for long dresses. Further, there is an episode in which Monchalbon, while attending a lecture by an Albanian Maoist, made a sketch in his notebook with a note that read, "Albania, theoretical desert". Though he threw it away, the paper was found and brought before the French delegate by the police, who were infuriated by the insult. The French delegation was sent back to France. See also Kessel, *Le mouvement "maoïste" en France*, p. 270.

116 See Hamon and Rotman, *Génération*, vol. 1, Chapter 10, pp. 329–366.

117 Interview with Thorn, April 2010, Paris.

118 See Thorn and Perron, *Le dos au mur*, p. 44.

119 Ibid.

120 Interview with Thorn, April 2010, Paris.

121 Thorn and Perron, *Le dos au mur*, p. 13.

122 Interview with Thorn, April 2010, Paris.

123 Ibid.

124 See *Dossier Penarroya, les deux visages du trust* (1972, 18 min.).

125 Thorn and Perron, *Le dos au mur*, p. 14.

126 Interview with Thorn, April 2010, Paris.

127 Linhart, *Volontaires pour l'usine*, p. 192.

128 Ibid.

129 Interview with Thorn, April 2010, Paris.

130 Linhart, *Volontaires pour l'usine*, p. 194.

131 Ibid.

132 See Thorn and Perron, *Le dos au mur*, p. 74: "the anniversary was in effect experienced as a kind of provocation by the majority of the employees of the site; if a lot of money had been spent on the event […] the employees were only offered the choice between a bottle of cognac, a corkscrew or a pen".

133 Ibid., p. 82.

134 Ibid.

135 Ibid.

136 Linhart, *Volontaires pour l'usine*, p. 190. 'The square brackets are present in the original text'

137 Interview with Thorn.

138 See *Mémoires d'usine, mémoires d'avenir*. Comité d'établissement Alstom Savoisienne, 1985.

139 Ibid.

140 See Thorn and Perron, *Le dos au mur*; Hennebelle, *CinémAction, 76. Le Cinéma "direct"*.

141 See *Le cinéma par dessus le mur*. Interview extra on Perron, Tangui and Thorn, Jean-Pierre, *Le dos au mur*. Montreuil, Scope édition - Périphérie, 2007.

142 See Thorn and Perron, *Le dos au mur*, p. 112.

143 Ibid., p. 77.

144 H. Bey, *T.A.Z.: The Temporary Autonomous Zone, Ontological Anarchy, Poetic Terrorism*. Brooklyn, NY: Autonomedia, 1991.

145 See P. Dauty. "Du documentaire à la fiction, l'itinéraire de Jean-Pierre Thorn". *Cinémaction, 76. Le Cinéma "direct"*. Paris: Cinémaction–Corlet, 1995, p. 121.

146 Ibid.

147 G.-P. Sainderichin, "Cinéma militant pas mort", *Cahiers du cinéma*, 321, 1981, pp. 61–62.

148 See Thorn and Perron, *Le dos au mur*, p. 85.

149 Ibid.

150 Bruno Muel was a cameraman for a number of militant groups and figures prominently in the history of Les groupes Medvedkine.

151 Interview with Alain Nahum, 5 December 2009, Paris.

152 See Thorn and Perron, *Le dos au mur*, p. 113.

153 Ibid., p. 120.

154 Ibid., p. 98.

155 Ibid., p. 110.

156 Ibid., p. 123.

157 Sainderichin, "Cinéma militant pas mort", pp. 61–62.

158 Ibid., p. 62.

159 Ibid.

160 See Thorn and Perron, *Le dos au mur*, p. 15.

161 Ibid., p. 95.

162 Ibid., pp. 140–141.

163 The CGT's magazine dedicated to issues faced by female union members.

164 Interview with Sainderichin.

165 Interview with Thorn, April 2010, Paris.

Chapter 3

1 Cinélutte collective, *2 ans ½ de pratique: Cinélutte*, internal circular, December 1975. Private collection of Alain Nahum.

2 Hennebelle, *Cinéma d'aujourd'hui*, p. 47.

3 See, in particular, section 2.1, "Jean-Pierre Thorn and *Oser lutter, oser vaincre*".

4 Louis de Funès was a Spanish-born actor who was very popular in French cinema. His many comedic roles in the postwar period were immensely successful.

5 Hennebelle, *Cinéma d'aujourd'hui*, p. 49.

6 Ibid., p. 47.

7 Bonan became an *établi* for a very brief period. "I decided to become an *établi* in the printing industry. But I was quickly found out because of my language, which betrayed my class origins. No one wanted to hire me. I ended up remaining a militant filmmaker outside of the factory." Correspondence with Bonan and the author June 29, 2011.

8 "Just after '68, I began to militate with Ligne rouge, after having seen *Oser lutter, oser vaincre*. I quickly became friends with a filmmaker named Jean Lefaux, who made *Écoute Joseph*. But the cinema group of Ligne rouge was more of a discussion group; we never really shot anything. And then it quickly became Drapeau rouge, and then it just kept splitting. I went to Secours rouge for a while, a bit of a split from GP." Interview with Bonan, May 2010, Paris.

9 Kébadian put Bonan in contact with a group of filmmakers aspiring to create a French film about the Black Panthers. Interview with Bonan, May 2010, Paris.

10 Ibid.

11 "Caroline was called Biri, because she lived in a Norwegian village called Biri. Despite the friendship and complicity that united us, she remained a mysterious figure, [and] we had even heard that she was Patrice Lumumba's mistress." Correspondence with Bonan and the author November 29, 2011.

12 GONG garnered some media attention as a result of a trial in which they had been charged with plotting against state security; ultimately they were acquitted. The trial had substantial coverage by *Le Monde*.

13 The film was never blown up, and was distributed in Super 8.

14 Interview with Bonan, May 2010, Paris.

15 "Ligne rouge wasn't a particularly large cell – it peaked at perhaps 100 militants – but it was extremely sectarian, and there was a quite distinct separation between what I could say in a Ligne rouge meeting and what I believed and how I lived in my everyday life." Interview with Richard Copans, November 2009, Paris.

16 Ibid. See also interview with Nicolas Dubost in *Voyages à l'usine*.

17 See interview with Nicolas Dubost in *Voyages à l'usine*..

18 On being a militant and a cinephile: "I was at the Cinémathèque. My father was a DJ on the radio, very well known, he loved cinema. My parents would take me to see films, political films. In '62 I saw *Octobre à Paris* in a clandestine screening; at that time, there was a clear relationship between cinema and politics largely because of that film. *Octobre à Paris* was an extremely powerful film for me, because at first I didn't see the repression; I was able to see the demonstration because quite simply it took place very close to where I was living. When I went with my brother to the clandestine screening, not even a year after, I was blown away. I saw something that was directly linked with my political engagement, and it was cinema that was doing it [creating the link]. So, from the beginning there is a link between being militant and being a cinephile." Interview with Copans, November 2009, Paris.

19   The SRF was created in 1968 and, in a sense, was the institutional attempt to realise the work of the EG. It is equally the organisation that established the Quinzaine des Réalisateurs at Cannes. See O. Thévenin, *La SRF et la Quinzaine des Réalisateurs: une construction d'identités collectives*. Montreuil: Éditions Aux Lieux d'Être et Éditions L'Harmattan, 2008. Copans was not a big supporter of the SRF, particularly given the fact that they did nothing to support *Histoires d'A* when it was banned, and that they largely supported film directors (i.e., there was an exclusion of a large body of film technicians within their union). See Hennebelle, *Cinéma d'aujourd'hui*, p. 47.

20   Interview with Copans, November 2009, Paris.

21   See S. Layerle, "Un cinéma de lutte pour des gens en lutte". In *Cinélutte, histoire d'un collectif* (PDF file), 2008. Text accompanying the DVD *Le Cinéma de Mai 68 - Volume 2 - L'Héritage*. Paris: Éditions Montparnasse, 2009.

22   Interview with Copans, November 2009, Paris.

23   Interview with Bonan, May 2010, Paris.

24   Ibid.

25   Internal circular, Cinélutte, March 1973. Private collection of Alain Nahum.

26   See Chapter 2 (section 2.1, on Jean-Pierre Thorn).

27   *Pour un front culturel révolutionnaire*, pamphlet, 1974, p. 34. Private collection of Alain Nahum.

28   Ibid.

29   Ibid.

30   Ibid.

31   "Un film sur le printemps des lycéens: *Chaud ! Chaud ! Chaud !*", *Le Monde*, 30 June 1973.

32   *Pour un front culturel révolutionnaire*. Catalogue, 1973, p. 35.

33   Ibid.

34   Ibid.

35   Ibid., p. 36.

36   "Sur le cinéma militant. Entretien de René Pierre avec Cinélutte", *Communisme*, 29–30, July–October 1977.

37   Internal circular, Cinélutte.

38   Ibid.

39   *Révolution!*, 60, 1974. Cited in internal circular, Cinélutte.

40   Hennebelle, *Cinéma d'aujourd'hui*, p. 50.

41   Internal circular, Cinélutte.

42   Ibid.

43   Hennebelle, *Cinéma d'aujourd'hui*, p. 52.

44   Internal circular, Cinélutte.

45   In the 1977 catalogue, for example, apart from the titles in Cinélutte's own *oeuvre*, we find *Oser lutter, oser vaincre, La reprise du travail aux usines Wonder* and projects created individually by members or "fellow travellers" of the group.

46   Internal circular, Cinélutte.

47   Cinélutte catalogue, 1977. Private collection of Alain Nahum.

48   Internal circular, Cinélutte.

49   Ibid.

50   Interview with Cinélutte, *Cinéma politique*, 11, p. 6.

51   Ibid., p. 8.

52   Ibid., p. 6. Italics in original, brackets are the author's.

53   Ibid.

54 Hennebelle, *Cinéma d'aujourd'hui*, p. 51.

55 Ibid.

56 *Cinéma et politique: actes des journées du cinéma militant de la Maison de la Culture de Rennes, 1977–78–79*. Paris: Éditions Papyrus, 1980, p. 32.

57 Interview with Bonan, May 2010, Paris.

58 Interview with Nahum, 5 December 2009, Paris.

59 See section 1.3: "Production eclipsed by theory".

60 Interview with Nahum, 5 December 2009, Paris.

61 The group is cited as Cinéluttes in the credits.

62 Internal circular, Cinélutte, 1974, p. 2.

63 Hennebelle, *Cinéma d'aujourd'hui*, p. 53.

64 Ibid.

65 Hennebelle, *Cinéma d'aujourd'hui*, p. 56.

66 Bonan in discussing direct cinema and Cinélutte has said: "Two things about the direct: first is that it wants to shoot reality as it is without transforming it; in this sense we can't say that even Rouch is direct. So there is a myth. When we recorded, we recorded in a way that was direct, given that ultimately we weren't even sure what we were going to do with what we shot. But then the editing is a reconstruction entirely. For instance, when we did the film of Credit Lyonnais, whoever was supposed to be doing the sound forgot to plug it in, so I used the music from a silent film. We started with the material to get somewhere else. In fact, I worked on that film the same way that later Alain Nahum worked on *À pas lentes*." Interview with Bonan, May 2010, Paris.

67 Hennebelle, *Cinéma d'aujourd'hui*, p. 55.

68 Ibid.

69 Ibid., p. 57.

70 Ibid., pp. 55–56.

71 "Entretien avec le collectif Cinélutte" *Cahiers du cinéma*, 251–252, 1974, p. 44.

72 In an interview with *Cahiers du cinéma*, Cinélutte addressed the issue of giving the camera to the workers. They recounted how, during the shooting of *Jusqu'au bout*, it happened that those participating in the strike began to help make the film (aiding with sound, shooting, and so on). Those aspects of the film created by the strikers were not, according to the group, treated differently from any other element of the film. "Entretien avec le collectif Cinélutte" *Cahiers du cinéma*, 251–252, 1974, p. 45. While this acknowledgment does in fact point to some sort of participation and transformation, these elements are not readily visible in the final product. The idea of transforming an event clearly suggests that the film is a carrier of this information, of this transformation; we will see the group engage in this practice, occasionally stumbling, as Cinélutte progressed as a film collective.

73 "When we finished filming *Jusqu'au bout*, I became friends with the Tunisian workers because of my background, and I ended up losing touch with them, but recently I was trying to find a guy named Najib, whom we see a lot of in the film. I found him after 30 years; we made a film about him because he's a painter. Najib reminded me that he was always behind the camera, and he wanted me to help him get into the business. I couldn't do much for him because I wasn't hooked up that way, but I set him up with a lab where he learned photography and earned his living with that for a long time. Now he's got a grocery store in Tunisia but paints 90 percent of the time." Interview with Bonan, May 2010, Paris.

74 Interview with Nahum, 5 December 2009, Paris.

75 For the production of the thesis, film students were allowed to ask for a supervisor, traditionally someone who was a professional in the film industry (Nahum chose Henri Alekan; Guy-

Patrick and François chose Vincent Blanchet). This idea was part of Copans' work to overhaul the programme at IDHEC, enabling the students to be trained not by professors but rather by those who had production experience. Interview with Sainderichin, November 2009, Paris.

76 Ibid.
77 Ibid.
78 Ibid.
79 Hennebelle, *Cinéma d'aujourd'hui*, p. 52.
80 Interview with Nahum, 5 December 2009, Paris.
81 Hennebelle, Cinéma d'aujourd'hui, p. 52.
82 Ibid.
83 Interview with Bonan, May 2010, Paris.
84 See J.-D. Bonan in Cinélutte collective, *2 ans ½ de pratique.*
85 See "Entretien avec le collectif Cinélutte" *Cahiers du cinéma*, 251–252, 1974,, and the catalogue *Pour un front culturel révolutionnaire* (photocopy from private collection of Alain Nahum).
86 See *Fiche technique Soyons tout,* (photocopy from private collection of Serge Le Péron), largely composed of excerpts from an interview with Le Péron in "Entretien avec Serge Le Péron". *Cahiers du cinéma*, 242–243, 1973, pp 75-86.
87 Ibid.
88 Ibid.
89 The film is considered lost.
90 *Fiche technique, Attention aux provocateurs*, November 1973.(Photocopy from private collection of Serge Le Péron).
91 Internal circular, Cinélutte, 1974.
92 A branch of the CGT.
93 One of the figures that emerges in this film is the principal organiser of the strike committee and future Lutte ouvrière president Arlette Laguillier.
94 Robert Nogrette was part of the management at Renault-Billancourt. He was kidnapped for two days by Nouvelle résistance populaire (a wing of the GP) in response to the killing of Pierre Overney. See Bourseiller, *Les Maoïstes*, pp. 307–311.
95 Interview with Sainderichin, November 2009, Paris.
96 A sometimes-violent Gaullist group, considered to be right-wing vigilantes. See F. Charpier, *Génération Occident: de l'extrême droite à la droite*. Paris: Éditions Seuil, 2005.
97 An ironic play on the "Mao-*Spontex*" epithet that was used pejoratively to describe the spontaneous tendency of organisations like La gauche prolétarienne.
98 *Darboy imprime Darboy* (fold-out poster from 1974 printed in Darboy), 1974, p. 1. Collection of the author.
99 Ibid.
100 Ibid.
101 Ibid.
102 Ibid., p. 2.
103 *Darboy imprime Darboy*, p. 3.
104 They lyrics to the song were printed in *Darboy imprime Darboy.*
105 *Darboy imprime Darboy*, p. 3.
106 Ibid., p. 2.
107 Ibid.
108 Interview with Nahum, 5 December 2009, Paris.

109 Hennebelle, *Cinéma d'aujourd'hui*, p. 50.

110 See Chapter 2, section 2.1, on Jean-Pierre Thorn.

111 "I rewatched the film about Darboy a couple of times and I was very shocked by the voiceovers. They're false. We speak in place of the people. When I saw it at Beaubourg, people loved it, they were enamoured with the people's speech. I intervened and said, no, it's not the people's speech, it's ours; the voices of the workers, they're our voices, we said what we wanted the workers to say. And there was a glacial silence." On a similar note, in discussing Linhart's book *L'Établi*, Sainderichin said: "I don't like that book at all. I mean it's incredible, but I find that book to be kind of phony. Linhart never says who he is. Not even in the book. AMBIGUOUS, MEANING HE WAS GOING BACK TO A RICH DISTRICT TO DO INTELLECTUAL WORK He never says that he returns to the 6th arrondissement with his books. He was the most brilliant *Normalien* of his generation, the *lycéens* saw the guy as a living god, as Mao himself. But at that moment he had a mental crisis, and that's when Levy sort of took the UJ and became leader of the GP. So it was no longer Marx, but it was still Engels. But what he says at the beginning is incredible, that he shows up at this factory and he realises that he is a fake worker, and that in fact everyone is a fake worker, that people came from all over. That part is true. But for me it is what Barthes referred to as a giant "Operation Margarine". Linhart starts by saying that he arrives with all his certitudes about the working class, and from there everything falls apart, none of it is true, there is no working class – but the last words of the book are 'working class'. 'Kamal is also the working class.'" Interview with Sainderichin, November 2009, Paris.

112 Interview with Le Péron. With author October 2011

113 Interview with Bonan, May 2010, Paris.

114 Interview with Nahum, 5 December 2009, Paris.

115 Interview with Bonan, May 2010, Paris.

116 Ibid.

117 Ibid.

118 K. Marx and F. Engels, *Selected Works, Vol. One*. Moscow: Progress Publishers, 1969, pp. 98–137.

119 Interview with Bonan, May 2010, Paris.

120 Interview with Sainderichin, November 2009, Paris.

121 Cinélutte catalogue, 1977, p. 4. Private collection of Alain Nahum.

122 In an interview with Sainderichin (November 2009, Paris), he remarked that the film almost cost them their graduation at IDHEC because of the missing stock: "I don't know what happened to the rushes. At IDHEC they measured the footage and they didn't want to give us our diploma. There was about 10,000 metres of stock missing. We signed a bunch of false papers to get out of it."

123 Cinélutte collective, *2 ans ½ de pratique*, pp. 2–3.

124 A Lebanese filmmaker mostly known for his films about civil war in Lebanon.

125 Interview with Sainderichin, November 2009, Paris.

126 Jean-Luc Melenchon's far-left party, which serves as a coalition of the PCF and other far-left groups.

127 Nouveau parti anticapitaliste, a continuation of the LCR.

128 Association pour la taxation des transactions financières et pour l'action citoyenne, an anti-globalisation organisation established in 1998.

129 Interview with Sainderichin, November 2009, Paris.

130 Interview with Marnix Dressen in the documentary *Voyages à l'usine* (Paul Douglas Grant, Bathysphere Productions, 2014).

131 Interview with Nahum, 5 December 2009, Paris.

132 Cinélutte collective, *2 ans ½ de pratique*, p. 8.

133 Interview with Copans, November 2009, Paris.

134 Ibid.

135 Interview with Bonan, May 2010, Paris.

136 American blacklisted filmmaker who worked in France during his exile from the United States.

137 Blacklisted screenwriter who worked with Berry.

138 Interview with Nahum, 5 December 2009, Paris.

139 Ibid.

140 The title is a play on the name of the region in Besançon where the Lip factory was, as well as meaning something along the lines of "one step at a time".

141 Internal circular, Cinélutte.

142 From the preproduction dossier on *Rien ne sera plus comme avant*. Photocopy from the private collection of Alain Nahum.

143 Ibid.

144 Ibid.

145 "When we went to Lip, the conflict had already been going on for a long time. The people participating were completely "particular" with a certain manner of living […] The women had never spoken, so they created *Lip au féminin*, which we filmed. When we began work on *À pas lentes*, these workers had experienced something different, and what they discovered was that their way of speaking was different, and that even their possibility of speaking was different, their capacity to interrogate themselves about what they had experienced. And the fact that Cinélutte arrived at this particular moment in the history of the Lip factory allowed them to capitalise on this population of self-actualised militants. This meant equally that the manner of approaching the production process was also different: they developed relationships with those whom they would film prior to shooting." Interview with Nahum, 5 December 2009, Paris.

146 Ibid.

147 See Collective. *Lip au féminin*. Paris: Éditions Syros, 1977.

148 The agreement that allowed new Lip director Claude Neuschwander to rehire the workers and restart manufacturing.

149 *Rien ne sera plus comme avant*, dossier.

150 *Cinéma vécu* was a term already in use by the Canadian documentary filmmaker Pierre Perrault, and this influence and appellation were not unmotivated. Nahum remarked, "Each of us asked ourselves different questions about our aesthetic predilections, and even if when Perrault films he's just being Perrault, for some of us his approach took on more importance, meaning that for instance if Richard [Copans] had filmed alone, perhaps he might have done it much more along the lines of Perrault." Interview with Nahum, 5 December 2009, Paris.

151 *Rien ne sera plus comme avant*, dossier.

152 Ibid.

153 Ibid.

154 Ibid.

155 *Lip au féminin*, p. 32.

156 Interview with Nahum, 5 December 2009, Paris.

157 Ibid.

158 Interview with Copans, November 2009, Paris.

159 Interview with Nahum, 5 December 2009, Paris.

160 Ibid.

161 Ibid.

162 Ibid.

163 Interview with Nicolas Dubost for the documentary *Voyages à l'usine*.

164 Interview with Cinélutte, *Cinéma politique*, 11, p. 5.

165 Ibid., p. 10.

Chapter 4

1 A more detailed account of Medvedkin's work, particularly after the Cine-Train years, can be found in E. Widdis, *Alexander Medvedkin*. London: I.B. Tauris, 2005.

2 Widdis, *Alexander Medvedkin*, p. 52.

3 See, in particular, C. Foltz, "L'expérience des groupes Medvedkine (S.L.O.N. 1964–1974), histoire d'une aventure cinématographique révolutionnaire".

4 See J. Bourrieau (ed.), *L'éducation populaire réinterrogée*. Paris: L'Harmattan, 2001.

5 For a discussion of this process, see J. Bourg, *From revolution to ethics: May 1968 and contemporary French thought*. Montréal: McGill-Queen's University Press, 2007.

6 K. Ross, *May '68 and its afterlives*. Chicago: University of Chicago Press, 2004, pp. 126–127.

7 D. Faroult, "Nous ne partons pas de zéro, car 'un se divise en deux'! (Sur quelques contradictions qui divisent le cinéma militant)". In C. Biet and O. Neveux (eds). *Une histoire du spectacle militant: théâtre et cinéma militants 1966–1981*. Vic la Gardiole: Éditions de l'Entretemps, 2007, p. 362.

8 K. Knabb, *Situationist International Anthology*. Berkeley, CA: Bureau of Public Secrets, 2007, p. 55.

9 The film takes its name from a campaign in the 1970s to try to reinvigorate a cinema-going public that was shrinking significantly, in large measure due to higher ticket prices.

10 M. Berchoud, *La véridique et fableuse histoire d'un étrange groupuscule: le CCPPO. Les cahiers des amis de la Maison du Peuple de Besançon,*, 5, 2003, p. 45.

11 Ibid.

12 Besançon was also home to the Lip watch factory.

13 M. Berchoud, *La véridique et fableuse histoire d'un étrange groupuscule: le CCPPO. Les cahiers des amis de la Maison du Peuple de Besançon,*, 5, 2003, p. 17.

14 Ibid., p. 13.

15 See Cèbe, P. *Culture en trois-huit: une mémoire militante 1959–1968. Les Cahiers des Amis de la Maison du Peuple de Besançon*, 7, 2009.

16 M. Berchoud, , *La véridique et fableuse histoire d'un étrange groupuscule: le CCPPO. Les cahiers des amis de la Maison du Peuple de Besançon*, 5, 2003, p. 19.

17 Ibid., p. 19.

18 Foltz, "L'expérience des groupes Medvedkine", p. 19.

19 Cited in M. Berchoud, *La véridique et fableuse histoire d'un étrange groupuscule: le CCPPO. Les cahiers des amis de la Maison du Peuple de Besançon*, 5, 2003, p. 28.

20 Ibid., p. 26.

21 M. Berchoud, *La véridique et fableuse histoire d'un étrange groupuscule: le CCPPO. Les cahiers des amis de la Maison du Peuple de Besançon*, 5, 2003, p. 36.

22 Ibid., p. 42.

23 B. Muel, "Les riches heures du groupe Medvedkine (Besançon-Sochaux 1967–1974)", *Images documentaires*, 37/38, 2000, p. 16.

24 M. Berchoud, *La véridique et fableuse histoire d'un étrange groupuscule: le CCPPO. Les cahiers des amis de la Maison du Peuple de Besançon*, 5, 2003, p. 29.

25 My translation.

26 For an eloquent discussion of the many ways montage and *détournement* were present in the arts during the 1950s and 1960s in France, see T. McDonough, *"The beautiful language of my century": reinventing the language of contestation in postwar France, 1945–1968*. Cambridge, MA: MIT Press, 2007.

27 P. Perrone. Obituary for Colette Magny, *The Independent*, 25 June 1997.

28 S. de Loppino, "Rhodia 4/8". *L'image, Le Monde*, 3, autumn 2002, p. 43.

29 J.-P. Thiébaud, *Hommage à Pol Cèbe*. Ville de Besançon: CCPPO, 1985. Cited in *Les groupes Medvedkine* (text accompanying DVD). Paris: Éditions Montparnasse, 2006, p. 31.

30 Ibid.

31 J. Chaban-Delmas, *Le discours de Jacques Chaban-Delmas sur la Nouvelle Société, un projet pour demain?* Economica, 2010.

32 It is interesting to note this film's striking resemblance to Roger Vailland's novel *325 000 francs*, in which a young amateur bicycle racer works overtime at a plastic factory to save money and purchase a small restaurant. He works himself ragged and eventually loses one of his hands in a factory press. See R. Vailland, *325 000 francs*. Paris: Éditions Corrêa, 1955.

33 J. Forni (director), *Trace de luttes* (2011, 60 min.).

34 H. Traforetti, "Les images-souvenirs", *Images documentaires*, 37/38, 2000, p. 41.

35 J. Forni (director), *Trace de luttes* (2011, 60 min.).

36 G. Binetruy, "Nous avons créé un lien…", *Images documentaires*, 37/38, 2000, p. 45.

37 Muel, "Les riches heures du groupe Medvedkine", p. 17.

38 Christian Corouge is the subject of a book-length interview by sociologist Michel Pialoux, recently published in its entirety as M. Pialoux and C. Corouge, *Résister à la chaîne: dialogue entre un ouvrier de Peugeot et un sociologue*. Marseille: Éditions Agone, 2011.

39 C. Corouge, quoted in Muel, "Les riches heures du groupe Medvedkine", p. 6.

40 Ibid., p. 24.

41 B. Duffort and M. Van Zele, Dynadia – SLON. *Image et Son – La révue du Cinéma*, 249, April 1971, p. 34.

42 Ibid.

43 Interview with Bruno Muel, 30 July 2008, Paris.

44 Cited in P. Cèbe, *Culture en trois-huit: une mémoire militante 1959–1968. Les Cahiers des Amis de la Maison du Peuple de Besançon*, 7, 2009, p. 7.

45 Ibid., p. 183.

46 B. Muel and F. Muel-Dreyfus, "Week-ends à Sochaux (1968–1974)". In *Mai–Juin 68* (prepared under the direction of D. Damamme, B. Gobille, F. Matonti and B. Pudal). Ivry-Sur-Seine, France: Éditions de l'Atelier, 2008, p. 335.

47 Ibid.

48 Portapak was an early lightweight video camera used by small crews in need of a mobility not provided by television-standard video cameras.

49 The latter shows the subjects' critique and response to being filmed and what they have seen. It then finally shows Rouch and Morin discussing the exchange, addressing their own feelings about the possible failings of the film (all as the sociologist and ethnologist wander the halls of the Musée de l'homme).

50 In the recent writing that has been published in French about Les groupes Medvedkine, Antonio Paleo has been the focus of some attention. Paleo was a Galician who had been imprisoned in Spain for his participation in the Republican Army and had clandestinely left Spain for France, eventually

arriving in Sochaux, where he worked in the foundry at Peugeot. He was an integral part of each film made at Sochaux, and in 1982 was a participant in Muel's film *Rompre le secret*, made for the broadcaster Antenne 2.

51 See Muel and Muel-Dreyfus, "Week-ends à Sochaux", p. 14.

52 Ibid., p. 17.

53 Ibid., p. 16.

Chapter 5

1 Cited by Jean-Paul Fargier in interview with Jean-Paul Fargier, 15 December 2010, Paris.

2 J.-P. Baudry, "Cinéma: effets idéologiques produits par l'appareil de base", *Cinéthique*, 7–8, 1970, pp. 1–8.

3 The weekly of the PSU split from the SFIO Parti Socialiste Autonome (PSA), left of the PS, in May '68. There were three leaders: Cohn Bendit, Geismar and President Jacques Savageot, who was from the PSU.

4 I saw that film on 4 August 1967 at the Festival de Avignon, where I was radicalised. I couldn't understand why people were booing the film, being very hard on it, yelling at *La Chinoise*. Then I got back to Paris to continue writing film criticism from a militant perspective.

5 Interview with Jean-Paul Fargier, 15 December 2010, Paris; interview with Gérard Leblanc, 1 April 2010, Paris.

6 Interview with Fargier, 15 December 2010, Paris.

7 See *Du Cinéma selon Vincennes (Cinema universite)*. L'Herminier, 1979.

8 The product of this study was eventually published in *Cinéthique* as "Vers le récit rouge", *Cinéthique*, 7–8, 1970, pp. 9–19.

9 Interview with Fargier, 15 December 2010, Paris.

10 Ibid.

11 Jean-Louis Comolli et al. (*Cahiers du Cinéma, Cinéthique, Tel Quel*), "Cinéma, littérature, politique", *Cahiers du cinéma*, 226–227, 1971, p. 115.

12 Ibid.

13 Interview with Fargier, 15 December 2010, Paris; interview with Leblanc, 1 April 2010, Paris.

14 Interview with Fargier, 15 December 2010, Paris.

15 J-P. Fargier "Politiques de la censure I", *Cinéthique*, 11/12, 1971, pp. 1–23; and J-P. Fargier "Politiques de la censure II", *Cinéthique*, 13/14, 1972, pp. 1–26.

16 J-P. Fargier "Politiques de la censure II", p. 25.

17 Censor board in France from 1920 to 1988.

18 J-P. Fargier "Politiques de la censure II", p. 26.

19 "'Quand on aime la vie, on va au cinéma' (decoupage de film)", *Cinéthique*, 17/18, 1974, pp. 53–103.

20 "Quand on aime la vie on va au cinéma" (presentation), *Cinéthique*, 19/20, 1975, p. 49.

21 Ibid., p. 53.

22 Ibid.

23 Interview with Leblanc, 1 April 2010, Paris.

24 Pierre Overney was a Maoist Renault factory worker who, after being fired, was shot by Jean-Antoine Tramoni, a Renault security guard, when Overney showed up for a demonstration at the factory in Billancourt on 25 February 1972. The photograph of the shooting became iconic, as it showed Tramoni firing against Overney while the latter held only a stick. See M. Sportès, *Ils ont tué Pierre Overney*. Paris: Grasset & Fasquelle, 2008.

25 Jean-Paul Fargier recounted, "At the time of the completion of the film my girlfriend was Danielle Jaeggi, who had made a film called *Pano ne passera pas* [1970, B/W, 67 min.], which was considered to be the only fiction film shot during May '68. Danielle studied at IDHEC, she had an editing table in the maid's quarters of her apartment, and it was there with Danielle that the film was edited. When we finished editing we showed *Quand on aime la vie* to François Truffaut and he ended up paying for copies to be made. Because his company also produced *Society of the Spectacle*. Because Truffaut's agent was also Debord's agent, Gérard Lebovici. What's strange though is that the film was almost finished by the time we saw *Society of the Spectacle* and the two really look similar, but we were great readers of Debord." Interview with Fargier, 15 December 2010, Paris.

26 "Quand on aime la vie on va au cinéma" (presentation), *Cinéthique*, 19/20, 1975, p. 48.

27 On the reception of the film Fargier noted: "The premier was at Grenoble, which was where the first attack from *Cahiers du cinéma* happened, because Toubiana was there and he came to the screening with his group Lou Sin, with Pascale Kane. They massacred us during the debate; they said the film was the *discours du maitre* [masters' discourse]. We said yeah, I guess it's the *discours du maitre*. That was the first moment that I was shaken a bit by criticism. After that there was the affair of Chili, and also Claude Menard left at that moment. Nineteen seventy-four. Right after that I left." Interview with Fargier, 15 December 2010, Paris.

28 Ibid., p. 50.

29 "Quand on aime la vie on va au cinéma" (presentation), *Cinéthique*, 19/20, 1975,, p. 52.

30 G. Hennebelle, "La vie est à nous: Entretien avec Cinéthique-Diffusion", *Écran*, 75(36), 1975, p. 85.

31 Ibid.

32 This film is discussed at length in *Cahiers du cinéma*, 242–243, in the text "Débat sur 'En renvoyant le dieu de la peste'", *Cahiers du cinéma*, 242–243, 1973, pp. 87–94..

33 The importance of revolutionary education for FRELIMO was evident in its referencing the armed struggle towards independence as a kind of education. See J. Marshall, "Making education revolutionary". In J.S. Saul (ed.), *A Difficult Road: The Transition to Socialism in Mozambique*, 1st ed. New York: Monthly Review Press, 1985, p. 78.

34 "'Étudier, Produire, Combattre' (avec decoupage)", *Cinéthique*, 19/20, 1975, p. 73.

35 G. Hennebelle, "La vie est à nous: Entretien avec Cinéthique-Diffusion", *Écran*, 75(36), 1975, p. 85.

36 Ibid., p. 86.

37 *Obstacles et difficultés dans la création d'un parti communiste en France et quelques éléments pour les surmonter: pour caractériser la ligne du PCR(ml)*. Paris: Cinéthique, 1977.

38 See Baiblble, Claude and Chapouillé, Guy. "La Guerre du lait". *Cinéthique*, 21/22, 1976, p. 51.

39 Ibid., p 52.

40 See the news report *Retour sur la Grève du lait*, 6 July 1982 (3 minutes, 32 seconds). Retrieved from http://fresques.ina.fr/ouest-en-memoire/impression/fiche-media/Region00266/retour-sur-la-greve-du-lait.html (accessed 25 June 2015).

41 See "Prendre part à la transformation de la réalité sociale". In Hennebelle, *Cinéma d'aujourd'hui*, p. 101.

42 Ibid.

43 Baiblble, Claude and Chapouillé, Guy. "La Guerre du lait". *Cinéthique*, 21/22, 1976, p. 56.

44 See B. Lambert, *Les paysans dans la lutte des classes*. Paris: Éditions du Seuil, 1970.

45 Quoted in Hennebelle, *Cinéma d'aujourd'hui*, p. 103.

46 See *Cinéthique*, 21/22, and Hennebelle, *Cinéma d'aujourd'hui*, p. 103.

47 Ibid., p. 104.

48 Interview with Leblanc, 1 April 2010, Paris.

49 See Koskas, Charles. "Mise au point", *Handicapés méchants*, 1, January 1975, p. 2.

50 See J.-L. Heridel, "Ames Charitables s'abstenir". In *L'écran handicapé: Cinémaction* (dossier compiled by Olga Beher). Paris: Cerf, 1984, p. 119.

51 Ibid., p. 120.

52 According to B.D.H. founder Jacques-Daniel Vernon, this organisation was established in 1977 during a UNESCO international persons with disabilities film festival. It was a group that sought to distribute and broadcast documentaries, particularly militant documentaries, about the special needs communities. See Vernon, Jacques-Daniel. "Le B.D.H." In *L'écran handicapé: Cinémaction* (dossier compiled by Olga Beher). Paris: Cerf, 1984, p 151.

53 Heridel, "Ames Charitables s'abstenir", p. 119.

54 Interview with Leblanc, 1 April 2010, Paris.

55 Ibid.

56 "Les cinq sens selon Kodak", *Cinéthique*, 25/26, 1980, pp. 106–110.

57 Ibid., 108.

58 Interview with Leblanc, 1 April 2010, Paris.

59 Interview with Leblanc, 1 April 2010, Paris.

60 Ibid.

Conclusion

1 See, among others, A. Martin, 'Turn the page: from *mise en scène* to *dispositif*', *Screening the Past*, 31, 2011, which even returned to the French term *dispositif*. Retrieved from http://www.screeningthepast.com/2011/07/turn-the-page-from-mise-en-scene-to-dispositif/ (retrieved 27 April 2014).

2 It should be remembered that Lebel was also a filmmaker, but his response to the *telquelians* and their ilk was expressed primarily in the medium that those writers established – namely, a particular kind of theoretical text.

3 In this sense, the filmmakers' discussions actually presaged the discussion of the *dispositif* in its more contemporary understanding.

4 See A.-M. Duguet, *Vidéo: La Memoire Au Poing*. Paris: Hachette, 1981.

5 F. Solanas and O. Getino, "Towards a third cinema." In B. Nichols (ed.), *Movies and methods: an anthology*. Berkeley: University of California Press, 1976, pp. 44–64.

6 G. Gauthier and T. Heller, *Le cinéma militant reprend le travail*. Condé-sur-Noireau: Éditions Corlet Télérama, 2004, p. 18.

Filmography

Filmography by Production Group

Atelier de recherche cinématographique (ARC)
Citroen–Nanterre 1968
Comité d'action 13eme 1968
Le droit à la parole 1968
Écoute Joseph, nous sommes tous solidaires 1968
Le joli mois de mai 1968
La reprise du travail aux usines Wonder 1968
Le Sergent Mikono 1968

Cinélutte
Chaud! Chaud! Chaud! 1973
Margoline 1973
Bonne chance la France 1974–75 (triptych):
L'autre façon d'être une banque
Portrait or *comité Giscard*
Un simple exemple
Petites têtes, grandes surfaces – anatomie d'un supermarché 1975
À pas lentes 1977–79

Cinéthique
Etudier, produire, combattre 1973
Même combat 1975
Quand on aime la vie, on va au cinéma 1975
Vive la lutte des peuples de Guinée–Cap Vert! Impérialistes dehors! 1975
Bon pied bon oeil et toute sa tête 1978
Tout un programme 1978
D'un bout à l'autre de la chaîne (Nicolas Stern) 1981

Le groupe Medvedkine Besançon
À bientôt j'espère (Chris Marker and Mario Marret) 1967–1968
La charnière (audio document) 1968
Classe de lutte 1968
Nouvelle société No. 5: Kelton 1969
Nouvelle société No. 6: Biscuiterie Bühler 1969
Nouvelle société No. 7: Augé découpage 1969
Rhodia 4/8 1969
Lettre à mon ami Pol Cèbe 1970
Le traineau-échelle 1971

Le groupe Medvedkine Sochaux
Sochaux, 11 juin 1968 1970
Les trois-quarts de la vie 1971
Week-end à Sochaux 1971–1972
Septembre chilien 1973
Avec le sang des autres (Bruno Muel) 1974

Thorn, Jean-Pierre
Emmanuelle (or *Mi-Vie*) 1966
BT.E4.10.N.103, No Man's Land 1967
Oser lutter, oser vaincre 1968
La grève des ouvriers de Margoline 1973
Le dos au mur 1980

Selected Filmography of Related Material

1913	Cinéma du peuple *Grève*
	Cinéma du peuple *Le vieux docker*
	Cinéma du peuple and Syndicat de l'habillement CGT *Les misères de l'aiguille*
1918	Pouctal, Henri *Travail*
1921	Champavert, Georges *Le porion*
1924	Chenal, Pierre *Visite aux usines de Pathé-Cinéma*; *Les usines de Joinville-le-Pont*
1926	Kaufman, B. *Les Halles de Paris*
1931	Clair, René *À nous la liberté*
1936	Collective: Becker, Jacques; Cartier-Bresson, Henri; Renoir, Jean, et al. *La Vie est à nous*
1938	CGT *La relève*
	CGT Syndicat de la Métallurgie de la Région Parisienne *Les métallos*
	Renoir, Jean *La Marseillaise*
1939	Anonymous *Luttes ouvrières*
1942	Clément, René, and Alekan, Henri *Ceux du rail*
1946	Carpita, Paul *Vers la lumière*
1947	Carpita, Paul *Nous voulons vivre*
	Collective *Mineurs de France* (17 min.)
	Collective *Renaissance du rail*
	Daquin, Louis *Les frères Bouquinquant*

1948   CGT *La grande lutte des mineurs*

1949   Daquin, Louis *Le point du jour*

1950   Franju, Georges *En passant par la Lorraine*

1951   Isou, Isidore *Traité de bave et d'éternité*

           Ménégoz, Robert *Commune de Paris*

           Ménégoz, Robert *Vivent les dockers*

           Vautier, René *Afrique 50*

1952   Debord, Guy *Hurlements en faveur de Sade*

1953   Ménégoz, Robert *La commune*

           Ménégoz, Robert *Ma Jeannette et mes copains*

1955   Carpita, Paul *Le rendez-vous des quais*

           Vautier, René, et al. *Une nation, l'Algerie*

1958   Chalon, Guy *58.2/B*

           Hanoun, Marcel *Une simple histoire*

           Pollet, Jean-Daniel *Pourvu qu'on ait l'ivresse*

1959   Debord, Guy *Sur le passage de quelques personnes à travers une assez courte unité de temps*

           Faurez, Jean *Quai du point du jour*

1960   Pollet, Jean-Daniel *La ligne de mire*

1961   Chartier, Jean-Pierre *Peinture à l'usine*

           Chartier, Jean-Pierre *L'usine sera loin*

           Debord, Guy *Critique de la séparation*

           Dhéry, Robert *La belle Américaine*

           Pollet, Jean-Daniel *Gala*

           Vautier, René; Le Masson, Yann; and Poliakoff, Olga *J'ai huit ans*

1962   Krier, Jacques *Budget d'un gréviste*

           Panijel, Jacques *Octobre à Paris*

1963   Marker, Chris *Le joli mai*

           Pollet, Jean-Daniel *Méditerranée*

1964   Pollet, Jean-Daniel *Bassae*

1965   Pollet, Jean-Daniel *Une balle au cœur*

           Pollet, Jean-Daniel *Paris vu par* (segment "Rue Saint-Denis")

1966   Pollet, Jean-Daniel *Le Horla*

           Pollet, Jean-Daniel *Les morutiers*

1967   Brault, Michel *Les enfants du néant*

           Krier, Jacques *Les matinales (Les femmes aussi)*

           Pollet, Jean-Daniel *Tu imagines Robinson*

1968   Chalon, Guy *La société est une fleur carnivore*

           Chardeaux, François *33 jours en mai*

           Comolli, Jean-Louis *Les deux marseillaises*

           Folgoas, Georg, and Carrère, J.P. *Boulevard Durand*

           Godard, Jean-Luc *Un film comme les autres*

           Kassovitz, Peter, and Otzenberger, Claude *Interview de M. Wolgensinger*

           Laguarda, Alain *Cléon*

1969   Cinéastes révolutionnaires prolétariens (CRP) / de Sardan, Jean-Pierre Olivier *Flins 68–69*

           Palestine vaincra

           Comolli, Jean-Louis *Comme je te veux*

CREPAC *La grève en service public*

Drach, Michel *Élise ou la vraie vie*

Groupe Dziga Vertov *British Sounds/See You at Mao*

Luttes en Italie

Pravda

Le vent d'est

Groupe SLON/ISKRA *L'ordre règne à Simcaville*

Libaud, David *La journée d'un métallo*

Zafirian, Christian *On voit bien qu'c'est pas toi*

1970   Chardeaux, François *33 jours en mai*

Ciné-Oc *Larzac, un païs que vol viure*

CREPAC *Les jeunes face à l'emploi*

Devart, Guy *On vous parle de Flins*

Groupe Dziga Vertov *Jusqu'à la victoire*

Handwerker, Marian *Têtes de Turcs*

Hondo, Med *Soleil O*

Jaeggi, Danielle *Pano ne passera pas*

Karmitz, Marin *Camarades*

Picon, André *Il se passe quelque chose aux Nouvelles Galeries de Saint-Étienne*

Pollet, Jean-Daniel *Le maître du temps*

Schmidt, Jean *L'Afrique des banlieues*

Paris des négritudes

Seban, Paul *Pourquoi la grève?* (44 min.)

Tresgot, Annie *El Ghorba*

Unicité *Les immigrés en France: le logement*

Vautier, René *Les ajones*

La Caravelle

Eux et nous

Les trois cousins

1971   Bonan, Jean-Denis, *Kimbe red, pa moli (Tiens bon, ne faiblis pas)*

Cinéma Rouge *L'entraînement des CRS*

Deligny, Fernand *Le moindre geste*

Duverger, Michel *La journée d'un docker*

Faraldo, Claude *Bof, anatomie d'un livreur*

Groupe Dziga Vertov *Vladimir et Rosa*

Lelouch, Claude *Smic, smac, smoc*

Le Péron, Serge *Soyons tout*

Pollet, Jean-Daniel *L'amour c'est gai, l'amour c'est triste*

Pollet, Jean-Daniel *Le Sang*

Vautier, René *Mourir pour des images*

Vial, Gérard *Grève chez Berliet-Bouthéon*

Vidéo Out *Grève de femmes à Troyes* (40 min.)

1972   Cazenave, Jean *Saint-Brieuc: la longue grève*

Cinéma Rouge *Le Joint français*

Dubosc, Dominique *Dossier Penarroya: les deux visages du trust*

Faraldo, Claude *Themroc*

Groupe Dziga Vertov *Letter to Jane*

Tout va bien

Karmitz, Marin *Coup pour coup*

Le Péron, Serge *Attentions aux provocateurs*

Torr e benn *Voici la colère bretonne: La grève du Joint français*

Vautier, René *Avoir vingt ans dans les Aurès*

Transmission d'expérience ouvrière

1973   Les cent fleurs: Caro, Annie; Jaeggi, Danielle; and Fargier, Jean-Paul *Cerisay: elles ont osé*

Chartier, Armand *Jacqueline*

Debord, Guy *La société du spectacle*

Dhouailly, Alain *Lip, réalités de la lutte*

Dubosc, Dominique *Penarroya, comment se mettre d'accord?*

Dumas, Claudy *Lip, 31 juillet 1973*

Groupe Cinéma de Vincennes *L'Olivier*

Le Masson, Yann *Kashima Paradise*

Macé, Yvon *Le temps des cerises vertes*

Marker, Chris *Lip 73* or *La lutte des travailleurs de Lip*

Pollet, Jean-Daniel *L'ordre*

Productions BZH *La femme agricultrice*

Torr e benn *Nous irons jusqu'au bout – Les Kaolins*

Vautier, René (with Unité production cinéma Bretagne [UPCB]) *Le Remords*

La Folle de Toujane

Vidéo Out and Roussopoulos, Carole *LIP 1: Monique*

LIP 2: La marche de Besançon

LIP 3: À la maison pour tous

Viénet, René *La dialectique peut-elle casser des briques?*

1974   ACET *Postiers en grève*

Anonymous collective *Les mézigris*

APIC *Mohamed Diab: pourquoi et comment on tue un travailleur immigré*

Aubier, Pascal *La mort du rat*

Belmont, Charles, and Issartel, Marielle *Histoires d'A*

Burch, Noël, and Fieschi, Jean-André *Nous sommes communistes*

Les cent fleurs *C'est tout pour nous et pour vous*

Les cent fleurs *Ceux de Pedernec*

Cinéma Rouge *Le charme discret de la démocratie bourgeoise*

Cinéma Rouge *Les enfants du gouvernement*

CREPAC and Scopcolor *S.O.S. Sahel*

Deloeil, Christian *La pointeuse et après*

Dubosc, Dominique *Lip, non au démantèlement*

Dugowson, Maurice *Lily aime moi*

Hondo, Med *Les bicots-nègres, vos voisins*

Julien, Daniel *Mohamed Diab*

Lawaetz, Gudie *Mai '68*

Legrand, Robert *La mort d'un cantonnier*

Srour, Heiny *L'heure de la libération a sonné*

Video OO *Des immigrés racontent*

Vidéo Out *Lip-Formation*

Viénet, René *Les filles de Kamare*

1975   Altman, Olivier *Nous sommes une force* (produced by IDHEC and distributed by Cinélutte)

Cinéma Rouge *L'invitation*

Collective *Garnier 75, non aux licenciements*

Collective *PTT*

Collective ADP *La lutte des femmes à Lip et ailleurs*

Comolli, Jean-Louis *La Cecilia*

Debord, Guy *Réfutation de tous les jugements, tant élogieux qu'hostiles, qui ont été jusqu'ici portés sur le film "La société du spectacle"*

Le Garrec, Nicole, and Vautier, René *Quand tu disais, Valéry*

Lilenstein, Nat *Les raisons d'une victoire* (25 min.)

1976   Bouchareb, Rachid *La pièce*

Chappedelaine, Soazic, and Vautier, René *Quand les femmes prennent la colère*

Chevalier, Laurent *Les apprentis se réveillent* (documentary)

Collective *Bretoncelles … et si un jour ça se passait ainsi?*

Collective ADP *Une autre façon de militer: le groupe femmes de Lip*

Dubosc, Dominique *Lip 1973* or *Le goût du collective*

Durandeau, Yves *Un goût de bonheur*

Stanojevic, Stanislas *Être jeune et travailler*

Tilly, Jean-Claude *Sera-t-il chômeur?*

Vautier, René *Quand tu disais Valéry*

Vidéo Out *LIP 6: Jacqueline et Marcel*

Vidéo Out and Roussopoulos, Carole *LIP 5: Monique et Christine*

1977   Alkama, Mohamed *Quitter Thionville*

Collective *Conflit "Les planchers Bourge" dans l'Essonne*

Gatti, Armand *Le lion, sa cage, ses ailes* (360 min.)

Gayrau, Michel *Ouvrières de Furnon*

Jussaume, Pierre *LIP 76*

Lévy, Denis, and Panayotatos, Dimitri *L'usine du vampire*

Paul, Bernard *Dernière sortie avant Roissy*

Philibert, Nicolas *La voix de son maître*

Vial, Gérard *Les cloutiers*

Viénet, René *Chinois, encore un effort pour être révolutionnaires*

1978   Andrieu, Michel *Le droit à la parole*

Brisseau, Jean-Claude *La vie comme ça*

Brunie, Patrick *La ville à prendre*

Collective *Les OS du fric*

Debord, Guy *In girum imus nocte et consumimur igni*

Gozlan, Gérard *Le choix du bon sens*

Le Masson, Yann *Pour demain*

Massin, Marie Hélène, and Quintart, Monique *Et si on se passait des patrons?*

Monsigny, Bernard *Merci monsieur Compas*

Philibert, Nicolas *La voix de son maître*

Pinel, Vincent, and Zafirian, Christian *Vues d'ici*

Pollet, Jean-Daniel *Pour mémoire*

Vautier, René *Marée noire, colère rouge*
1979   Atelier 16, Toulouse le Mirail *Carmaux 48*
Ciné-Oc, *La raison de la colère*
Collective *Chômage 78–79, des témoignages, des luttes*
Collective *Les états généraux pour l'emploi et le mieux vivre*
Dubosc, Dominique *Mémoires ouvrières: François et Bubu LIP*
Dubosc, Dominique *Mémoires ouvrières: Marcel et Jacqueline LIP*
Dubosc, Dominique *Mémoires ouvrières: Monique et Christiane LIP*
Les films de l'Églantine *Nos quat'sous*
Le Tacon, Jean-Louis *Cochon qui s'en dédit*
1980   Augerm, Thierry *Le carreau glacé*
Collective *Alès, la mine*
Faraldo, Claude *Deux lions au soleil*
Lefaux, Jean *Morts à 100%*
Le Masson, Yann *Regarde, elle a les yeux grands ouverts*
Piel, Jean-Louis *L'affaire Boussac*
Serres, Jean *Lorraine cœur d'acier*

Bibliography

Anderson, P. *Considerations on Western Marxism*. London: Verso, 1976.

Anon. *Pour un front culturel révolutionnaire*, pamphlet, 1974, p. 34. Private collection of Alain Nahum.

Anon. Internal circular, Cinélutte, March 1973. Private collection of Alain Nahum.

Barthes, R. *Le degré zéro de l'écriture*. Paris: Seuil, 1972.

Baudry, J.-P. Cinéma: effets idéologiques produits par l'appareil de base, *Cinéthique*, 7–8, 1970, pp. 1–8.

Baiblble, Claude and Chapouillé, Guy. "La Guerre du lait". *Cinéthique*, 21/22, 1976,

Berchoud, M. *La véridique et fableuse histoire d'un étrange groupuscule: le CCPPO. Les cahiers des amis de la Maison du Peuple de Besançon*, 5, 2003, p. 45.

Bertin-Maghit, J.-P. *Une histoire mondiale des cinémas de propagande*. Paris: Nouveau Monde éditions, 2008.

Bey, H. *T.A.Z.: The temporary autonomous zone, ontological anarchy, poetic terrorism*. Brooklyn, NY: Autonomedia, 1991.

Biet, C. and O. Neveux (eds). *Une histoire du spectacle militant: théâtre et cinéma militants 1966–1981*. Vic la Gardiole: Éditions de l'Entretemps, 2007.

Binetruy, G. "Nous avons créé un lien…", *Images documentaires*, 37/38, 2000, p. 43-6.

Bourg, J. *From revolution to ethics: May 1968 and contemporary French thought*. Montréal: McGill-Queen's University Press, 2007.

Bourrieau, J. (ed.). *L'éducation populaire réinterrogée*. Paris: L'Harmattan, 2001.

Bourseiller, C. *Les Maoïstes: la folle histoire des gardes rouges français*. Paris: Éditions Seuil, collection "Points", 2008.

Brody, R. *Everything is cinema: the working life of Jean-Luc Godard*. New York: Metropolitan/ Henry Holt & Co., 2008.

Buchsbaum, J. *Cinema engagé: film in the Popular Front*. Urbana, IL: University of Illinois Press, 1988.

"*Les Cahiers* aujourd'hui", *Cahiers du cinéma*, 250, May 1974, pp. 5–10.

Carpita, P., and P. Tessaud. *Paul Carpita: cinéaste franc-tireur*. Montreuil: Échappée, 2009.

Cèbe, P. *Culture en trois-huit: une mémoire militante 1959–1968. Les Cahiers des Amis de la Maison du Peuple de Besançon*, 7, 2009.

Chaban-Delmas, J. *Le discours de Jacques Chaban-Delmas sur la Nouvelle Société, un projet pour demain?* Economica, 2010.

Charpier, F. *Génération Occident: de l'extrême droite à la droite.* Paris: Éditions Seuil, 2005.

Cinélutte collective. *2 ans ½ de pratique: Cinélutte*, internal circular, December 1975.

Cinélutte catalogue, 1977. Private collection of Alain Nahum.

Cinéma et politique: actes des Journées du cinéma militant de la Maison de la Culture de Rennes, 1977–78–79. Paris: Éditions Papyrus, 1980.

"Cinéma Libre: une experience de diffusion (1971–1975)". *Cahiers du cinéma*, 257, 1975, pp. 44-52.

Coffret le cinéma de mai 68 (DVD). Paris: Éditions Montparnasse, 2008.

Collective. *L'image, Le Monde*, 3, autumn 2002.

Collective. *Lip au féminin.* Paris: Éditions Syros, 1977

Comité d'action cinématographique. Rencontres internationales pour un nouveau cinéma (conference). Agence de Presse Libre de Québec, Montréal, 1975.

Comité d'Etablissement Alsthom Savoisienne, *Mémoires d'usine, mémoires d'avenir*, 1985.

Comolli, J.-L. Technique and ideology: camera, perspective, depth of field. In P. Rosen (ed.), *Narrative, apparatus, ideology: a film theory reader.* New York, NY: Columbia University Press, 1986.

Comolli, J.-L., J.-P. Fargier, G. Leblanc, J. Narboni, M. Pleynet and P. Sollers (*Cahiers du Cinéma, Cinéthique, Tel Quel*). Cinéma, littérature, politique, *Cahiers du cinéma*, 226–227, 1971.

Daney, S. *Postcards from the cinema.* Trans P. Grant. Oxford: Berg Publishers, 2007.

Darboy imprime Darboy (fold-out poster from 1974 printed in Darboy), 1974. Collection of the author.

Dauty, P. "Du documentaire à la fiction, l'itinéraire de Jean-Pierre Thorn". *Cinémaction, 76. Le Cinéma "direct".* Paris: Cinémaction–Corlet, 1995, pp. 117–131.

Dauvé, G. *Eclipse and re-emergence of the communist movement.* London: Antagonism Press, 1997.

de Baecque, A. *Les Cahiers du cinéma: histoire d'une revue.* Paris: Cahiers du cinéma, 1991.

de Baecque, A. *Godard.* Paris: Grasset, 2010.

"Débat sur 'En renvoyant le dieu de la peste'", *Cahiers du cinéma*, 242–243, 1973, pp. 87–94.

de Loppino, S. "Rhodia 4/8". *L'image, Le Monde*, 3, autumn 2002

Dressen, M. *De l'amphi à l'établi: les étudiants Maoïstes à l'usine 1967–1989.* Paris: Belin, 2000.

Dubost, N. *Flins sans fin.* Paris: Maspero, 1979.

Duffort, B. and Van Zele, M. Dynadia – SLON. *Image et Son – La révue du Cinéma*, 249, April 1971, p. 34.

Duguet, A.-M. *Vidéo: La Memoire Au Poing.* Paris: Hachette, 1981.

"Entretien avec le collectif Cinélutte" *Cahiers du cinéma*, 251–252, 1974, pp. 44-52.

"Entretien avec Serge Le Péron". *Cahiers du cinéma*, 242–243, 1973, pp 75-86.

Estrade, L. Pour un cinéma éthique: Hervé Le Roux, *Critikat*, 20 May 2008. Retrieved from http://www.critikat.com/Herve-Le-Roux.html (accessed 15 June 2009).

"'Étudier, Produire, Combattre' (avec decoupage)", *Cinéthique*, 19/20, 1975, pp. 73-83.

Fairfax, D. "Yes, we were utopians; in a way, I still am…": an interview with Jean-Louis Comolli (part 1), *Senses of Cinema*, 62, April 2012. Retrieved from http://sensesofcinema.

com/2012/feature-articles/yes-we-were-utopians-in-a-way-i-still-am-an-interview-with-jean-louis-comolli-part-1/ (accessed 1 May 2012).

Fargier, J.-P. "Politiques de la censure I", *Cinéthique*, 11/12, 1971, pp. 1–23.

Fargier, J.-P.. "Politiques de la censure II", *Cinéthique*, 13/14, 1972, pp. 1–26.

Fargier, J.-P. Vers le récit rouge, *Cinéthique*, 7–8, 1970, pp. 9–19.

Faroult, D. Nous ne partons pas de zéro, car "un se divise en deux"! (Sur quelques contradictions qui divisent le cinéma militant). In C. Biet and O. Neveux (eds). *Une histoire du spectacle militant: théâtre et cinéma militants 1966–1981*. Vic la Gardiole, France: Éditions de l'Entretemps, 2007, pp. 355–368.

Fiche technique, Attention aux provocateurs, November 1973, (photocopy from private collection of Serge Le Péron).

Fiche technique Soyons tout, no date (photocopy from private collection of Serge Le Péron).

Foltz, C. L'expérience des groupes Medvedkine (S.L.O.N. 1964–1974), histoire d'une aventure cinématographique révolutionnaires. Université Paris I, Panthéon Sorbonne, UFR 03 (thesis advisor: Nicole Brenez), 2001.

Gauthier, G., and T. Heller. *Le cinéma militant reprend le travail*. Condé-sur-Noireau, Paris: Corlet Télérama, 2004.

Godard, J.-L.. *Des années Mao aux années 80*. Flammarion, 2007.

Hamon, H., and P. Rotman. *Génération*, 2 vols. Paris: Seuil, 1990.

Harvey, S. *May '68 and film culture*. London, UK: BFI, 1978.

Hennebelle, G. *Cinémaction, 76. Le Cinéma "direct"*. Cinémaction–Corlet, 1995.

Hennebelle, G. *Cinéma d'aujourd'hui: Cinéma militant*, 5–6, March–April 1976. Rumont: Film Editions.

Hennebelle, G. *Guide des films anti-impérialistes*. Paris: Éditions du Centenaire, 1975.

Hennebelle, G. Letter to the editors, *Cahiers du cinéma*, 248, 1973, p. 57.

Hennebelle, G. *Quinze ans de cinéma mondial, 1960–1975*. Paris: Cerf, 1975.

Hennebelle, G. La vie est à nous, *Écran*, 78(74), 1978, p. 75.

Hennebelle, G. La vie est à nous. *Écran*, 79(86), 1979, p. 71.

Hennebelle, G. La vie est à nous: Entretien avec Cinéthique-Diffusion, *Écran*, 75(36), 1975.

Hennebelle, G. *Vous avez dit : "Cinéma d'intervention" ?*", Ecran, N°80, 1979, pp. 17-32.

Hennebelle, G and Leblanc, G. (1972) *"Coup pour coup*. Polémique entre Gérard Leblanc et Guy Hennebelle"*Écran*, 72(4), pp. 41–44.

Hennebelle, Guy and Martin, Marcel. "Les Cinéastes révolutionnaires prolétariennes". *Cinéma*, N° 151, 1970, pp. 100-104.

Hennebelle, G. and Serceau,D. "L'Irresistible ascension du cinéma militant". *Écran*, N° 31, December 1974.

Heridel, J.-L. Ames Charitables s'abstenir. In *L'écran handicapé: Cinémaction* (dossier compiled by Olga Beher). Paris: Cerf, 1984.

Hogenkamp, B. "Film, propagande et Front Populaire: à la défense des intérêts des cinéastes et des spectateurs", in: Jean-Pierre Bertin-Maghit (ed.), *Une histoire mondiale des cinémas de propagande*, Paris: Nouveau monde éditions, 2008, p.215-232.

Interview with Cinélutte, *Cinéma politique*, 11.

Kessel, P. *Le mouvement "maoïste" en France – 1*. Paris: Union Générale d'Édition, 1972.

Knabb, K. *Situationist international anthology*. Berkeley, CA: Bureau of Public Secrets, 2007.

Koskas, Charles. "Mise au point", *Handicapés méchants*, 1, January 1975,

Lambert, B. *Les paysans dans la lutte des classes*. Paris: Éditions du Seuil, 1970.

Layerle, S. *Caméras en lutte en mai '68: par ailleurs le cinéma est une arme*. Paris: Nouveau Monde, 2008. Text accompanying the DVD *Le Cinéma de Mai 68 - Volume 2 - L'Héritage*. Paris: Éditions Montparnasse, 2009.

Layerle, S. "Les murmures du monde. L'Atelier de recherche cinématographique en Mai '68", 2008, p. 2. Text accompanying the DVD *Le cinéma de Mai '68, une histoire. Volume 1: 1968– 1969*. Paris: Éditions Montparnasse.

Layerle, S. … Que rien ne passe pour immuable entretien avec Jean-Pierre Thorn, *Cinémaction*, 110, January 2004.

Lebel, J.-P. *Cinéma et idéologie*. Paris: Éditions Sociales, 1971.

Le Dantec, J.-P. *Les dangers du soleil*. Paris: Presses d'aujourd'hui, 1978.

Lenin, V.I. *What is to be done? Burning questions of our movement*, rev. ed. New York: International Publishers, 1969.

"Les cinq sens selon Kodak", *Cinéthique*, 25/26, 1980,

Linhart, V. *Le jour où mon père s'est tu*. Paris: Points, 2010.

Linhart, V. *Volontaires pour l'usine: vies d'établis (1967–1977)*. Paris: Seuil, 2010.

Lunn, E. *Marxism and modernism: an historical study of Lukács, Brecht, Benjamin, and Adorno*. Berkeley, CA: University of California Press, 1982.

Maarek, P.J. *De Mai '68 aux films x: cinema, politique et société*. Paris: Dujarric, 1979.

MacCabe, C., and S. Shafto. *Godard: a portrait of the artist at seventy*. New York: Faber and Faber, 2005.

McDonough, T. *"The beautiful language of my century": reinventing the language of contestation in postwar France, 1945–1968*. Cambridge, MA: MIT Press, 2007.

Mannoni, O. *Clefs pour l'imaginaire ou l'autre scène*. Paris: Éditions Seuil, 1985.

Manchette, J.-P. (2008). *Journal: (1966-1974)*. Gallimard.

Mao, T. Speech at the Chinese Communist Party's National Conference on Propaganda Work, 12 March 1957. *Selected works of Mao Tse-Tung*, vol. 3. Peking, China: Foreign Languages Press, 1975.

Marshall, J. Making education revolutionary. In J.S. Saul (ed.), *A Difficult Road: The Transition to Socialism in Mozambique*, 1st ed. New York: Monthly Review Press, 1985.

Martin, A. Turn the page: from *mise en scène* to *dispositif*, *Screening the Past*, 31, 2011. Retrieved from http://www.screeningthepast.com/2011/07/ (retrieved 27 April 2014).

Marx, K., and F. Engels. *Selected Works, Vol. One*. Moscow: Progress Publishers, 1969.

Muel, B. Les riches heures du groupe Medvedkine (Besançon-Sochaux 1967–1974), *Images documentaires*, 37/38, 2000, p. 16.

Muel, B., and F. Muel-Dreyfus. Week-ends à Sochaux (1968–1974). In *Mai–Juin 68* (prepared under the direction of D. Damamme, B. Gobille, F. Matonti and B. Pudal). Ivry-Sur-Seine, France: Éditions de l'Atelier, 2008, p. 14.

Obstacles et difficultés dans la création d'un parti communiste en France et quelques éléments pour les surmonter: pour caractériser la ligne du PCR(ml). Paris: Cinéthique, 1977.

Oudart, J.-P. Cinema and suture, *Screen*, 18(4), 1977–1978.

Perron, T. "À la recherche du cinéma ouvrier: périodisation, typologie, definition", *Les cahiers de la cinémathèque* (Cinémathèque de Perpignan), 71, 2000. Retrieved from http://www.peripherie.asso.fr/patrimoine_activites.asp?id=15&id=2. (accessed 10 February 2011.)

Perron, Tangui and Thorn, Jean-Pierre, *Le dos au mur*. Montreuil, Scope édition - Périphérie, 2007.

P. Perrone. Obituary for Colette Magny, *The Independent*, 25 June 1997.

Pialoux, M., and C. Corouge. *Résister à la chaîne: dialogue entre un ouvrier de Peugeot et un sociologue*. Marseilles: Éditions Agone, 2011.

"Politique et cinéma". *Cinéma*, N° 151, 1970, pp 81-104.

Pour un front culturel révolutionnaire (Photocopy from private collection of Alain Nahum)

Proust, J.-M. Nicolas Sarkozy, le plus soixante-huitard des presidents, Slate.fr, 26 October 2011. Retrieved from http://www.slate.fr/story/45451/sarkozy-mai-68.

"'Quand on aime la vie, on va au cinéma' (decoupage de film)", *Cinéthique*, 17/18, 1974, pp. 53–103.

"Quand on aime la vie on va au cinéma" (presentation), *Cinéthique*, 19/20, 1975, pp. 48-54.

Ragon, M. *Histoire de la littérature prolétarienne de langue française*, revised and expanded edition. Paris: Le Livre de Poche, 2005.

Rancière, J. *Les Scènes du peuple*. Lyon: Horlieu, 2003.

Rien ne sera plus comme avant. Photocopy from the private collection of Alain Nahum.

Ross, K. *May '68 and its afterlives*. Chicago: University of Chicago Press, 2002.

Roud, R. *A passion for films: Henri Langlois and the Cinémathèque Française*. New York: Viking Press, 1983.

Roussopoulos, P. In *Cinéma et politique: actes des journées du cinéma militant de la Maison de la Culture de Rennes, 1977–78–79*. Paris: Éditions Papyrus, 1980, pp. 25-7.

Ryan, M. "Militant documentary: *Mai '68 par lui-même*", *Ciné-tracts*, 8(3–4), Summer–Fall 1979, pp. 1-20.

Sadoul, G. *Dictionnaire des cinéastes*. Paris: Microcosme/Éditions du Seuil, 1965.

Sainderichin, G.-P. Cinéma militant pas mort, *Cahiers du cinéma*, 321, 1981, pp. 61–62.

Saul, J.S. (ed.). *A Difficult Road: The Transition to Socialism in Mozambique*, 1st ed. New York: Monthly Review Press, 1985.

Schneider, P. *Lenz*. Köln, Germany: Verlag Kiepenheuer & Witsch, 2008.

Shafto, S. *Zanzibar. Les films Zanzibar et les dandys de mai 1968*. Paris: Paris Experimental Editions, 2006.

Solanas, F., and O. Getino. Towards a third cinema. In B. Nichols (ed.), *Movies and methods: an anthology*. Berkeley: University of California Press, 1976, pp. 44–64.

Sportès, M. *Ils ont tué Pierre Overney*. Paris: Grasset & Fasquelle, 2008.

"Sur le cinéma militant. Entretien de René Pierre avec Cinélutte", *Communisme*, 29–30, July–October 1977.

Tartakowsky, D. Le cinéma militant des années trente, source pour l'histoire du Front Populaire, *Les Cahiers de la cinémathèque* (Cinémathèque de Perpignan), 71, December 2000, pp. 15–24.

Thévenin, O. *La SRF et la Quinzaine des Réalisateurs: une construction d'identités collectives*. Montreuil: Éditions Aux Lieux d'Être et Éditions L'Harmattan, 2008.

Thiébaud, J.-P. *Hommage à Pol Cèbe*. Ville de Besançon: CCPPO, 1985. Cited in *Les groupes Medvedkine* (text accompanying DVD). Paris: Éditions Montparnasse, 2006.

Thorn, J.-P., and T. Perron. *Le dos au mur*. Montreuil: Scope éditions, Périphérie, 2007.

Traforetti, H. "Les images-souvenirs", *Images documentaires*, 37/38, 2000, pp. 37-42.

"Un film sur le printemps des lycéens: *Chaud! Chaud! Chaud!*", *Le Monde*, 30 June 1973.

Vailland, R. *325 000 francs*. Paris: Éditions Corrêa, 1955.

Vautier, R. *Caméra citoyenne: mémoires*. Rennes: Apogée, 1998.

Vernon, Jacques-Daniel. "Le B.D.H." In *L'écran handicapé: Cinémaction* (dossier compiled by Olga Beher). Paris: Cerf, 1984.

"Vive le cinéma, arme de propagande communiste !" *Cahiers du cinéma*, 245–246, 1973, pp. 31–42.

Warren, J.-P. *Ils voulaient changer le monde: le militantisme marxiste-léniniste au Québec*. Montréal: VLB, 2007.

Weil, S. *La condition ouvrière*. Paris: Éditions Gallimard, 2002.

Widdis, E. *Alexander Medvedkin*. London: I.B. Tauris, 2005.

Zimmer, C. *Cinéma et politique*. Paris: Seghers, 1974.

Žižek, S. *The fright of real tears*. London, UK: British Film Institute, 2001.

Index

Berto, Juliet 117

Besançon 4, 111, 113, 119–20, 123–6, 130, 132, 134, 136–7, 140–9, 166, 174, 196n.140

Bey, Hakim 68

Binetruy, Georges 124, 134, 142–3

Biscuiterie Bühler 140

Blanchet, Vincent 84, 93, 194n.75

Boisset, Yves 3, 178n.12

Bonan, Jean-Denis 29, 30–4, 44, 77–82, 84, 91–2, 96, 101, 105–6, 108–9, 116, 184n.115, 185n.127, 191n.n.n.n.7,8,9,11, 193n.66, 193–194n.73

Bonfanti, Antoine 42, 123, 133, 138, 141

Bonneau, Pierre 27

Bonne chance la France 61, 98–9, 105–6, 109

Bon pied, bon oeil et toute sa tête 155

bourgeoisie 3, 15, 41, 46–7, 49, 51, 55, 85, 87, 99, 106, 113, 117, 147, 156–8, 160, 163, 165, 173; bourgeois class 38, 51; bourgeois culture 122; bourgeois elite 36; bourgeois line 96; bourgeois film practice 19; bourgeois ideology 34, 151, 155, 173–4; bourgeois journalists 50; bourgeois right wing 100; inner bourgeois 28; modern bourgeois revisionists 78; petit-bourgeois deformation 49; petit-bourgeois intellectual 160

Branco, Paulo 117

Brecht, Bertolt 18, 35, 37, 44, 68, 125–9, 170

Bresson, Robert 30

BT.E4.10.N.103, No Man's Land 35

Cahiers du cinéma (journal) 2, 7, 13–15, 17–22, 24, 28, 45, 74, 88, 152–4, 173, 177n.5, 180n.n.28,34, 193n.72, 200n.27;

caméra sous la botte, La 24

Caméra III 131

Cannes film festival 2, 161, 183–184n.109, 192n.19

capitalism 9, 69, 73, 159, 170, 183n.107, 184n.116

Carpita, Paul 24, 26

Carrefour 93–5, 110

Carré, Jean-Michel 8

cause du peuple, La (newspaper) 48

CCPPO 120, 122–43, 165

Cèbe, Pol 124–6, 130–1, 141, 143–5

Centre culturel populaire de Palente-les-Orchamps *see* CCPPO

Centre d'études de recherches et de formation institutionnelles *see* CERFI

Centre national de la recherche scientifique (CNRS) 26

Centre national du cinéma et de l'image animée *see* CNC

CERFI 31, 183n.107

CFDT 36, 38, 61, 64–5, 70, 73–4, 79, 98, 101, 115, 143

CGT 12, 24, 27, 29, 30, 36, 38–42, 44, 46, 60–1, 65, 67–8, 70, 73–5, 78–9, 83, 86, 98–103, 143–5, 167

CGT(G) 79

CGT-PC 70

Chaban-Delmas, Jacques 138–9

Chabrol, Claude 2–3

Chaillo, Yvonne 66

charnière, La 133

Charvein, Jean 45

Chaud! Chaud! Chaud! 81–3, 86, 88–9, 92

China 4, 9, 46, 59, 65, 108, 123, 185n.2, 187n.36

Chinoise, La 2, 108, 152, 199n.4

Chronique d'un été 37, 147

Cineaste (journal) 16

Cinéastes révolutionnaires prolétariens 17, 48, 178n.12; *see* CRP

ciné-clubs 7, 49, 55, 152

Cinélutte 4, 11–13, 22, 28, 30, 45, 52, 54, 56, 61, 71, 73–4, 77–117, 82, 122, 130, 145, 161–2, 165, 167, 170–1, 174, 183n.104, 193n.n.66,72, 196n.145

CinémAction (journal) 8, 19, 22–3, 27, 179n.5

cinéma d'intervention 7–9

cinéma direct 43, 93, 133, 136

cinéma du peuple 24

Cinéma et politique (book) 19–22

Cinéma-Liberté 35–6

Cinéma Libre 47, 52, 54–8, 86, 88, 116

Cinéma ligne rouge *see* ligne rouge

cinéma militant: Octobre à Paris 26

Cinéma national populaire (CNP) 152

cinema of propaganda 12, 88

cinéma parallèl 7–8, 19

Cinéma politique (journal) 19, 116

cinémas de rupture 7

Cinémathèque Française 2

cinéma vécu 112, 196n.150

cinéma vérité 37, 43

Cinéthique (Groupe) 4, 85, 88, 91, 122, 151–71, 174

Cinéthique (journal) 7, 13–15, 17–19, 21–2, 28, 34, 88, 151–6, 161–3, 167–8, 173, 177n.5, 179n.4, 180n.34

Cinétracts 29

Ciné-tracts (journal) 16, 81

Cine-Train 119–21, 134, 141